KU-686-705

Tessa Cubitt

LATIN AMERICAN SOCIETY

CHESTER COLLEGE

ACC. No.	DEPT	X
872925		
CLASS No.		
918		
LIBRARY		

Copublished in the United States with
John Wiley & Sons, Inc., New York

Longman Scientific & Technical,
Longman Group UK Limited,
Longman House, Burnt Mill, Harlow,
Essex CM20 2JE, England
and Associated Companies throughout the world.

Copublished in the United States with
John Wiley & Sons, Inc., 605 Third Avenue, New York, NY 10158

© Longman Group UK Limited 1988

All rights reserved; no part of this publication
may be reproduced, stored in a retrieval system,
or transmitted in any form or by any means, electronic,
mechanical, photocopying, recording, or otherwise,
without either the prior written permission of the
Publishers or a licence permitting restricted copying
issued by the Copyright Licensing Agency Ltd, 33–34
Alfred Place, London, WC1E 7DP.

First published 1988

British Library Cataloguing in Publication Data

Cubitt, Tessa
    Latin American society.
    1. Latin America – Social conditions –
    1945 –
    I. Title
    980′.038   HN110.5

    ISBN 0-582-30164-5

ISBN 0-582-30164-5

Library of Congress Cataloging-in-Publication Data

Cubitt, Tessa, 1944 –
    Latin American society.

    Bibliography: p.
    Includes index.
1. Latin America – Social conditions. 2. Economic
development – Social aspects – Latin America. I. Title.
HN110.5.C8   1988   306′.098   87-3871
ISBN 0-470-20862-7 (Wiley, USA only).

Set in Linotron 202 10/11pt Ehrhardt Roman

Produced by Longman Group (FE) Limited
Printed in Hong Kong

For David and Christian

Contents

List of figures and tables

Acknowledgements

I am especially indebted to Michael Redclift for all his encouragement in getting the project off the ground and the invaluable assistance he gave me over the text. For their helpful comments on the script, I would also like to thank Caroline Ramazanoglu, David Corkill, Sue Cunningham, and David Lehmann. I am particularly grateful to Sundra Winterbotham for her thoroughness in typing the manuscript and all the trouble to which she went to get it done on time. Special thanks are due to David, my husband, for all his support and help with sources and style. Finally I want to thank my students at Portsmouth Polytechnic, who for 15 years have made my Latin American Sociology class a stern testing ground of ideas and theories.

Tessa Cubitt
January 1987

We are grateful to the following for permission to reproduce copyright material:

Allan Publishers for table 1.4 (Colman & Nixon, 1978); CEPAL Review for tables 6.4 (ECLA 1985, adapted) and 6.5 (PREALC 24, adapted); Mary Glasgow Publications for tables 1.2 & 1.3 from *Geofile*, No. 1, Sept. 1982, (c) Mary Glasgow Publications Ltd, London 1982; Journal of Area Studies for fig. 3.1 (Cubitt D. & T., 1980); Latin American Research Review for table 7.2 (Portes 1985, adapted); Longman Group UK Ltd for fig. 1.1 from fig. 5.6 of *Economic Development in the Third World* (Todaro, 1981); Methuen & Co. for table 6.3 (Armstrong & McGee, 1985); Unidad Coordinadora de Politicas, Estudios y Estadisticas del Trabajo for table 4.1 (Jiménez, 1979).

Introduction

This book is intended to be introductory. As it covers the very broad topic of Latin American society, the aim is to acquaint the reader with some of the major issues and debates concerning Latin American society, offering references, which can be used to follow up points in more detail if desired. The chapters, therefore, relate to distinct social areas, but there are also clear themes linking the sections of the work and providing a general, overall picture. Although the principal perspective is sociological, the material and theory used are taken from a variety of social science disciplines and the volume is therefore intended as a starting point for any study of Latin America within the context of development. I am concerned to discuss Latin America, not in isolation, but very much in relation to the Third World in general and to relate its social organisation to general development problems.

The first two chapters discuss development in general, firstly the meaning and implications of the term and then evaluating the theories available for analysis. At the end of the first chapter, some general points are made about Latin America in relation to other less developed regions. Development is defined in terms of movement towards a complex of welfare goals and the extent to which Latin America is achieving these goals, such as a reduction in poverty, inequality and unemployment, and improved standards in education are referred to throughout the various chapters on the different sectors of society.

Chapters 3–8 turn specifically to the region, but not losing sight of broader implications. One of the themes of the volume is that despite very impressive economic growth rates in some areas, little progress has been made in the achievement of certain welfare goals, such as the reduction of poverty and underemployment and in one area in particular, inequality, the situation, if anything, has worsened. It is argued that the benefits of development, which are very real, are only enjoyed by a minority, who maintain a very high standard of living, while the gap between the wealthy and the poorest in society becomes wider.

Chapters 3 and 4 demonstrate an increasing integration of society, as ethnicity gives way to class, when peripheral groups become more closely involved in the national economy, and then as a universal value system becomes more widely accepted through the expansion of education and the spread of mass media. This does little to reduce inequalities and often only serves to heighten awareness of them. Chapter 5 also shows an increasing integration, this time of the peasantry into the national economic system, but again the benefits are often only felt by a few, the majority suffering from underemployment, which has become so characteristic of rural Latin America. Many migrate to the towns, only to find similar problems of underemployment, as most end up working in the informal sector (Chapter 6). For some, this presents opportunities; for the majority, although conditions are poor, poverty is not as great as in the rural areas.

Chapter 7 provides an overall picture of Latin American society, in terms of class structure, showing the general situation which has been brought about by the changes described in previous chapters. Combining class analysis and income distribution figures, reveals the way in which social inequality has become entrenched. The middle class have promoted economic growth, which has given them a style of life similar in some ways to that in industrialised countries, but have been reluctant to see any radical reordering of society. The role of the state towards development is discussed in Chapter 8, particular attention being paid to the growth of the authoritarian state, whose policies have exacerbated the growth-without-redistribution pattern.

Despite the continuation of some problems associated with underdevelopment, Latin America is very much a dynamic society and emphasis in this volume is placed on the positive action of different sectors of society. The high levels of production are themselves an indication of economic dynamism. The response of other sectors to problems has also been positive. The peasantry migrate long distances in search of work, they have responded to economic opportunity where this has presented itself and they have at times formed political movements. Many of the urban poor put up their own homes, because standard housing is not available and create economic activities from very little. Trade unions have brought about some advances for the working class. Recently this dynamism has manifested itself in the growth of social movements, which cover a very wide social area: urban movements; rural groups; gender-based associations; church groups, which although they have all so far been limited in their achievements, seem to be gaining in strength and scope.

Latin America is by no means static, but the changes taking place bring mixed results in terms of development goals. The conclusion discusses the development based on industrialisation models that so many Latin American countries have followed and its implications for other Third World countries.

1

Development

The year 1985 marked a high point in relations between the poor and the rich countries of the world. Why? Because consciousness of the horrors of starvation and poverty was aroused universally by the tireless efforts of an Irish pop singer. It was the music of the bands and the involvement of international stars that made people aware of the destitution that some fellow citizens of the world experienced.

For Sahel Africa, which includes some of the poorest countries in the world like Upper Volta and Chad, 1985 was as disastrous a year as 1984, both of which witnessed suffering and starvation on a massive scale due to drought and the resulting shortage of cereals. Since the poor harvest proved insufficient to satisfy basic nutritional requirements, attempts were made to bring emergency supplies of sorghum to the area, but these were often frustrated by bureaucracy, inefficiency and problems of transport. Aid workers commented on the futility of feeding the women and children who came to their clinics, some of whom had to be fed through tubes because they were too weak from malnutrition to feed themselves, since, once recovered, they would have to return to their villages where there was no millet and, therefore, to starvation. Both 1984 and 1985 were particularly bad years, but starvation is continually with the people of the Sahel.

At the same time, in the most industrialised parts of the world, there are increasing numbers of people who suffer from the opposite condition – an excess of food and drink. Obesity and an increasing incidence of disease connected with an over-indulgence of rich and fatty foods and alcohol, have led to a boom in the slimming business.

While one-half of the world's population is desperately short of calories, others are searching for the low-calorie version of foodstuffs and drinks. Supermarket shelves abound with slimming aids, and health farms attend to those for whom the problem has reached a more advanced stage. The affluence of the industrialised world and its resulting comfortable lifestyle have also led to a greater concern for fitness in general, so that jogging has become an accepted part of contemporary life in Europe and the USA.

Are these stark contrasts inevitable or is it possible to improve the living standards of the poor countries of the world and, if the latter is the case and the potential to reduce their problems exists, why has this not already happened? This book aims to examine these problems, in an attempt to understand how and why they have come about and what solutions are available. The book, therefore, concentrates on the notion of development which, although often used very differently by various writers, is usually seen as the means to improved living conditions. Development issues are discussed in general, though the book focuses on Latin America as the particular unit of study.

WHAT IS DEVELOPMENT?

'Development never will be, and never can be, defined to universal satisfaction. It refers, broadly speaking, to desirable social and economic progress, and people will always have different views about what is desirable.' (Brandt 1980: 48). This comment from the Brandt Report sums up the essence of the controversy in the notion of development. It must, by definition, mean progress, but this implies a value judgement, and what constitutes an improvement varies considerably according to views and ideology. Having defined development as 'a process of improvement with respect to a set of values', Colman and Nixon come to the conclusion that 'the rate or the relative level of a country's development are normative concepts whose definition and measurement depend upon the value judgements of the analysts involved'. (Colman and Nixon 1978: 2). Colman and Nixon also point out what is widely supported among social scientists today that 'value judgements are inescapable elements of factual study in the social sciences'. (Colman and Nixon 1978: 3). This problem, therefore, should by no means be a stumbling block to further analysis, but should serve to keep us alert to ideological frameworks within which judgements are made. Moreover, despite different viewpoints, there is often considerable agreement over the major goals of development. The objectives for development identified by Seers (in Baster 1972), for instance, would probably meet with widespread acceptance. These are: (1) family incomes should be sufficient to provide food, shelter, clothing and footwear at subsistence level; (2) jobs should be available to all family heads; (3) education and literacy rates should be raised; (4) the people should be given the opportunity to participate in government; (5) national independence is an important aim for each country. These objectives cover economic factors necessary for survival, cultural factors relating to the satisfaction of non-material needs, and political factors allowing for the greater involvement of people in the running of their own affairs.

Attempts have been made to escape from an ideological standpoint in defining this area. Norman Long, in his *Introduction to the sociology of rural development*, refers to the focus of his book in the following words, 'my basic subject matter is sociological work that deals with the processes by which rural populations of the Third World are drawn into the wider national and international economy and with the accompanying social transformation and local-level responses'. (Long 1977: 4). Here, attention is centred on processes and social changes of a particular nature, that is, the involving of people in the wider society, without any reference to whether or not this can be judged 'better' for them.

Social and economic progress refers to a very wide arena, the component parts of which may not all be progressing at the same rate. Can the changes that have been taking place in Brazil in the last few decades be called development? Transnationals, using advanced technology, operate in São Paulo producing cars for the wealthy, modern buildings tower above the cities and the luxury goods on sale are a testimony to an affluence that exists in some sectors of society. In the same country, however, live people who have some of the most simple forms of technology to be found in the world. The Amazonian Indians, many of them living in hunting-gathering bands, exist today in the same way that they have done for centuries. Since some of these tribes have had no contact at all with outsiders, their existence is only known to us through aerial pictures showing their dwellings in clearings in the jungle. Tribes such as the Nambikwara, live on fruit, honey, roots, spiders, grasshoppers, snakes and lizards, which the women collect, and game, if the men are successful with their hunting (Brain 1973). The implements needed for this subsistence economy are minimal. How does one, then, categorise a country harbouring such extremes in terms of development? Development for whom? is a critical question that arises. Whether or not it is possible to bring about improvements for all is highly debated but, for most people, the concept of development means better standards of living for at least the majority of people, if not the mass of society.

Implied in the term is an economic element and, indeed, many would argue that economic changes are necessary to bring about other desired aims. It is important, however, to distinguish at this early stage between economic growth, which usually refers to some quantifiable index like increase in per capita income, and economic development which involves some kind of structural and organisational transformation of society. Thus, development does not just mean a little more of everything, it also includes a rather deeper change in societal arrangements.

In order to examine further all these issues in the Third World, it is worth taking a fairly general definition, which does imply a value judgement, but bearing in mind the implications of this. Brookfield says that 'the popular trend is to define development in terms of progress toward a complex of welfare goals, such as reduction of poverty and unemployment, and diminution of inequality' (Brookfield 1975: xi). How far do the changes that have been taking place in the Third World bring the countries concerned closer to these goals?

The whole essence of progress is change and, in the case of the Third World, the main changes that have been taking place are linked to the growth of modern society, in most cases based on the development of capitalism, though in a very small number of countries, notably China, Cuba and North Vietnam, revolution has brought about a move to a socialist society. Therefore, for the vast majority of the Third World's population, it is the growth of modern capitalist society which brings about alterations in their lives. It is the contention of this book that these processes, which draw different social groups into national society, have brought about both improvements and major problems. This uneven development is a major characteristic of non-industrialised countries. In the case of Latin America, uneven development is reflected in an increasing polarisation of society. Improvements have been concentrated among the 'haves', while the problems for the poor, far from being alleviated, become more onerous. In attempting to understand this, it is first necessary to clarify the multiplicity of terminology that has been applied to the part of the world under discussion.

Interest in the Third World was first aroused in a meaningful way in the post-war period, when nations came together to discuss the future of world development. The non-industrial countries were then referred to as 'underdeveloped' in a famous UN report, which attempted to produce measures for economic development in the Third World, in 1951. Later, however, the term 'underdeveloped' came to be thought of as derogatory, as if it implied that lack of development was due to a weakness or failure within these countries. Emphasis shifted from 'underdeveloped' to 'developing', which has a more positive ring about it since it suggests that, although these countries may not be as economically advanced as the USA or Europe, this is not so much due to intrinsic inability as lagging progress, and the implication is that movement forwards is taking place.

'Developing' held sway for some time until what may now seem a rather obvious criticism gained considerable ground and that is that many of these countries are, clearly, not advancing, and they have been unable to produce sustained autonomous economic growth. The rather more subtle term of 'less developed' then appeared and has since become very widely used. Many development economists refer to LDCs when talking about this part of the world, since the term points out the disparity between the industrialised and non-industrialised world but, at the same time, tries to avoid value-loaded expressions. The terminology discussion has now gone full circle, because 'underdeveloped' has become the appropriate term for radical scholars, who view the problems of the Third World as a direct result of the development of the industrialised countries.

Recently an attempt has been made to escape all the problems of value judgements, relativity and the direction of processes, by using terminology that includes no reference at all to development. The Brandt Report chose to depict these areas in the geographical terms of North and South, pointing out that the vast majority of LDCs are in the southern hemisphere, while industrialised societies predominate in the North (Brandt 1980). Although this terminology is attractively neutral in value terms, it does entail other difficulties, notably that it is not precise. Australia and New Zealand are very definitely southern countries, but not normally considered within the rubric of 'less developed'. Since the term LDCs has achieved such common currency, that is the one used primarily in this book.

CENTRAL ISSUES – POVERTY AND RELATED PROBLEMS

The question that needs to be answered then, is, have the changes in the LDCs brought about progress towards the complex of welfare goals mentioned earlier? In order to answer this we have to decide which welfare goals are important and then if and how progress in these can be measured.

One of the most obvious welfare goals that would be widely accepted is to alleviate poverty. The Brandt Report estimated that there were 800 million 'absolute poor' in the world, suggesting that almost 40 per cent of the population of the LDCs are only just surviving (Brandt 1980: 50). Though there is poverty in the developed nations, it bears no comparison with the deprivation experienced in the LDCs. What absolute poverty means, is living life totally preoccupied with day-to-day survival. For the destitute, there is very little work available and what is, is extremely poorly paid. The major business of the day is finding sufficient food to keep a family alive.

Housing is usually constructed by the poor themselves out of any available materials, including rubbish and, since these dwellings are not standard housing, they are invariably not serviced by urban facilities, such as roads, electricity, water supplies and sewage systems. Life is short for all, not only do people die young, but families can expect to lose at least one child in infancy. Diseases that could be cured in developed countries prove fatal because medicines are just too expensive.

The problems of poverty are expressed in a number of ways. Hunger and starvation are, perhaps, the most acute expressions of extreme poverty. Susan George very graphically points out that, in the time it takes to read her book (about six hours), 'somewhere in the world 2,500 people will have died of starvation or of hunger-related illnesses' (George 1986: 19). In LDCs, 40,000 children suffer avoidable death daily (UNICEF 1981). Certain regions of the Third World experience these problems particularly forcefully. In the North East of Brazil, ten million people, the majority of whom were children under the age of five, died in the four-year period from 1980–84, of hunger and malnutrition (*Uno Mas Uno* 23 April 1984, quoting a document produced by *Asociación Brasileña de Reforma Agraria*). The problem is not one of a shortage of food, but of distribution, for the resources and the technical skills are available in the world today to feed the population of our planet (George 1986, Redclift 1984).

Thus, hunger persists because poor people can not afford to buy food or produce it, rather than because supplies are inadequate in any absolute sense. Although the wealthier nations do eat considerably more than the poor, this is only a part of the problem. According to Susan George:

> in recent years, the world has produced about 1,300 million tons of food and feed grains annually, and the DCs eat half although they account for only about a quarter of the world's population. Their animals eat fully a quarter of all the grain or . . . the equivalent of the total human consumption of China and India put together – some 1.3 billion people (George 1976: 24).

Part of the problem, therefore, is that grain that could be used to nourish hungry populations of the poor countries is being used to feed livestock which, in turn, will provide meat for the wealthy nations. There is not only an uneven pattern of global distribution of food, but this inequality is often reflected within nations. In the cities of Latin America, the wealthy can obtain luxury imported foods, while hunger reigns in the countryside.

Malnutrition has various long-term effects on a population. Children are often the most vulnerable. In Latin America, approximately

55 per cent of them suffer from malnutrition (*Uno Mas Uno* 23 April 1984, quoting statistics from the *Banco Interamericano de Desarollo* and the International Food Policy Research Institute). It is, perhaps, at its most crucial in the first few weeks of life, for babies who are malnourished in their first two months may feel the effects throughout their lives. Since one child in four in LDCs is seriously undernourished (UNICEF 1981), its influence on an adult population is extensive.

Malnutrition affects both mental and physical development. Experiments have shown that adults who were undernourished as babies have lower IQs than those who have had sufficient calories, often to the extent of not being able to hold productive jobs (George 1976). This mental underdevelopment is passed on to children and also hampers the way in which mothers care for their infants. There is, therefore, some physiological basis for the apathy so often associated with the poor, though the extent of this apathy can be and often is exaggerated.

Apart from hunger-related illnesses, so often given visual coverage by the media in the form of pathetic children with swollen stomachs, undernourishment leads to physical weakness and a greater vulnerability to disease in general. Illnesses which most children expect to get and recover from in industrialised societies often prove fatal among the very poor. In Guatemala, in 1965, the childhood death rate from measles was one thousand times the rate in the United States (Murdoch 1982). 'Malnutrition is probably the biggest single contributor to the high childhood mortality in underdeveloped countries.' (Murdoch 1982: 99.) These rates are exceptionally high. In the 1970s, the non-communist LDCs had an infant mortality rate of 140 per 1,000 births, as compared to twenty-seven in the rich countries (Murdoch 1982).

Since malnutrition is not due to inadequate supplies, this is a problem which, in theory, could be solved. However, hunger has always been present in the world and, as pointed out, is still widespread. Thus, an important aspect of development must be a better-fed population. Attempts to bring this about, in terms of the Green Revolution and food aid projects, will be examined in the chapter on rural society.

Apart from malnutrition, people in the LDCs suffer from poor health in many ways. The population of Chad can expect to live a shorter life than anywhere else in the world, with a life expectancy of forty-one years. The average person in Nepal, Somalia and Malawi is not much better off, with a life expectancy of forty-four, and in Zaire, Mozambique, Sierra Leone and the Ivory Coast the population can expect to live to forty-seven (World Development Report 1982). This is less startling when one realises that less than 5 per cent of the rural population in developing countries is within easy reach of medical care (UNICEF 1981).

As well as the lack of adequate food, poverty means an inability to acquire the other basics of life – clothing, shelter, access to health facilities and education, and sources of mental and spiritual sustenance. What makes poverty particularly glaring is the existence, so often, of wealthy groups within the same country. Gross inequality within nations is very much a characteristic of the underdeveloped world in general, though more pronounced in Latin America than elsewhere.

Absolute poverty is not just shown up by these contrasts, but is also closely related to this issue which is, in itself, another problem of underdevelopment, that of inequality. Todaro argues that 'the magnitude of absolute poverty results from a combination of low per capita incomes and highly unequal distributions of that income' (Todaro 1981: 131). There are, therefore, the two problems of the low level of the total earnings of a nation and the way these are distributed among its members. At first sight, it may seem that they could both be solved by increasing a society's Gross National Product, that is, the sum total of a nation's wealth. If this were the case, then attention could be focused on increasing productivity, assuming that the new wealth would 'trickle down' through society, enriching the population in general. However, there is now considerable evidence to show that increased productivity does not necessarily benefit the mass of the population and, therefore, it is not enough just to attempt to raise GNP and hope that a redistribution of income will follow, or even that the majority will experience some improvement. What is more important than the increase in production, is the character of economic growth. This refers to the way in which growth is achieved, which groups in society participate, which sectors are given priority and what institutional arrangements are emphasised.

Todaro offers some useful evidence for this. He has examined the relationship between economic growth, based on increased GNP and the distribution of income, in Third World countries. Taking thirteen developing countries, he plots on a graph their rates of growth of GNP on the horizontal axis and the growth rate of increase of the poorest 40 per cent of their population along the vertical axis. Each country's data, calculated for a period of about six to seven years, are plotted on the graph at a point which reflects the intersection of the two variables concerned. The countries above the 45° line have experienced an improved distribution of income, i.e. the incomes of the poorest 40 per cent grew more rapidly than the overall GNP rates, while countries below the 45° line are those where distribution has worsened.

What the diagram reveals is that there is no obvious relationship between GNP growth and the distribution of income. Countries are fairly evenly scattered above and below the line, showing that increased GNP does not, of necessity, lead to either an improvement or a deterioration of income distribution (see Fig. 1.1).

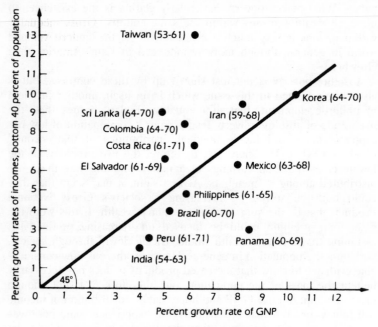

Fig. 1.1   A comparison of rates of GNP growth and income growth rates of the bottom 40 per cent in selected LDCs. (Todaro, 1981)

Another study, which was wider ranging, analysed the relationship between the shares of income accruing to the poorest 60 per cent of the population and the country's economic performance, in forty-three developing nations. The main conclusion that can be drawn from this is that the impact of economic development on income distribution has been, in general, to decrease both the absolute and the relative incomes of the poor. Todaro suggests that growth tends to lead to a 'trickle-up' process rather than the reverse (Todaro 1981).

There are some economists who, following the pioneering work of Professor Kuznets, suggest that in the early stages of economic growth, the gap between the rich and the poor becomes wider, but will narrow in later stages. Others develop this point by arguing that a widening of the distribution of income levels is not necessarily economically undesirable in the long run because it provides a basis for further economic growth. This view is supported by the argument that inequality is necessary to provide savings for investment of a sufficient magnitude to promote industrial growth. It is necessary to have some concentration of wealth available for capital investment.

Clayton argues that a preoccupation with the redistribution of income has distracted academics from the important issues of development. He suggests that this attitude is economically harmful and politically unacceptable, especially where smallholder agriculture predominates, as it does in much of Asia and Africa. Believing that in this sector, great disparities of income do not exist anyway, he argues that the differences that do exist can only serve to stimulate entrepreneurial activity. In a free market economy, the incentive of wealth is necessary to draw out the talents and abilities of the population. He concludes that 'Income redistribution within smallholder agriculture is therefore unnecessary, undesirable and unachievable' (Clayton 1983: 19).

Various counter-arguments can, however, be made to show that inequality is not only socially unjust but also economically undesirable. For a start, Third-World elites do not plough surplus wealth back into businesses at the rate that Europeans did during the early stages of their industrialisation. This potential capital is often spent on luxuries and imported goods. These facts should not be viewed in any unctuous way by the industrialised world, because our European forebears did not experience, as do LDCs, the temptation of consumer goods produced by more advanced societies, since Europe was leading the industrialisation process. Secondly, gross inequalities will affect both the supply of effective labour and demand for goods produced locally. If we take the figure suggested earlier, as the proportion of the Third World's population which is just surviving, 40 per cent of a country's population will be so poor that they will have no purchasing power and, therefore, make no contribution towards a market for locally produced goods. Clearly, this offers no stimulation to production, because the poor have no money for home-produced goods and the rich prefer imports. Finally, a lack of material welfare is not likely to encourage participation in the development process, only an apathetic acceptance of what life has to offer.

One explanation for inequitable growth that received wide coverage in the late 1970s, is Lipton's thesis of urban bias (Lipton 1977). Lipton argued that the persistence of rural poverty was the result of the concentration of political and economic resources in urban areas. Although subject to considerable general debate, the thesis has not been applied much in Latin America, where the considerable uneven development that does exist has been explained mostly in terms of dependency and internal colonialism.

POPULATION, UNEMPLOYMENT AND EDUCATION

Although, as already pointed out, poverty and hunger are due more to maldistribution than inadequacy in an absolute sense, the solution is often seen in terms of reducing population levels. If there were fewer of the poor, then feeding them would be an easier task. The population debate that has arisen over this focuses on the relationship between population and the problems of underdevelopment.

The populations of the Third World are increasing at growth rates which are unprecedented in history. Every year, between seventy-five and eighty million people are being added to the world population and about sixty-five million of these are born each year in Third-World countries (Todaro 1981). Of the world's population in 1981, about three-quarters lived in LDCs (UNICEF 1981). In these areas, the average rate of population growth is now about 2.1 per cent, whereas most of the industrialised countries have a growth rate of 0.6 per cent (Todaro 1981). The explanation for the high rate in LDCs lies in the reduced death rates, and in increasingly high birth rates. The improved medical knowledge and better health facilities which have resulted from contact with the economically developed world mean that people can expect to live longer than in the past but, at the same time, there has been no reduction in the rate at which children are born. This becomes especially apparent when looking at the age structure of LDCs. There, almost one-half of the total population are children under the age of fifteen, while the corresponding age group make up one-quarter of the population of industrialised societies.

But to what extent is rapid population growth a serious development problem? It is true that high birth rates are usually found in poor countries, but many economists would see this as a result of poverty rather than a cause. Historically, falling birth rates have tended to follow a rise in the standard of living of a poor society.

The main argument supporting the rapid population increase as a major problem view, is that fewer people would ease the pressure on resources and improve the quality of life for the population in general. However, a closer look at statistics for population and resources suggests that there is no clear correlation between population density and food supply. Famine exists in countries with small populations, such as Bolivia with five inhabitants per square kilometre, and also in densely populated countries, such as India with 172 inhabitants per square kilometre. On the other hand, some heavily populated countries, such as Holland with 326 inhabitants per square kilometre, do not know famine (George 1976). Indeed, the most densely populated continent is Europe with a population of sixty-six per square kilometre, closely followed by Asia with sixty-one. The continents of Africa and Central and South America, together come a long way behind, with sixteen and twelve, respectively (UNICEF 1981). Perhaps the best example of this point is China, a country which, when it had a population of 500 million frequently experienced famine but now, with a population of 800 million feeds each inhabitant over 2,300 calories a day (George 1976).

Many, in fact, argue that rapid population increase is not a major problem and to emphasise this takes attention away from the crucial issues. Susan George takes the argument a step further by asking why it is that the rich are so keen to promote population control and to see this as a way of solving development problems. She suggests that this is a deliberate attempt to encourage adaptation to existing structures rather than alleviating poverty and inequality through changing institutions and the organisation of society (George 1981).

In economic terms, it may be argued, too, that for some countries and regions, population growth is necessary for development, mainly because people provide a labour force which is an essential ingredient of economic growth.

What is often forgotten in this debate, is the view of the poor themselves, who are frequently seen as unable or unwilling to exercise any control over the situation but who, in reality, are often positively in favour of large families. A few extra hands can make a great difference to the output of the family unit, so the peasant, who has children to help him, can produce more for both the market and home consumption. Moreover, in countries where the state offers no provision or help for the old, parents must turn to their children for security, when they are unable to support themselves. The greater the number of adult children, the greater is the security in old age.

The main conclusion to emerge from this is that rapid population increase is not a major development problem, so that attention should first be focused elsewhere, but that it is clearly linked to problem areas and, therefore, can not be ignored.

Unemployment is always a very real problem in any society, but in underdeveloped countries its magnitude is emphasised by the lack of welfare systems. Where there is no social security to fall back on, unemployment causes very substantial hardship. In economic terms, this reflects a distinct under-utilisation of a factor of production. Labour power is something that LDCs have in abundance yet, if unemployment levels are high, it is clearly not being used to anything like its full capacity.

Although unemployment is considerable, it bears no comparison with underemployment which is very widespread. Underemployment refers to work which is not full-time and does not provide the worker with any real security or substantial income. He/she is not unemployed because he/she has some sort of job but not sufficient to support him/her fully. LDCs are full of people in this category, who may be street sellers, shoe-shine boys or, perhaps, the sons or daughters of farmers, whose plot of land is too small to support a peasant family. In some Latin American countries, underemployment has reached the 60–70 per cent level. Unemployment is clearly linked to the other problems mentioned for, with no work, poverty follows. 'There is a close relationship between high levels of unemployment and underemployment, widespread poverty and unequal distribution.' (Todaro 1981: 208).

One important question that emerges is why are there so many people without proper work, even in LDCs which have experienced economic growth? The 1950s and 1960s saw industrial development and the accumulation of capital in many LDCs and yet the modern sector failed to generate significant opportunities for labour. So, where economic growth has taken place, it has not automatically reduced poverty, nor has it increased employment significantly. The following chapter will offer explanations for this.

Education is important, not only because it leads to wealth, power and status in society, but also because it enhances the quality of life. Low levels of education and literacy are another characteristic of LDCs, with illiteracy rates being as high as 73.7 per cent in Africa, 73 per cent in the Arab states, 46.8 per cent in Asia and 23.6 per cent in Latin America, compared to levels of 1.0 per cent and 2.0 per cent in North America and Europe (Todaro 1981). This, again, has been viewed as both a cause and a result of underdevelopment. On the one hand, it is argued that the increased knowledge, skills and ability gained from improved educational systems would contribute to the development of the society and, on the other hand, where there is considerable poverty, education is often a luxury that cannot be afforded. The higher the level of education, the greater likelihood of it being fee-paying and, therefore, beyond the reach of the poor. Even when primary school is free, as it often is, there are other costs which may be incurred. Children may have to provide their own paper, pencils, books and other equipment, or to wear more formal and, therefore, more expensive clothing than usual. But, perhaps, most important of all, is the 'opportunity cost' of a child's labour which is high for the poor. By going to school the child may be forfeiting some earnings, albeit meagre, from cleaning shoes, selling chewing gum or even begging. Moreover, the expected benefits of education are lower for the poor than the rich. The advantage of the three Rs to the peasant, struggling to grow enough to feed his family, is minimal but, for the wealthy, it is the foundation of a career which will lead to wealth, power and status. This has led to suggestions that primary education in the Third World should be less academic and linked more to the real resource needs of the nation. If the content were oriented more towards agricultural problem-solving, or day-to-day household management, education may be seen to be more valuable than it is currently.

One of the major problems within education is that of illiteracy. This is an area, however, where some significant improvements have taken place usually because of massive national-level campaigns. One of the most spectacular was the Cuban one after the 1959 revolution. Prior to the revolution, the mass of the rural population had been illiterate, but in 1961, the year of education, the literacy campaign was launched. The previous year Castro had called on all Cubans, who had an education beyond the second year of secondary school, to volunteer to go into the most remote areas of the countryside to teach reading, writing, hygiene and nutrition. Five thousand people from different walks of life answered the call, with the result that over one million adults were taught to read (Huberman and Sweezy 1969). Following their slogan 'the people should teach the people', the Cubans rapidly improved literacy levels.

The difficulties of raising literacy levels are exacerbated by rapid population increases. Some countries have managed to reduce their illiteracy rates over the decades, but still find the absolute numbers of illiterates increasing. In LDCs, the percentage of adults (over fifteen) who are illiterate fell from 60 per cent in 1960, to 51 per cent in 1980. However, the absolute number of adult illiterates rose in that period by nearly 70 million to an estimated total of over 850 million (Todaro 1981).

Literacy is a basic skill which makes it possible to continue to higher levels of education. This raises the question of the balance between different levels of education in poor countries. Is it more desirable to give large numbers the benefit of primary education, or to spend a substantial proportion of the education budget on higher education for the benefit of a few? The former offers limited development for the masses while the latter creates an intellectual elite and the opportunity for an educated leadership. Most Third World countries, when faced with this issue, have made primary education the first priority (Goldthorpe 1975).

MEASURING DEVELOPMENT

This chapter has suggested that the various problems associated with underdevelopment are clearly interlinked, but it is difficult to identify distinct causal relationships. If improvements are to be made in these areas, we need to have some way of measuring progress, some indicators which can be used to show whether or not life is improving for the poor. Although, as we have seen, there is some debate over what are the major problems, the attempt to measure development is even harder. The difficulties are very similar to those encountered in attempts at defining development. There are differences of opinion over which are the important criteria and, then, many of the criteria are qualitative ones. How can one measure standard of living, health levels, participation in society and the quality of life in general? The only way to approach this is to measure them indirectly, but using indicators which can be directly quantified. Health, for instance, is often judged by using infant mortality or life-expectancy statistics. A wide variety of indices are used to compare living standards, since this is such a complex factor. Average national income per person is very commonly used and does provide some sort of universal yardstick, though, as we shall see, it does have its drawbacks. Many indices relate to housing facilities, such as access to piped water or electricity, others to aspects of diet or clothing. In Mexico, since many of the peasants go barefoot because they can not afford shoes, the proportion of the population wearing shoes is often used as an indicator. Indices referring to housing, clothing and diet vary according to country and region.

The difficulties can, therefore, be best summed up as follows:

1. No quantitative indicator can exactly measure a qualitative criterion.
2. Bearing in mind all the component parts of development, no one indicator can successfully sum these up and represent them.
3. It is difficult to bring together different sets of statistics, measuring qualitatively different factors, into a single index of development (Colman and Nixon 1978).

Despite these problems, as the 'concept of development only acquires substance through a process of measurement' (Colman and Nixon 1978: 6), it is important to examine the strengths and weaknesses of the various indicators that are used.

The desire to use one single index is understandable since it simplifies the process of measurement and comparison. When analysts have relied on only one, it has usually been economic since, as we have seen, an economic element is considered essential to any general progress. One indicator in particular has been widely accepted as an estimation of a country's level of development and that is national income or gross national product (GNP) per capita. Since GNP is calculated in every nation on the basis of the same set of rules, it has the advantage of offering information that can be compared across national boundaries. It is a statistic which measures the overall level of income or production of a society and, therefore, does identify a key activity, the provision of goods and services, an increase which reflects economic growth. These advantages make it particularly attractive to economists who see economic growth as the essential motor for development. On the other hand, the disadvantages reveal serious criticisms of relying too heavily on this one index. For a start, it takes no account of non-economic factors such as health, education, quality of life, etc. Secondly, the rules for measurement were devised in the industrialised societies and, therefore, make it difficult to measure income and production in poor countries where produce does not necessarily go through the market system nor is recorded on any official documents. Finally, while GNP provides a general picture at national level, it gives no indication of different income levels within countries and, therefore, may be quite inadequate in revealing poverty and inequality. Thus, for example, in the Philippines 1961–65, India 1954–63 and Peru 1961–71, GNP increased, but so did inequality, showing that GNP in this case is of no value in estimating changes in poverty levels or income distribution (see Fig. 1.1). Other countries, such as Nigeria in the 1970s and Brazil in the late 1960s and early 1970s, have experienced substantial economic growth and high rates of GNP but, at the same time, supported very poor and backward regions.

The latter problem can be tackled by using indicators of income distribution though comparison, in this case, becomes more complex. Income distribution tables are usually constructed by dividing a country's population into ten groups, according to their income level and then indicating what proportion of national income accrues to each group. Comparing the proportion going to the wealthiest 10 per cent with that earned by the poorest groups, will reveal the gap between the rich and the poor. Cross-nation comparisons of a country's wealth, showing what proportion the rich receive, also indicate different levels of inequality. Table 1.1 shows that the wealthy in poor countries receive a bigger share of the national 'cake' than they do in the richer countries.

Many economists and sociologists link development to an expanding industrial sector and would, therefore, use indices relating to the growth of this sector. The percentage of labour employed in urban occupations is sometimes used to show the move from an agriculturally based society to a more industrial one.

The most accurate, but also most complex, way of assessing levels of development or measuring changes is to use a group of indicators selected from a range of social areas. There have been various attempts to do this, mainly by international organisations who are concerned with aid or loans to LDCs. The number and range of the indices used reflect the aims of the exercise, namely, whether the assessment is being made for the purposes of financial assistance, improved trading relationships or welfare programmes.

Table 1.1 Income distribution

	Percentage of income received by lowest 20 per cent			Percentage of income received by highest 5 per cent		
	1960	1970	MRE	1960	1970	MRE
Industrialised countries	4.3	6.2	5.1	19.2	14.0	–
Developing countries by region						
Africa south of the Sahara	5.2	4.1	6.2	27.8	26.4	–
Middle East and North Africa	4.9	5.0	5.3	23.9	22.0	21.4
East Asia and Pacific	5.3	6.0	6.2	–	27.9	–
South Asia	4.5	7.0	–	24.6	24.3	–
Latin America and the Caribbean	3.7	3.4	2.9	30.5	29.2	23.7
Southern Europe	5.5	4.3	5.0	21.5	29.8	–

Source: Adapted from *World Tables 1980 Social Indicators.*
MRE most recent estimate

A good example of this is the way indicators are used to make distinctions within the Third World in order to identify the most needy countries, which have come to be called the 'Least Developed Countries'. In the late 1960s, the gap between the very poor countries in the world and those which, though in the Third World, were industrialising, was becoming more apparent and international organisations felt a need to identify those areas requiring urgent assistance. The UN Conference on Trade and Development (UNCTAD) in 1968, and the UN General Assembly in November 1971, picked out the countries with severe long-term constraints on development, by using three criteria:

1. Gross Domestic Product (GDP) per capita of $100 or less in 1970. (This figure has since been up-dated; it was $250 in 1976–78.)
2. Manufacturing making up 10 per cent or less of GDP.
3. A literacy rate of 20 per cent or less of the population aged fifteen years or more.

Originally, these indicators led to the inclusion of twenty-four countries in the least developed category but, by 1981, the number had risen to thirty-one with a total population of 275 million (see Table 1.2).

Table 1.2 The thirty-one least developed countries

Afghanistan	Lesotho
Bangladesh	Malawi
Benin	Maldives
Bhutan	Mali
Botswana	Nepal
Burundi	Niger
Cape Verde	Rwanda
Central African Republic	Somalia
Chad	Sudan
Comoros	Tanzania
Ethiopia	Uganda
Gambia	Upper Volta
Guinea	Western Samoa
Guinea-Bissau	Yemen Arab Republic (AR)
Haiti	Yemen People's Democratic
Laos	Republic (PDR)

Source: *Geofile* Sept. 1982 No. 1

The indices in this case are predominantly economic, but do include literacy rates as a non-economic indicator of quality of life. If other commonly used indices were added, these countries would still appear at a low level of development, suggesting that, although the original criteria are only three in number, they are crucial ones.

Because the World Bank makes loans to poor countries it, too, needs a working definition. In this case, they are referred to as 'low-income countries' and comprise a larger group than the UN's 'Least Developed Countries' because the criterion used here is GNP per head below $500 in 1979. 'Low-income countries', therefore, include, as well as the original thirty-one, those in Table 1.3.

Table 1.3 Countries considered by the World Bank (in addition to those in Table 1.2) as being low-income countries

Angola	Kenya	Sierra Leone
Burma	Liberia	Solomon Islands (Br)
Djibouti	Madagascar	Sri Lanka
Dominica	Mauretania	Togo
Egypt	Mayotte	Tonga
Equatorial Guinea	Mozambique	Vietnam
Ghana	Niue Island	Zaire
India	Pakistan	Zimbabwe
Indonesia	St Vincent	
Kampuchea	Senegal	

Source: *Geofile* Sept. 1982 No. 1

Taking the UN's thirty-one countries as the poorest in the world, what do they have in common? By definition, their earning capacity is very low. In 1979 the average GDP/CAP was $183, compared to $674 in the rest of the developing world and $8,217 in the market economy industrial countries (*Geofile* Sept. 1982 No. 1). By definition, too, the contribution of manufacturing to the society's economy is small and literacy rates are low. In addition, these countries all have a heavy dependence on foreign aid and, therefore, have increasing debt problems. In December 1981, the total of this debt was estimated at $5.4 billion (*Geofile* Sept. 1982 No. 1). For the inhabitants of these countries, life is short, for life expectancy rates are low and infant mortality high.

This would suggest five suitable criteria, the three used plus dependence on foreign aid and infant mortality rates or life expectancy. The only unusual one here is dependency which, although acknowledgd as being a feature of the LDCs, is not used as an indicator. Indeed, countries which would be categorised as more developed according to all the criteria suggested, are also those with greater debts. The debts of the least developed countries are minimal in comparison with those of countries like Brazil, which have embarked on considerable industrialisation programmes.

Other international organisations have resorted to a greater number of indicators in attempts to assess socio-economic development. The sixteen used by UNRISD, United Nations Research Institute for Social Development, would give a very comprehensive picture of the development of a nation. The more indicators that are used, the closer the analysis comes to a genuine understanding of the situation, but the more difficult it is to produce figures that can easily be compared either country with country, or one period in the development of a society with another.

Table 1.4 UNRISD list of core indicators of socio-economic development

Expectation of life at birth
Percent population in localities of 20,000 and over
Consumption of animal protein, per capita, per day
Combined primary and secondary school enrolment
Vocational enrolment ratio
Average number of persons per room
Newspaper circulation per 1,000 population
Percent economically active population in electricity, gas, water, etc.
Agricultural production per male agricultural worker
Percent adult male labour in agriculture
Electricity consumption, KWh per capita
Steel consumption, kg per capita
Energy consumption, kg of coal equivalent per capita
Percent GDP derived from manufacturing
Foreign trade per capita, in 1960 US dollars
Percent salaried and wage earners to total economically active population

Source: Colman, D., Nixon, F. (1978) *Economics of change in less developed countries* p. 13

One other method of assessing development is worth mentioning, though, in this case, the indicators are selected not in order to measure degrees of development, but to assess an absolute, that is the minimum level of income at which people can reasonably be said to conduct their lives. This is an attempt to identify the minimum consumption needs of families, so that any family whose consumption pattern falls below this can be said to be living in poverty. The indicators that contribute to a Poverty Datum Line (PDL) vary from country to country, according to regional requirements, but the definition used in 1974, in *The urban poverty datum line in Rhodesia*, has the essential elements of any definition. It is defined as 'The income required to satisfy the minimum necessary consumption needs of a family of given size and composition within a defined environment in a condition of basic physical health and social decency'. (Cubitt and Riddell 1974: 5).

The PDL focuses on the family rather than the individual as the unit of study, so that the final calculation relates to family size and ages of children. An important aspect of the definition is the inclusion of social decency along with physical health. The latter is, clearly, an essential element and relates to the food, housing and clothing considered necessary for the maintenance of physical efficiency. Social decency is more complex, but refers to socially defined necessities, at a minimum level, such as education, fuel and lighting, maintenance of personal hygiene and the replacement of household goods for cooking, washing and eating. The final Rhodesian PDL was made up of nine components – food, clothing, fuel and lighting, personal care and health, household goods, transport, education, accommodation, and provision for post-employment consumption (Cubitt and Riddell 1974). The last item is interesting for it rests on the argument that in LDCs, where there is no real state provision of pensions, families must save during their working lives to support themselves after retirement.

Once the items have been selected for the PDL, researchers then work out the cost of these for families of different sizes and the final figures can be used to assess how many and which families are living below a poverty line. It is, of course, a static concept for, in a sense, it is only truly valid at one moment in time, given changing costs, but it can provide a guideline for action, especially if it is updated. In practice, too, there are certain basic assumptions which have to be made for the PDL to hold validity:

> These are (i) that is is possible to estimate in monetary terms the basic needs of a family; (ii) that families of similar size and composition and in the same environment have exactly the same needs; (iii) that the money available to a family is spent in the most rational way and only on PDL items; (iv) that there are no economic obligations beyond the basic nuclear family (Cubitt 1979: 3).

These poverty studies owe their origin to the pioneering work of Booth in London (Booth 1889), but have been adapted in several African situations to assess poverty in the context of development. This approach makes provision for social needs and focuses on the family, unlike the economic indicators which operate at national level. Poverty studies demonstrate the human face of underdevelopment.

BROAD TRENDS

Considerable research has been carried out on identifying, assessing and measuring the problems of LDCs. The important point is how these are to be solved and here the answers are varied and numerous, stemming partly from the different interpretations of the problems themselves. The most important contribution in recent years is the Brandt Report because it did bring about international discussion at the highest level, though the practical results of this have been limited (Brandt 1980).

The Brandt Report is the result of the work of an independent Commission on International Development Issues under the chairmanship of Willy Brandt and made up of representatives from both the industrialised and the developing world. The report deals with the world's needs in the 1980s and offers some practical solutions. Its main emphasis is on the integration of the world, the fact that the countries of the North and the South have mutual interests. The poor countries of the world need to trade with the richer on improved terms and need aid from them to develop their own economies, but the industrialised countries will benefit from this because a wealthier South will mean more markets for their goods and more trading opportunities in general. The thrust of the document is to promote trade and aid between North and South arguing that in the long run this can only benefit the North as well as the South. Indeed, one of the points made is that without development, the problems of the poor countries of the world will become so critical as to be disruptive on an international level. Apart from the problems already discussed in this chapter, the report deals with disarmament, energy, transnational corporations, trade and international finance, making several specific recommendations.

Willy Brandt and his colleagues were concerned with long-term development and restructuring the world order, but they also realised that some immediate relief was necessary to solve the worst problems. In order to alleviate the scale of human suffering in the short term, and in order to ease increasing debt problems, massive resource transfers were thought to be necessary. The proposal was that the wealthier countries should increase their government aid to 0.7 per cent of GNP, preferably by 1985 (Brandt 1980).

On the surface, aid would seem to offer some solution, depending on the extent of 'generosity' of the donor nation. However, a closer look reveals that aid is more complex, involving various disadvantages. Aid, apart from that in the form of grants, involves the recipient nation in indebtedness. Borrowing is a basic way of acquiring capital and often promotes capital accumulation to the benefit of the borrower in the long term. But many LDCs have not achieved these successes through aid and so are now not only unable to pay off their debts, but also the interest on these loans. Aid is very rarely given without strings, either economic or political, being attached to it. From the donor's viewpoint, they offer some influence over the way money is spent but, for the LDC, this may well impose severe limitations. Economically, the loan package may require a change in economic policy not necessarily desired by the recipient nation. The IMF often insists on wage controls, which may cause considerable hardship, as a condition for a loan. The assistance may be directed towards certain projects or industries, not necessarily favoured by the Third World nation, but which will provide some economic advantage for nationals of the donor country. Even food aid is by no means disinterested and can be promoted to serve the interests of the developed world as well as the LDCs. Susan George quotes a 1966 USA report which states 'this food aid has improved the diets of forty million of the world's school children . . . *and built bigger cash markets* for American farm products . . . . Over the past twelve years these rising commercial sales have brought tangible returns to the American farmer and businessman' (George 1977: 199).

Political strings are of two kinds. There are those which relate to the nature of the political system of the recipient nation and, secondly, those which impose conditions about political support in an international arena. In the first case, donor nations do not give aid to countries with ideologies which they believe to be antipathetic to their own way of life. In 1985, the USA's aid to El Salvador, which was run by a dictatorship under the guise of democracy, was massive, while instead of helping neighbouring socialist Nicaragua, the USA gave aid to the country's guerrilla enemies. Political stability is often deemed an important condition, the argument being that stability is necessary for economic development to take place. There is, indeed, a case here for, without economic stability, aid may well be counterproductive. No bank or financial organisation lends money if it feels that the recipient's situation is unstable and, therefore, likely to jeopardise the project. The problem, however, is that some of the most stable regimes amongst the LDCs are those dominated by the military, since they can enforce law and order, and these often have the worst human-rights records. Some of the most brutal situations cited by Amnesty International, such as in Argentina and Chile in the late 1970s, and in Uganda in the 1970s, have occurred under the aegis of military governments. Political support in the international arena usually takes the form of following the lead of the donor country in UN debates.

In practice, both the industrialised and developing countries often have a preference for earned income over handouts. Trade, however, depends on the capacity of the countries concerned to produce appropriate commodities and is often subject to tariffs, quotas and taxes.

The nature and extent of development problems, the way they are examined and the solutions tried, vary between different countries, regions and continents of the Third World. Nevertheless, some general statements can be made about development.

Using single economic indicators, some broad trends can be identified. World Bank statistics show that in the period 1960–78, in terms of GNP per capita, the world in general experienced economic growth. The rate of growth of the lowest-income underdeveloped countries was 1.6 per cent, for the middle-income countries and the industrialised capitalist countries it was 3.7 per cent, and the socialist countries grew at 4.0 per cent per year per head (Griffin 1981). This, too, was a period of political independence for many small nations and so might appear to be a time of political and economic progress. However, following the arguments in this chapter, large catch-all statistics need to be questioned in terms of their component parts. Although these figures show that there was general economic growth, the economic gap between the rich and the poor countries was growing wider, both in absolute and relative terms. It is clear from the statistics that, although the economies of the poor countries are expanding, they are not doing so at the rate of the rich. Moreover, the low level at which the poor countries start, means that a percentage increase on that baseline will mean an absolute improvement that is much smaller than that brought about by the same percentage increase in an industrialised country with a much higher starting point. Equivalent percentage increases only increase the absolute gap between the two.

Singer and Ansari, writing in 1982, estimated that within the following thirty years the gap between the rich and poor countries might widen by between three and four times, with disastrous political and economic consequences. They suggest that 'the average Indian, Pakistani or African will in the year 2000 have a much lower standing of living *in comparison* to the standard of living enjoyed by the average British, American, or USSR citizen' (Singer and Ansari 1982: 141).

Not only has inequality increased within the world in general, but also the differences between Third World countries themselves have become greater. This means that the poorest countries, such as Bangladesh, Chad and Niger are, in real terms, worse off today than they were two decades ago (Griffin 1981). On the other hand, some Third World countries have experienced programmes of such rapid economic growth, that their levels of industrialisation are approaching those of some First World countries, with the result that they are referred to as newly industrialising countries.

This pattern is also reflected within individual countries, where the gap between rich and poor has been widening. Even in countries where incomes on average have risen, the standard of living of the poor has fallen. Keith Griffin has provided considerable evidence to demonstrate this point in Asia (Griffin 1981).

Apart from this situation being morally unacceptable, it clearly has implications for stability in the world. Brandt and Singer and Ansari, have predicted social unrest at an international level in the future (Brandt 1980, Singer and Ansari 1982), but there is considerable evidence of social conflict today which has arisen from these tensions. At national level, events such as the civil wars in Ethiopia and Afghanistan, the Muslim insurgency in the southern Philippines and the revolution in Nicaragua bear witness to this. Brazil, which has enjoyed high economic growth rates in recent years, but has since been through a recession, is experiencing a considerable upsurge in urban violence promoted by the increasing army of the hungry.

If conflict and inequality are on the increase, despite an increase in economic growth rates, what has gone wrong? The different welfare goals, which are considered to be the object of development, are interlinked, but there is no evidence to show that progress in one will automatically lead to progress in another area. So often the debate on development has focused on growth versus distribution; is it preferable to make the cake larger or to distribute what there is more equitably? Explanations for this uneven development are dealt with in the next chapter, which examines the various theories that have arisen to aid an understanding of the issues.

Finally, we need to look more closely at the position of Latin America within the Third World. To what extent does it share the same problems as Asia and Africa? In what ways are its problems unique?

A quick glance at some of the tables in this chapter reveals that Latin American countries barely feature at all amongst the poorest in the world. In the UN's thirty-one least developed countries, there is only one Latin American nation, that is Haiti, and there are none in the extra twenty-eight, considered by the World Bank as also being low-income countries (see Tables 1.2 and 1.3). Latin America, therefore, almost totally falls within a middle-income category. In fact, any discussion which refers to the wealthier Third World countries, apart from high-income oil exporters, usually refers to Brazil and Argentina. The two decades of prosperity in the 1960s and 1970s resulted from very substantial economic growth, for during these years average annual economic growth reached 5.5 per cent, compared to 4.2 per cent in the developed countries (Hurtado 1986). Latin America is more urbanised than other parts of the Third World. Some nations, such as Chile, Argentina and Venezuela, are highly urbanised, since the percentage of their inhabitants living in towns is in the eighties. In 1984, 69.2 per cent of Latin America's population was urban (Inter-American Development Bank 1985). It follows from this that fewer Latin American than other Third World populations work in the agricultural sector (see Table 1.5).

Table 1.5 Percentage of labour force in agriculture

	Percentage of labour force in agriculture		
	1960	1970	MRE
Developing countries by region			
Africa south of Sahara	84.6	80.6	77.6
Middle East and North Africa	57.6	49.1	42.6
East Asia and Pacific	63.5	53.1	50.5
South Asia	73.3	70.5	66.3
Latin America and the Caribbean	42.8	34.1	30.2

Source: Adapted from *World Tables 1980 Social Indicators*. MRE most recent estimate

Latin America, therefore, is richer, more urban and has fewer people employed in agriculture than other Third World regions, all factors which have been suggested by researchers as indicators of development. This might imply that Latin America is more developed than many African and Asian societies. However, other welfare goals have not been achieved and, in some areas, in particular equality, the situation has worsened. Table 1.1 shows that, as a region, Latin America and the Caribbean have a more unequal distribution of wealth than any other Third World region. Felix has shown that Latin American development is characterised by considerably greater income concentration than is the development of other LDCs and the industrialised countries (Felix 1983). Therefore, despite economic growth and overall *relative* wealth, the gap between rich and poor is great. Latin America also excels itself when it comes to problems of indebtedness. The major development issues that, therefore, occur in a discussion of Latin America are inequality, poverty and unemployment/underemployment. This book aims to show how increasing polarisation of society has come about and what attempts have been made by the different sectors of society to bring about development. It is clear that social changes are taking place in that continent and that these are linked to the growth of modern capitalist society. This process has meant urbanisation and industrial growth in some areas, but poverty and hunger in others. Development issues in this case are, therefore, clearly linked with industrial growth. Although the focus of the book is Latin America, two important points need to be made about how this relates to development issues in general.

Firstly, Latin America demonstrates the fallacy of the *simple* economic-growth-leads-to-development formula most clearly because it is the most industrialised area. This is not to deny the value of economic growth as one of a number of welfare goals. This point has been emphasised because, although many may believe the 'trickle-down' theory has been long buried, there is still a tendency to suggest that Latin America, because it includes some highly industrialised countries, will benefit overall from their levels of economic growth. Instead, polarisation has taken place not only within countries, but also between republics in the one continent. The discrepancies in development between Latin America's newly industrialising countries and the rest is reflected in the rate of growth of manufactures from the area, as a whole, from 3 per cent in 1960 to over 18 per cent in 1978, but with three countries in the region registering an equivalent rate from 5 to 30 per cent (Parkinson 1984).

Secondly, if low-income countries are to follow in the path of middle-income countries, suggested by many development models, then they can learn from the mistakes of others. 'Latin America must not be seen in isolation but as a microcosm of the developing world in all its diversities.' (Parkinson 1984: 133.)

The question, then, is how to achieve industrial growth without increasing inequality? Can development be seen in terms that are not so centred on unequal economic growth, for example, basic needs, social equality or ecological balance? In which case, what kind of economic development is necessary to enable these goals to be achieved?

FURTHER READING

Development in general

Brandt, W. (1980) *North:South a programme for survival.* Pan Books, London

Colman, D, Nixon F. (1978) *Economics of change in less developed countries.* Allan Publishers, Oxford

Foster-Carter, A. (1985) *The sociology of development.* Causeway Press, Ormskirk

George, S. (1976) *How the other half dies. The real reasons for world hunger.* Penguin, Middlesex

Singer, H., Ansari, J. (1982) *Rich and poor countries* 3rd edn. Allen and Unwin, London

Todaro, M. P. (1981) *Economic development in the Third World* 2nd edn. Longman, New York

World Bank world development reports and UN publications for recent statistics

Latin America
The best introduction to Latin America is through the publications
of the Latin America Bureau. Their special brief series presents
current information and recent developments for each Latin American
country, while other books focus on particular problems and issues.

Theories of development

Theory is often treated apprehensively by students as being some sort of unintelligible construct devised by academics to score points against each other. In reality, this fear is misplaced because theory is devised to organise, in a coherent form, some body of information and, in so doing, to offer an explanation. Good theory should make a set of apparently dissociated events intelligible to the observer, because it attempts to explain causes and interrelationships.

In order to understand the numerous problems and issues of the LDCs, a vast body of theory has emerged in the post-war period. This chapter summarises the main schools of thought and the way they have developed and offers a critical appraisal, paying particular attention to recent ideas. Although, in general, the theory discussed explains the relation between the Third World and the rest of the world, those points which are particularly relevant to the under-standing of the development of Latin America are emphasised. Variations in the theoretical frameworks applied to different regions relate particularly to features such as the levels of urbanisation and industrialisation.

It is understandable that social scientists, in their early attempts to explain the process of development and, correspondingly, the reasons for lack of development or uneven development, should look to the experience of the so-called developed world for ideas. In trying to understand change, it would seem useful to first analyse the historical data of countries that had gone through a period of change that resulted in societies, which have been conceptualised as industrial or capitalist. Thus early development theory leaned heavily on the European experience, for which there already existed a considerable body of social theory. Elements of nineteenth-century evolutionary theory, with various modifications, found their way into modernisation theory, while Marx's ideas were taken up later with the development of more radical theories.

THE MODERNISATION APPROACH

Since the main change taking place in the LDCs was the growth of modern industrial societies, social scientists in the 1950s assumed LDCs would follow a similar path of development to that of the industrialised world. Moreover, in the climate of the post-war period, there was a world emphasis on reconstruction and development, which was encouraged by the burgeoning international organisations. The LDCs appeared backward and those in Latin America were thought to have a traditional oligarchic system. The USA focused their hopes of social change on an emergent dynamic middle class, which would act as an agent of change. This view was shared by the orthodox communist parties who, following Marx, argued that the LDCs must go through the stage of bourgeois capitalism before they would be ready for the proletarian revolution. This general political and philosophical climate gave rise to the modernisation school of thought, which developed in the USA in the post-war period.

This approach relied heavily on the prolific work of Talcott Parsons, who saw the economic changes involved in capitalist growth as bringing about a modern society. He drew together elements of the work of Weber and Durkheim to produce an analysis of the development of modern society, which provided a springboard for the growth of modernisation theories of the Third World (Parsons 1949). Parsons, drawing on Weber, saw modernisation being characterised by an increasing rationalisation of life and, following Durkheim, thought that it also meant a decrease in mechanical solidarity. The implication for modernisation theorists was that industrialisation, because it involved a standardisation of economic structures and technology, would bring about a corresponding uniformity in social structures. Differences in societies and cultures across the world would fade as industrialisation brought about a shift to modern society. 'To what degree does industrialism create a common culture for all peoples?' (Kahl 1970: 3) was the sort of question posed.

Modernisation theorists, therefore, thinking that all societies progress along a path of development from a traditional state, constructed models of development based on the processes that had taken place in the industrialised world and then applied these to situations in the

LDCs (Rostow 1960, Kahl 1970). In this way, it was argued, a Third World country could be identified as being modern, traditional or at some in-between stage on this path of development. The theorists of the modernisation school were agreed on the general processes that made up development, though there were considerable variations in the models representing these changes.

With modernisation theory, there was an emphasis on values which, because of the approach's roots in structural functionalism, were seen to be interdependent with other aspects of society. Thus economic change would alter values but, more importantly, a change in values would mean a change in the economy. These ideas are well expressed in the work of Redfield who, although writing before Parsons, embodied some of the fundamental notions of modernisation theory (Redfield 1941). His emphasis on the diffusion of culture stressed that change could result from changing values emanating from culture contact. Redfield was concerned with the transition from folk to secular societies, a transition which in his analysis reflected the evolutionary process of Tonnies' *gemeinschaft/gesellschaft* and Durkheim's mechanical/organic solidarity. Redfield's study of four Mexican villages revealed a relationship between urban contact and disorganisation of the folk culture. The implication was that the more prolonged the contact of a folk culture with a more technologically advanced one, the more the values of the former changed and approximated those of the urban centre. Thus for Redfield, it was increasing contact with urban culture that brought about a diffusion of values and, so, change in the rural community.

The general argument was that the economic process of the growth of industry would produce particular arrangements in society, which are appropriate for running modern industry, in particular the growth and expansion of a middle class. European industrialisation had produced a middle class, whose interests were tied to industry and commerce, who had often experienced upward social mobility and whose values, therefore, were different from those of the traditional land-owning elite. They had successfully challenged the political hegemony of this elite and, having done so, brought about social reforms such as the 1832 Reform Act. Modernisation theorists felt that in the LDCs, too, the growth of capitalist industrialisation would bring about a modernising middle class which would, in its turn, bring economic development and democracy to the poorer and more peripheral parts of their countries. Modernisation, which was lacking in Latin America, could be spread from the industrialised world to the LDCs, through the transference of technology and consumer goods and through trade. The middle classes would import these and, with them, the values of achievement and entrepreneurship, along with other so-called modern values, and spread both these and the benefits of Western technology to the rest of society. In general, they expected a diffusion of social, political and cultural forms associated with industrial societies. One of the major aspects of this was the 'trickle-down' effect of wealth, mentioned in the previous chapter, which they thought would follow increasing affluence from economic growth.

Assuming this to be the path of development, modernisation theorists constructed models in an attempt to analyse the processes more closely. A model comprises generalisations of empirical processes and so, to produce this, the social scientist needed to abstract what were considered to be the stages of the development process. In order to isolate these stages, a version of Weber's Ideal Type was used (Weber 1947). The simplest model was the two-category one, with the Ideas Types being modern society and traditional society, but most social scientists went beyond this to a model comprising modern and traditional as polar types with a number of stages in between. Variations occurred in the nature of the criteria used to define traditional, modern and the stages. Some used Talcott Parsons' pattern variable approach (Parsons 1951), but selecting variables which they considered characteristic of modern society on the one hand and traditional on the other. Kahl, for example, identified six pattern variables which he felt were the critical criteria for modern and traditional polar types (Kahl 1970). These were activism/fatalism; perception of low stratification of life chances/perception of high stratification of life chances; low community stratification/high community stratification; occupational primacy/lack of occupational primacy; low integration with relatives/high integration with relatives; individualism/security in the community (Kahl 1970: 18–20).

Since Kahl's aim was to measure the extent of modernisation in a society, he used the variables as polar types in a set of scales, marking off degrees in between the poles. Then, large numbers of people were given scores according to their ratings in terms of the variables mentioned. In this way, Kahl tried to assess the degree of modernisation in a community. His research in Mexico and Brazil suggested that both these countries were near the modern end of the scale. In this work, he came to the conclusion that modernism correlates more highly with social status than anything else (including the rural-urban dichotomy). Since the extremes in social status, that is, the elite and the peasants, were deliberately excluded from Kahl's sample, this would suggest that, in line with modernisation theory in general, modernisation was associated with the middle class. It is worth noting that Kahl's variables made some use of Weber and Durkheim's earlier works. Durkheim's ideas are reflected in the strength of community ties associated with traditional society. Kahl's modern man was 'heir to Weber's protestant businessman, although in modern times he is just as likely to be a striving bureaucrat in a socialist enterprise, or a skilled worker in a large factory' (Kahl 1970: 117).

Others, in defining modern and traditional, turned to criteria based on historical data (Johnson 1958, Germani 1972). Germani's four-stage model relates only to Latin America, since the stages were based on the events of the continent's past. Germani identified four stages; firstly, traditional society which refers to the period of discovery, conquest and colonisation; secondly, the beginnings of the break-down of traditional society, during which time the American and French revolutions provided the stimulating ideology; thirdly, dual society and outward expansion which is influenced by the industrial revolution abroad and foreign ideologies; finally, the phase of mass social mobilisation from the 1930s to the present. In this way, Germani linked the stages of development to external factors. With this model, he suggested that there was a similar pattern of devel-opment for Latin American countries, but that each of them went through this at different rates so that, while Argentina was well into stage four, Bolivia might still be emerging from stage three (Germani 1972).

These models, however, are descriptive, and how useful is it to be able to say that one country has so many degrees of modernism and another is modern to such-and-such an extent? The value of any theory of development must lie in its ability to explain problems and uneven development and, therefore, to point a finger in the direction of solutions.

Modernisation theory defined development in terms of the econ-omic and cultural characteristics of the USA and Europe and explained Latin America's lack of these characteristics in terms of obstacles to change. The reason why the LDCs had not progressed further along the path of development was the existence of obstacles, and development policies should, therefore, be oriented towards identifying and removing these obstacles. In Latin America, one of the major obstacles was the *hacienda* which was viewed as a feudal institution blocking the spread of modern capitalism from the town to the countryside. It was this thinking that influenced many of the agrarian reform programs, as will be seen in Chapter 5.

One of the many difficulties with this notion of a smooth unilinear path of change, is the existence at the same time of both modern and traditional institutions in the one society. This uneven development was explained by modernists in terms of dualism.

Dualism was an attempt to combine, in one system, theory appro-priate for both an advanced society and a traditional one (Brookfield 1975, Bourricaud 1967, Lambert 1967). The argument is as follows: in many countries in Africa, Asia and Latin America, two socio-economic systems operate within one nation's borders. The modern, based on a Western lifestyle, is materialist, rational and individualist and rooted in a capitalist economy. A middle class, who cultivate a Western lifestyle and culture, have emerged, industry is developing and employment is based on qualifications. The traditional is pre-capitalist and characterised by fatalistic attitudes and a labour-intensive and overwhelmingly agricultural economy. Social structure is rigid, allowing for no mobility, and traditional methods of agriculture are used. With continual change, the former dynamic sector moves further away from its traditional, static counterpart. Dualism is a term that has frequently been used to explain apparent contradictions in society and to describe this co-existence of modern and traditional in LDCs of different continents.

In the 1950s and early 1960s, modernisation theory was important, not only because it was the guiding light of research in the social sciences, but also because of its practical implications and, in some places, it still acts as a methodological reference point for development projects. It has had considerable influence on international aid, as exemplified by the stance taken in the Brandt Report in encouraging aid for industrialisation (Brandt 1980).

In the case of Latin America, the first important contribution to the social sciences was made by ECLA (Economic Commission to Latin America). As well as forging ahead in terms of theoretical developments, they used these significant advances to make policy proposals. The ECLA analysts, like modernisation theory in general, stressed the importance of industrialisation for development in the LDCs, but they argued that the existing pattern of the world economy was not beneficial to the non-industrialised countries. This was because most LDCs relied heavily on exporting natural resources to the USA and Europe and then importing manufactured goods from those countries. Since the economy of LDCs was based on agricultural produce and extractive industries for export and they could import the necessary consumer goods, this inhibited the development of manufacturing industry within the LDC itself. What was important for the LDCs was to achieve autonomous self-sustained economic growth but this was being hindered by the existing pattern of trade which benefited the industrialised world more than the LDCs, since the former could develop their own industries on the basis of cheap imported resources. (This is an argument that will be developed later in the chapter.) As the industrialised world benefited, these countries were likely to impose external obstacles on countries attempting an independent path of industrialisation. ECLA, therefore, not only suggested that the state should intervene in the economy, but also proposed specific economic policies to put their theories into practice. These policies of protectionism, exchange controls, attracting foreign investment to home industries, encouraging national investment and raising wages in order to provide an effective demand, were all aimed at stimulating the production of goods locally to replace imports, that is, import substitution or IS. As well as attaching importance to external obstacles to development, ECLA writers advocated the removal of internal obstacles as being necessary to promote industrialisation. One of the main obstacles for the ECLA team was the continent's pattern of land ownership.

It is worth pointing out that the Marxist writers of the time also stressed the removal of obstacles as being essential for development, but for different reasons.

By the early 1960s, a mood of pessimism had set in among development social scientists of all schools of thought, because of the 'developmentalism crisis', as the economic problems of the period were called. Palma has since pointed out that the error made by everyone at the time was to ignore the cyclical nature of capitalism (Palma 1981).

In both economic and political terms, the 1960s failed to fulfil the predictions of the modernisation theorists and, therefore, critics began to cast doubt on the value of their theories. Despite the implementation of policies based on modernisation theory, such as the initiation of agrarian reform in order to remove the obstacle of the feudal-like estate, the economic situation was disappointing, since self-sustained autonomous development had failed to take place. Politically, a power vacuum had developed because the traditional oligarchy had declined, but the new industrial bourgeoisie, partly because of the stagnation of the economy, was too small and weak to become a dominant political force. They were also hindered in this because they were reluctant to enlist the support of the working class for fear that this might lead to too much social mobility.

To add fuel to this crisis in capitalist development, a major event had taken place in 1959 which had considerable repercussions throughout Latin America and influenced the thinking of scholars and politicians during the 1960s. The Cuban revolution made Latin Americans aware of an alternative form of development. It revitalised Marxist thinking in the area which had, until then, in general followed a Moscow line and had not been oriented towards the specific situation of the LDCs.

By the 1970s, it was very clear that the expectations of the modernists had not been fulfilled. Although there had been some economic growth, the 'trickle-down' effect had clearly not taken place. No real diffusion of consumer goods from urban centres to rural areas had occurred. Far from a redistribution of income taking place, the opposite had happened and the gap between the wealthy and the poor had widened (Graciarena, Franco 1978). Moreover, in many Latin American countries by this time, the political vacuum had been filled by the authoritarian state in the form of military regimes which were a far cry from the liberal democracies that the modernisation theorists had expected industrialisation to produce.

These economic and political events of the 1960s had a profound effect in shaping the ideas of academics and in shifting the emphasis away from modernisation and towards the dependency school. The new radical theorists were quick to point to the weaknesses in the theory itself, as well as its failure to aptly portray the empirical reality. Modernisation theory does tend to be descriptive, a weakness admitted by some modernists themselves (Germani 1972) in that much of the so-called theory refers to describing modern and traditional and stages in between. What it never really explains is the mechanism of social change, it is forced to accept economic change without explaining it sociologically. Even the explanation of developmental problems in terms of obstacles is not very useful. Everyone would probably agree that the feudal estate is an obstacle to change, but the point is, why? By just seeing it as an obstacle, we are brought no nearer to understanding the process of change, nor to what constitutes development.

But perhaps the major criticism to arise was the failure of modernisation theory to take into account fully enough the global situation. The obstacles to change were identified as primarily internal, the industrialised world was seen as a promoter of industrial development. It is this last point that the dependency school focused on in particular, for they felt the reverse to be the case. According to them, it was precisely involvement in world trading and economic relationships with the USA and Europe that had brought about underdevelopment in the LDCs. Many Latin American academics were critical of the use of Western models of development for LDCs. Why should these countries not develop their own path, rather than just following in the footsteps of the USA and Europe? The North American model of development is not necessarily the 'best' for the LDCs (see Frank 1969 for useful criticisms of modernisation theory).

DEPENDENCY

The Cuban revolution not only instigated a profound structural transformation of society, it also severed the country's ties of economic dependency with the USA. Previously, Cuba's economy had been almost totally based on sugar and, for this, both the market and the technology were supplied by the USA, thus tying Cuba's fortunes to the wishes of her northern neighbour. Many LDCs still have economies which are based on the export of raw materials and the import of manufactured goods, which makes them dependent and, therefore, vulnerable in various ways. For a start, natural resources, in the form of agricultural produce, are unreliable because forces outside man's control, such as drought, floods, blight, etc., can destroy the basis of the economy. This is unlike an economy based on manufacturing, where man is in control of the complete process. Moreover, in most LDCs, only a small number of products are produced, so that a poor harvest in one will severely affect the economy as a whole. But most important, the LDCs are dependent on the advanced nations to provide the skills and technology to develop the produce and to buy the goods. If these markets do not materialise, then the LDC will have no income with which to buy manufactured goods which are so necessary because they are not produced at home. It might seem as if both advanced nations and LDCs are dependent in this trading relationship, but a closer look shows that the advanced nations have a much more strategic position. The exports of the LDCs, for the most part, are not essential or can be bought from another country. If Ecuador were to withold her bananas, or Ghana her cocoa, Europe and the USA would buy elsewhere or could do without. The technology and manufactured goods, however, provided by the advanced nations are essential to the LDCs and leave them in a weak bargaining position. It was the difficulties of this dependent position and the way in which Cuba attempted to throw off the yoke of a dominant power that led radical thinkers to focus on global interactions, an approach which gave rise to the dependency school.

Taking its lead from theories of imperialism, dependency dominated development thinking during the late 1960s and 1970s. The vast majority of LDCs had experienced imperialist control, leaving a legacy of economic imperialism, though in the case of Latin America, political control had been cast off two centuries before. Taking into account the historical experience of the LDCs would suggest an analysis of theories of imperialism was required. The main theory of imperialism which emphasises economic aspects of development is the Marxist theory.

Apart from some comments on India, Marx himself wrote little about imperialism, which was not surprising since he was writing mostly before the late nineteenth century imperialist expansion. His basic ideas on capitalism were developed by Lenin who articulated a theory of imperialism that forms the starting point for later Marxist ideas (Lenin 1970). Lenin's view is that imperialism is a new stage in capitalism, in fact he defined it as 'the monopoly stage of capitalism'. (Lenin 1970: 736). From his treatise on this highest stage of capitalism, the following arguments emerge, which have formed the basis for so many later writers on imperialism. The capitalist economy in its advanced stage involves a concentration of capital and production, which is the result of increasing capital accumulation, advanced technology, economies of scale and the growth of big business. This concentration results in a monopolist market replacing the competitive one. (These are all points made by Marx.) The final stage is reached when the monopolies grow so vast that they look beyond national boundaries for expansion. This growth takes place in three major areas: to expand there must be a constant supply of raw materials, so there is a search for sources of resources; as finished products must be sold, the companies have to find new markets; and as capitalism generates a surplus, new outlets for investment have to be found. This expansion must take place to ensure the continuity of capitalist advance and accumulation, but the only areas available for it are those of the Third World, where the raw materials are to be found. In many cases expansion to new territories must be preceded by political domination in order to reshape local institutions so that they can accommodate production for profit and the economic forces of international pricing, marketing and financial systems. At the core of this economic expansion is the super profit gained by the industrialised countries.

According to Marxist theory, then, the motor force of imperialism is economic. But, for both Marx and Lenin, the main concern was for industrialised society, their interest in the nations in the periphery of the globe was in terms of their relationship to the central powers. It was not until the 1950s that social scientists began to use this theoretical approach with a focus on the LDCs rather than the industrialised nations.

Paul Baran, referred to by Palma as the 'father' of the dependency approach (Palma 1981: 401), develops Lenin's argument further, showing how economic imperialism has an inimical effect on the economies of the LDCs, primarily because the economic surplus of these countries is being expropriated by the centre. This point has been developed by Frank in his well-known thesis that the underdevelopment of the LDCs is a result of their integration in the world capitalist system and, therefore, the solution would be socialist revolution (Frank 1967). He argues that Latin America has been capitalist since the conquest, because its involvement in the world economy since the colonial period through the export economy has transformed it into a capitalist society itself, a point which has since been much criticised. He goes on to suggest that this integration in the world economy creates a metropolis-satellite chain stretching from the industrial nations through the towns of LDCs and, finally, reaching the rural areas. The point about this chain of integration is that at each point the surplus generated is, successively, creamed off towards the centre. It is through these metropolis-satellite links that the centre develops at the expense of the periphery, suggesting that the development of capitalism at the centre requires underdevelopment in the periphery. Frank's work in the 1960s was a major contribution to development theory in that he drew attention to the exploitative forces in operation, which generated considerable research by other social scientists. His weakness lies in the over-simplification of his views, perhaps because he was trying to cover large quantities of material across time and space.

One of the major criticisms of Frank's work is that his insistence on Latin America being capitalist since the colonial period is not well founded, a point that is well articulated by Laclau (Laclau 1971). He argues that the basis of Frank's view that Latin America has always been capitalist lies in the continent's integration into a world capitalist market system. But for Marx, definitions of capitalism, feudalism, etc. were not in terms of the market, but in terms of the mode of production. It is the latter which determines the capitalist or feudal nature of the economy. In Latin America's case, there have always been non-capitalist modes of production, which have played a significant part in the economy of the region.

The peasant mode of production has been a characteristic feature of rural areas, especially in Central America and in the Andean countryside. The plantations in Brazil and parts of Venezuela grew up using a slave mode of production. Thus, using a strict Marxist definition of capitalism, the view that Latin America has always been capitalist, does not carry much conviction. But Laclau points out that this does not necessarily contradict the major thrust of Frank's argument, that development of the centre has led to underdevelopment in the periphery. Laclau strongly supports this point, saying that it is not just the development of capitalism that creates underdevelopment, but a more complex process in which capitalism interacts in a dominating way with indigenous modes of production.

The inspiration provided by Frank's writing led to a proliferation of dependency theses and, like most schools of thought, there are considerable variations between them, but Frank's main theme of underdevelopment resulting from the development of the advanced nations, is adhered to by all.

Dependency theory was taken up with enthusiasm and developed by Latin American academics, who welcomed theories that were focused on the LDCs rather than taking the USA or Europe as their model for development. Many of them pointed out that although the dependency situation was important, this analysis must be linked with one of the internal social structure. It was not sufficient to blame Latin America's problems solely on external forces, for these factors must be examined in terms of their relationships with internal factors (Dos Santos 1973, Quijano 1971, Cardoso, Faletto 1979). Dos

Santos argues that dependence is a conditioning context for certain kinds of internal structure. It is not determinist, in that it defines internal structures, as Frank suggests, but it creates a general condition, in which a society operates. It, therefore, does alter the internal functioning and articulation of the elements of the dependent formation, but will create different types of relations of dependency in different societies. These relationships may be colonial, industrial-financial or, more recently, industrial-technological, and will generate different internal structures. While Frank emphasised similarities in the effects of dependence throughout Latin America, Dos Santos stresses discontinuities and differences (Palma 1981).

In dismissing a mechanical determinist approach, Dos Santos allows for a more dynamic role for Latin American classes, for he says it is the internal relationship between classes which makes possible the form that dependency takes. He makes the important point that economic imperialism is only possible where it finds support among those local groups who profit by it. It can only occur where there is a coincidence between dominant local and foreign interests. Local elites compromise and dependency is structurally linked to the internal situation (Dos Santos 1973). This compromise has occurred where Latin Americans have worked as managers for foreign-run plantations or businesses, or where they have themselves invested in foreign enterprises. Clearly, their fortunes were then linked to overseas interests.

Dos Santos is primarily concerned with the dominant social classs and their relationships with external forces but, as Frank has suggested with the metropolis-satellite model, the influence of dependence stretches to the poorest and most peripheral groups in society. This theme has been developed to apply dependency theory to rural areas through the concept of internal colonialism (Stavenhagen 1970). Internal colonialists take, as their starting point, the position of the dualists for, while accepting that on the surface many LDCs appear to have two distinct systems, they argue that this merely reflects gross differences in society. These differences are not due to the social distance between the modern and traditional, but precisely the opposite, that is, the integration of these sectors of society into one system in a manner in which the rural traditional sector is exploited. Backwardness is, therefore, not due to lagging development, or being left behind by the modern sector, but exists because of the relationship with the modern sector. Urban areas advance at the expense of the rural, a process that replicates the underdevelopment of LDCs that has taken place as a result of the development of the advanced nations. The term internal colonialism implies that colonial relationships, similar to those between nations, exist within individual countries (Stavenhagen 1970).

The work of Dos Santos, Quijano and others on the one hand, and that of the internal colonialists on the other, link the dependency relationship with internal social structure. The influence of dependence can be traced through to different sectors of society. One of the weaknesses of the dependency approach is that, while this is done admirably in theory, these academics have not produced much in the way of empirical studies on this theme. With a few notable exceptions, such as Quijano on Peru (Quijano 1971) and Petras and La Porte on rural Latin America (Petras, La Porte 1971), very little good material has been collected using this as a framework for research. Despite the importance attached to internal factors by Dos Santos and others, the approach is not so easy to operate at the level of field work.

As we have seen, one of the premises of dependency theory is the international division of labour in which LDCs supply raw materials for the industries of Europe and the USA, who produce consumer goods that are then imported by the LDCs. In recent years, this situation has altered, which has led to some new lines of thought among the dependency school.

The classical dependency situation in the form of the enclave economy is one where natural resources are developed by foreign technology for export, thus providing no benefit to the LDC. Profits go abroad and, because of the use of technology, there is little influence on employment structure, therefore not even providing the benefit of jobs. The effects are harmful in that the economic surplus of the nation is being lost, without the nation developing its own autonomous and self-sustaining economic growth.

This situation has changed due to the greater involvement of foreign capital with the LDC itself. Essentially, there are three main processes in these new forms of dependency (Cardoso 1972). Firstly, there is a shift in investment from traditional sectors to industrial areas, in particular in technologically and organisationally advanced sectors. This is only a shift, not a complete transfer, but foreign investment in primary resources has been on the decline, while it has been increasing in dynamic and expanding industries. Secondly, there has been a move to multinational corporations, which have been replacing North American businesses. Since multinational companies involve three different types of capital – local state capital, private national capital, and monopoly international capital, which is under foreign control, the LDC, both on a private and a state level, becomes involved with foreign capital in a joint venture. Finally, there is a general process of increased local participation. Managers of branches of multinationals are selected more from the host society, local industries become more closely linked through the provision of supplies, the purchase of finished products and the use of foreign technology and local markets are cultivated more for the end products of the multinationals.

The result of this is that the most modern and dynamic sector of the LDC's economy becomes integrated with the international capitalist system, thus benefiting all involved. But this is only a small minority of the society, the remainder, the backward social and economic sectors, become subordinated to the advanced one.

In summary, then, processes of differentiation and integration are taking place. Differentiation is taking place in the pattern of invest-ment since it is going into a wider variety of both foreign and indigenous industries, in the forms of capital and in foreign owner-ship since there is less North American investment than previously and more European and Japanese. On the other hand, integration is taking place through the increasing identification of some sectors of the LDCs with foreign interests. This leads to an increasing polar-isation of society.

The explanation of the dependency school for problems and uneven development is, clearly, very different from that of the modernisation theorists and expressed in the use of the term under-development. For them, underdevelopment is the direct result of involvement in the world capitalist system, trade with the advanced nations does not bring autonomous industrialisation and devel-opment, as the modernisation theorists suggested, but instead it hinders this process. This is for several reasons. Firstly, as the invest-ment necessary for economic growth has an external source, the surplus from economic activity goes abroad, thus depriving the local community of an opportunity to build up its own savings and capital. Imported technology limits employment opportunities, so inhibiting the well-being of a large sector of society; the existence of multinationals in agribusiness is having the same effect on rural social structure and depriving the peasant of a livelihood, often by taking over his land. This leads to rural-urban migration on a massive scale which only serves to exacerbate the urban problem of unemployment. The exist-ence of foreign enterprises hinders the growth of a local bourgeoisie, because it makes it difficult for local industries to accumulate capital. Entrepreneurial activity is stifled since local businessmen can not compete with the capital, the technology and the economies of scale of the multinationals. Local industrialisation and the middle class associated with this, who modernisation theorists predicted would be the primary agent of change, do not get a chance to develop if they cannot expand investment. Finally, the general process described leads to a polarisation of society, in which a small minority, linked to foreign interests, prosper at the expense of the vast majority, who are unable to find work, while profits flow abroad. (For an excellent dependency analysis of the historical development of Latin America see Stein, Stein 1970.)

Modernisation theorists explained these contrasts between rich and poor, urban and rural in terms of dualism and lagging development, the backward sectors lagging behind the advanced. The dependency school explains uneven development in terms of the subordination of the backward sectors to the advance of the dominant ones. The latter can only develop by accumulating capital, which means extracting the surplus from the dependent countries. The 'trickle-down' effect from the latter's wealth has not taken place because of the combination of dependence and class structure.

CRITICISMS OF DEPENDENCY, AS A THEORY

Dependency has been criticised from different perspectives. Some economists, who have inherited many of the principles of the modernisation school, disagree with it because they argue that LDCs have benefited from contact with the industrialised world.

> Far from the West having caused the poverty of the Third World, contact with the West has been the principal agent of material progress there. The materially more advanced societies and regions of the Third World are those with which the West established the most numerous, diversified and extensive contacts .... The level of material achievement usually diminishes as one moves away from the foci of Western impact. The poorest and most backward people have few or no external contacts; witness the aborigines, pygmies and desert peoples. (Bauer 1981: 70)

Equality as a goal has been attacked as being discouraging to initiative and dynamism. Skewed income distribution in a free society is seen as a method of rewarding merit and productivity and thus the mechanism for drawing out the talents and abilities that exist and harnessing them to the needs of society. Inequality is therefore necessary if progress is to be made (Bauer 1981, Clayton 1983).

Many contemporary criticisms, however, move on from a dependency position, rather than totally discarding these ideas. The basic point dependency makes about industrialised countries developing on the basis of capital accumulation from the surplus derived from LDCs, provides a starting point for understanding the process of development. Nevertheless these critics point to crucial weaknesses which flaw the logic of the argument. There is a tautology built into the thinking from the very beginning. Development is defined as self-sustaining or autonomous industrial growth and yet development requires underdevelopment, as countries need to extract the surplus from others in order to develop. 'Dependent countries are those which lack the capacity for autonomous growth and they lack this because their structures are dependent ones.' (O'Brien 1975: 24.) This circular argument leads to research which provides the historical evidence to prove the obvious (see O'Brien 1975, Booth 1985 for a useful discussion of this argument).

Aspects of the theory do not always stand up to the test of evidence. The implication that the stronger the ties between advanced and non-advanced regions, the greater the underdevelopment of the latter, is not easily empirically sustained. Indeed, the areas that now have the closest links through transnationals, such as São Paulo and Mexico City, represent the most advanced sectors of the economy.

Another problem is that the connection between dependency and the socio-economic problems of the periphery has never been adequately demonstrated. Attention has been focused on the dominant classes and their relationship with international capital, the inference being that the poor are exploited by this situation, but the mechanics of this situation are rarely identified. There is some evidence to show that foreign investment encourages capital-intensive industrialisation, which leads to high levels of unemployment/underemployment. Industrialisation attracts labour from the countryside, despite the lack of real opportunities, thus aggravating the pressure on urban facilities. Agribusiness, too, encourages labour mobility, usually in the form of semi-proletarianising the peasantry. But little attempt has been made at in-depth analysis of the relationship between social class, apart from the bourgeoisie, and dependence. A notable exception here is Hamilton, whose analysis includes the working class, not just as the passive receivers of history but as an active force in proceedings (Hamilton 1982). Are these problems solely the result of a dependent situation or are they the outcome of the growth of industrialisation and its resulting concentration of capital and machinery?

Following on this point, Lall argues that for dependency to be a theory of underdevelopment, it should specify particular features of dependent economies which are not characteristic of non-dependent economies and that these characteristics should be shown to affect adversely the development of the dependent economies. But no such factors can be clearly identified, most dependency theorists refer to characteristics, which Lall sees as being aspects of modern capitalism in the Third World. She goes on to demonstrate that it is impossible to show a causal relationship between underdevelopment and the characteristics associated with dependent economies (Lall 1975), a finding which is supported by empirical data (Palma 1973).

Booth argues that the explanation for these limitations in theory lies in the determinist nature of much of its thinking. 'Behind the distinctive preoccupations, blind spots and contradictions of the new development sociology there lies a metatheoretical commitment to demonstrating that the structures and processes that we find in the less-developed world are not only explicable but necessary under capitalism.' (Booth 1985: 776.)

Warren has developed one of the most comprehensive critiques, based on the view that dependency is no longer a relevant concept because uneven development in LDCs today is not attributable to imperialism, but to capitalism, which has always had a contradictory and exploitative element (Warren 1973). Warren does not deny the role of imperialism in the past, but suggests that this is now declining and no longer responsible for the problems of LDCs. He agrees with the dependency theorists that the extension of capital into the Third World created an international system of exploitation called imperialism, but makes the point that this process also created the conditions for the destruction of imperialism by sowing the seeds of capitalist social relations and productive forces. Imperialism was, in fact, necessary to initiate the process of industrialisation and, having done so, is now retreating leaving capitalist societies. Capitalism's contradictory and exploitative element is responsible for the problems of LDCs. This thesis relies on a 'pure' Marxist analysis, for uneven development is attributed, not to Third World imperialist relationships, but almost entirely to the internal contradictions of Third World capitalism itself. Thus imperialism is seen as progressive because it moves history closer to socialism.

Warren demonstrates this by referring to the characteristics of Latin American economies, which were referred to earlier as the new forms of dependency, only for him these represent the growth of independent industrialisation. Referring to Sutcliffe, he sets out the main criteria for economic development. 'These are that development should be based on the home market; that development should encompass a wide range of industries; that development should not be reliant on foreign finance except where the underdeveloped country can control the use of foreign funds; and that analogously to having a diversified industrial structure there should be "independent technological progress".' (Warren 1973: 17).

From empirical observation and from the new forms of dependency material, he suggests that there has been an increase in manufacturing for the home market; there has been a diversification in industrial development; local investment is on the increase, as well as Latin American countries having greater influence over foreign capital through multinationals; and, finally, there is some indigenous technological development, though this is the criterion which is least developed of the four. Warren points out that the imperialist theory of the international division of labour is breaking down because of the LDCs' move away from natural resources to manufacturing. In global terms, this means that the distribution of power in the capitalist world is becoming less uneven.

Warren's view represents a departure from other criticisms because he lays the blame for problems squarely on the shoulders of capitalism itself, rather than dependent capitalism. Most other critics attach some importance still to an unequal relationship between developed and underdeveloped.

CHANGE SINCE DEPENDENCY

In addition to criticisms of the theory, economic developments began to challenge the dependency position. Even while the many dependency theorists were writing, events were taking place which would lead to a rethinking of these ideas. In the late 1960s and early 1970s the terms of trade were changing in favour of some of the LDCs exporting minerals and agricultural products, a situation which some countries were able to take advantage of and use to promote economic growth. As well as this, as their middle classes grew, some Latin American countries were beginning to develop as important markets for the industrial nations. Large corporations producing cars and electrical items, were finding that profits could be made by selling these within the Latin American countries. The 1973 oil crisis was a particularly critical occurrence for the LDCs, since it demonstrated a dramatic reversal of the dependency relationship on the part of a small number of countries. Although this situation only occurred in the case of one natural resource, it did show that dependency could be shaken and that some LDCs were capable of turning the tables on the industrialised world and making them dependent, with all the vulnerability that that implies, on the LDCs for a short while. The discovery of oil in countries like Ecuador, which had hitherto depended on exports such as bananas, did give a boost to the economy.

These events tended to confuse the straightforward dichotomous picture of one set of countries, the LDCs, being dependent on another. Some LDCs, such as Brazil, appeared to have economies more like those of the industrialised world than those of LDCs such as Nepal, Upper Volta, and Bolivia, for example. These changes led to a rethinking of the dependency approach.

Cardoso sees these economic changes as being distinctly beneficial to Latin America and, for these processes, he uses the term associated-dependent development, specifically to imply the two notions of dependence and development which, he says, have hitherto been seen as contradictory. The key institution in linking development with dependency is the multinational, since it brings into play a new international division of labour and is responsible for the injection of capital into Latin American economies, which provides the dynamics for development. Therefore, there is an increasing identity of interests between foreign corporations and Latin American states. Because of the multinational, the relationship between the developed country and the underdeveloped one no longer exploits and perpetuates stagnation but promotes growth in crucial and dynamic sectors of the economy. Development in the contemporary capitalist world requires the technology, finance and organisation that only multinational firms can supply. Cardoso, basing his analysis on Brazil, sees the growth of multinationals in Latin America as being a stimulant to development, but he also accepts that as long as the technology necessary for production comes from outside the LDC, there is still a relationship of economic dependence (Cardoso 1973).

Muñoz suggests that LDCs may be able to use these improved conditions to give them greater bargaining strength in world trade (Muñoz 1981). His concept of 'Strategic dependency does not denote simply a state-to-state dependency; rather it characterizes a situation in which the *international* segment (that sector associated with multinational corporations) of the dominant structure of advanced capitalist societies depends for its continued prosperity upon access to the cheap natural resources, labour, and markets of, principally, underdeveloped societies' (Muñoz 1981: 4). The way that the economic significance of Latin America has increased can be seen in the three main components of strategic dependency – cheap raw materials, low-priced labour, and markets.

A good deal of the world's raw materials are found in LDCs, so it is important for the multinationals to maintain a cheap supply with easy access. Competition tends to put up the prices of goods, so a monopolistic situation is preferred. Thus the industrialised world comes to depend, in a general way, on the suppliers of raw materials. This situation reached a peak in 1973 in the energy crisis, when the wealthier nations of the world stepped up aid towards the resource-rich nations of Latin America. Muñoz points out that 'Differences in degrees of cooperation were found to be dependent upon variations in the levels of strategic dependency of the center nations involved' (Muñoz 1981: 8).

In the case of labour, Muñoz suggests that a world market has developed, in which it may be profitable for a large corporation to reorganise itself, so that production takes place in a part of the world where labour is cheap. Clearly, this will depend on the technology employed by the firm, it is more appropriate for those using labour-intensive processes rather than for capital-intensive corporations. The advantage of cheap labour can be seen in the USA's companies which have set up in northern Mexico, because labour is much cheaper there than in the USA but, at the same time, it is not far to transfer the goods to the home place of the corporation. It could be argued, however, that although the Mexicans gain employment through this, their advantage is small, i.e. low wages, as compared to the big profits the North American company receives.

As mentioned earlier in the chapter, foreign investment has been shifting out of natural resources and into manufacturing, and these manufactured goods are being sold locally. Volkswagen, for example, have expanded their markets by setting up factories in Latin America which assemble the cars and then sell to the local bourgeoisie. These markets throughout the continent become important for the prosperity of the giant corporations.

The increasing importance, then, of some LDCs for multinationals and other large corporations, which gives them greater bargaining power, has been encouraged by contemporary world economic problems. The oil crisis, inflation, trade rivalry, and the international monetary crisis, sharpen industrialised nations' need for cheap and reliable sources of raw materials and labour, and expanding markets.

Muñoz is very aware of limitations that exist on the negotiating power of the LDCs, for he points out that while, in theory, this strategic dependency may exist, the core nations of the world economy usually have the upper hand in negotiations for political reasons (through greater political experience and political power). The importance of his argument is that he demonstrates the fallibility of a simple dependency model and suggests that countries like Brazil, Mexico and Venezuela have some economic importance to the countries at the centre of the world economy and should, therefore, be considered semi-peripheral, rather than on the periphery or dependent in terms of the world economy.

For a period in the 1970s, the terms of international trade seemed to be swinging in favour of Latin America, but this did not last. One of the major problems is that although Latin America has experienced periods of economic growth and development, the region has not been able to produce *sustained* economic development. These periods of growth have often been financed by foreign capital, thus preventing the region from generating its own investment capital and have frequently ended in stagnation or crisis. The most recent example of this is the debt crisis, which has displayed the vulnerability for LDCs of this type of development. Economic growth was achieved on the basis of borrowing, a very acceptable principle in a capitalist system, but the debt has now become so exorbitant that some countries are unable to meet the debt servicing payments, let alone repay the original loan. Resources must now be used to finance repayments rather than fuel new development projects. Countries like Mexico and Ecuador borrowed on the strength of their oil reserves, only to find themselves in a crisis situation when the oil bonanza ended. Some economists believed that, by the end of the 1970s, Latin America was beginning to overcome certain difficulties, such as employment problems but, with the world-wide economic troubles of the 1980s, this work has been undone (PREALC 1981, Tokman 1982, Garcia 1982). The issue, then, is how can self-sustained development be brought about?

THEORY SINCE DEPENDENCY

The result of these changes in both ideas and socio-economic developments is that no one global theory enjoys the eminence that dependency did in its heyday. Instead, attention has focused more on specific rather than general issues and a number of theories and approaches have arisen to explain particular problems.

Social class

One area which the dependency school has never really got to grips with is internal class relations, which are so vital to an understanding of any social formation. In order to remedy this and attempt to analyse the nature of class, social scientists refer back to Marx's original formula. For him, class relations stemmed from the mode of production and this, therefore, should provide the focus for further study. Here, they are following the line of thought developed by Laclau in his criticism of Frank and shifting the emphasis away from market exchange and the relationship between dependent and advanced societies, to modes of production as the source of class relations.

The modes-of-production debate picks up Laclau's point about the articulation of the capitalist mode of production with pre-capitalist modes and develops this further (Long 1977, Foster-Carter 1978). The argument is that capitalism has allowed pre-capitalist modes, such as peasant production, to remain in Latin America because the former benefits through increased capital accumulation. For example, in parts of Central America and the Andean countries, peasants manage farms that are too small to support a family and, therefore, the farmer and members of his family are compelled to find seasonal wage-work on large estates to boost their earnings to a subsistence level. This system suits the capitalist estate owner who can pay low wages, since the peasants are desperate for work, and pay piece-rates, rather than maintaining an agricultural labour force throughout the year during periods of little activity, as well as peak times. The existence of infra-subsistence peasant holdings, therefore, makes possible a source of cheap labour, thus allowing greater profits for the capitalist and so contributing to capital accumulation. Articulation between capitalist and pre-capitalist modes of production benefits the former and leads to the dominance of capitalism over other modes but not, of course, to their exclusion. As can be seen in Chapters 5 and 6, this approach has been used quite successfully in the analyses of rural society and the urban poor.

World systems approach

The approach which has the closest affinity with dependence is world systems (Wallerstein 1974, 1980, Hopkins, Wallerstein 1982). This suggests that, in order to understand what is happening in the Third World, we should look at the world as one capitalist system with capital accumulation in the core countries and surplus extracted from the periphery. The participation of other areas has been in different forms to suit the needs of capitalist accumulation. The historical development of this world system involves a stage of dependent capitalism, but analysis in terms of a dependent/non-dependent dichotomy is no longer useful. With the growth of the newly-industrialising countries, this theory argues that it is more instructive to use the terms core, periphery and semi-periphery, for the following reasons. Firstly, this terminology solves the problem of the dyadic relationship implied in dependency since it has a global perspective. Secondly, it eases the difficulty of the dichotomy of developed/underdeveloped, since countries such as Brazil and Argentina may be identified as being on the semi-periphery. Finally, following on from the previous point, this form of analysis takes into account the industrialisation and development that is taking place in the Third World. This allows us to emphasise the distinctiveness of countries on the semi-periphery, which are sometimes referred to as newly industrialising countries. As pointed out in the previous chapter, the gap between the newly industrialising nations and the poor societies of the world is becoming wider. However, this approach makes use of the advances made by dependency by emphasising the importance to the development of LDCs of involvement in the world capitalist system.

Like dependency, however, this approach is more attractive at an abstract level than in implementation as a problematic. Difficulties arise as to which countries should be considered as semi-peripheral; there is no agreement over the placement of countries in this and the periphery categories.

Theories of the state and development problems

As a result of the critical thinking outlined and also socio-economic changes, theories with very few links with the dependency tradition have emerged in the 1970s and 1980s. These have centred either on the role of the state in promoting economic growth or basic development problems.

In the first category are those which have taken into account the growth of the strong state and wave of military regimes that characterised Latin America in the 1970s and early 1980s. These theories, which will be discussed in Chapter 8, attempt to explain the power structure and policies of the more industrially-advanced Latin American countries. These republics are predominantly urban, highly industrialised in parts and harbour a middle class, whose lifestyle is modelled on that of the industrialised world. They have, at times, achieved high levels of economic growth and yet the problems that dependency exposed some years back are still apparent, namely the lack of self-sustained growth and the social costs of this path of development.

The social costs have been in the areas of income concentration, poverty and unemployment/underemployment, some of the problems of underdevelopment identified in the previous chapter. Approaches which have focused more on these social costs in terms of either a local level analysis or a development from below angle are very varied. In the mid-1970s, a Basic Needs strategy was developed by the ILO and the Institute of Development Studies at Sussex to tackle specific development problems. Its aim was to eradicate the worst aspects of human poverty by the year 2000, by changing the structure of production and distribution as well as consumption. Specific targets were set, which included: increasing the productivity of employment and therefore the incomes of the poor; financial and other assistance for those in the traditional sectors of the economy; progressive taxation to finance the provision of basic consumer services for all; reduction of inequality of household consumption of goods and services; expansion of trade; involving people in popular participation through the setting up of organisations such as trade unions. The plan was also to incorporate the redistribution with growth idea. Although promising and appealing in its directness, the Basic Needs strategy has had little further attention from sociologists. Perhaps this is because a basic weakness is the failure to address the issue of power structures, which must affect any attempts at development projects.

Another area of interest is that of social movements. Increasingly, research is being carried out on the expanding number of local level groupings which are appearing in town and country as a response to low incomes, food shortages, lack of urban facilities and numerous other day-to-day problems. Particularly evident among these are local-level church-sponsored groupings and women's groups, which have given an added impetus to Third World gender-based research. These are examined in Chapters 4 and 7.

Ecology issues have also started coming to the fore with Redclift's work linking development and environment, in which he points out that the political aspect of the resources issue has so far been neglected (Redclift 1984b). This is a more sophisticated version of the view that criticises the assumption that development needs to be industrially oriented. It has been argued that uneven development is the result of urban bias, which goes hand-in-hand with industrialis-ation, urban society advances at the expense of rural (Lipton 1977). The implication, which is more relevant for the less urbanised areas of Asia and Africa than Latin America is that development could at times be based on agricultural productivity and rural advance instead of industrialisation.

CONCLUSION

It is a long theoretical path from modernisation to social movements and ecology issues and it encompasses a wide range of theories and ideas. The modernisation school saw development resulting from new internal values which, because LDCs lacked them, had to be encour-aged by external factors emanating from the industrialised countries. For the dependency theorists, these external factors were the root of the problem of underdevelopment. Although a compromise has been suggested by Streeten, who argues that the industrialised world propagates both positive and negative impulses (Streeten 1981), in general, these two schools have produced opposing sets of ideas.

The legacy of dependency that has been taken up by later theorists is the emphasis on capital accumulation and the theme that the centre can only develop by capital accumulation, which is dependent on extracting the surplus from the periphery. The large profits made in Third World countries are frequently exported abroad. Would it, then, be possible for Latin America to extract itself from the network of international relationships in which it is involved? Kitching argues that whether or not LDCs choose a capitalist or socialist model of development, industrialisation is necessary and that is not possible without investment capital. Since these countries are too small and poor to produce savings from internal sources, investment must come from outside. Simple nationalism therefore, he claims, is not very constructive (Kitching 1982). Problems of generalisation arise again, since a country like Brazil has pockets of great wealth and capital investment and also areas of extreme poverty.

The decline of a dominant global theory has stimulated a greater interest in empirical issues. Theory can not just be discarded, however, it shapes the choice of subject for research and is essential in providing a framework for analysis. In recent years, theoretical developments have taken different paths, relating to specific topics, rather than operating at the macro-level. These ideas can be examined further by closer analysis of the empirical material.

FURTHER READING

Booth, D. (1985) Marxism and development sociology: interpreting the impasse. *World Development* vol. 13 No. 7

Cardoso, F. H., Faletto, E. (1979) *Dependency and development in Latin America* trans. from the Spanish by M M Urquidi. University of California Press, Berkeley

Foster-Carter, A. (1978) The modes of production controversy. *New Left Review* 107

Frank, A. G. (1969) Sociology of development and underdevelopment of sociology. In **Frank, A. G.** *Latin America: underdevelopment or revolution. Essays on the development of underdevelopment and the immediate enemy.* Monthly Review Press, New York and London

Long, N. (1977) *An introduction to the sociology of rural development.* Methuen, London

Muñoz, H. (1980) *From dependency to development: strategies to overcome underdevelopment and inequality.* Westview Press, Boulder, Colorado

Palma, G. (1981) Dependency: a formal theory of underdevelopment or a methodology for the analyses of concrete situations of underdevelopment? In **Streeten, P., Jolly, R.** (eds) *Recent issues in world development. A collection of survey articles.* Pergamon Press, Oxford

Redfield, R. (1941) *The folk culture of Yucatan.* University of Chicago Press, Chicago

Roxborough, I. (1979) *Theories of underdevelopment.* Macmillan, London

Ethnicity and race relations

The twenty Latin American republics share a common heritage in that they were all conquered by peoples who spoke languages derived from Latin. Despite this, these Latin American societies have long been racially and culturally mixed, which makes the delineation of tenable boundaries between groups, on the basis of race or ethnicity, very difficult. This diversity is largely the result of historical-demographic developments. Over the four-and-a-half centuries since the discovery of America, successive waves of immigrants have entered the region and settled over the basic Amerindian stock of the original inhabitants. Nor, despite the early appearance of cross-racial unions in the colonial period and the rapid development of a largely *mestizo* population from the seventeenth century onwards, has the process of homogenisation of populations proceeded very far. This has been thanks to the facts of social structure: relatively rigid class societies set in the mould of deeply traditionalist social orders have imposed white and Hispanic (and, from the late nineteenth century onwards, North American) cultural characteristics as the values to which the individual should aspire, at least in the material lifestyle. Large masses of the population, excluded from the arena of social esteem by their inability to meet the demands of the hegemonic cultural system, have remained alienated from the dominant system in their country. Thus Latin American societies have emerged racially and culturally mixed.

The population originated from three racial stocks – the Amerindians, the indigenous people of the continent, the European Caucasoid, who came to dominate the New World and the African Negro who was brought over as a slave. All three have contributed to the cultural heritage of the continent, though it is European traditions and lifestyle which have come to be the prevailing influence in Latin American society. The contribution of the non-European groups varies in strength and kind across South and Middle America, according to the historical incidence and development of the different ethnic groups (see Figure 3.1).

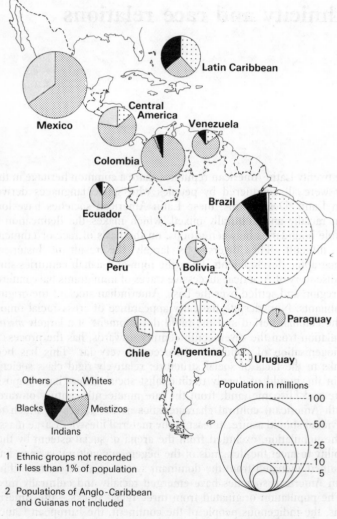

Fig. 3.1 Latin America: ethnic groups. (Cubitt D and T, 1980)

Since ethnicity refers to culture and race, this concept is frequently more relevant than race in the context of Latin America. One of the themes of this chapter is that cultural criteria are often used in an attempt to identify racial groups. The numbers of the Indian population of Mexico are, for example, assessed on the basis of language, those speaking only an indigenous language are identified as being Indian. Miscegenation has taken place to such an extent that any attempt to distinguish racial groups on any biological basis would be virtually impossible. Nevertheless, ethnicity, often expressed in racial terminology, plays a very important part in the social ordering of life.

This role of ethnicity varies according to different areas of Latin America. Analyses of the cultural background point to three regions, with their own particular characteristics. Wagley names the three regions Indo-America, Afro-America and Ibero-America, but insists that the names are only symbolic and that the main characteristics of each region are the result of human ecology (Wagley 1968). The basic institutions have derived from the relationship between man and his social and physical environment. For instance, the institution which distinguishes Afro-America from the other two regions is the plantation, which was manned by slave labour and later wage labour and produced cash crops for the export market, thus linking slavery and the demand for the African Negro with the economy and land-use. It was the plantation that set the cultural pattern, that was to last for generations, for the area.

Beals, identifying three regions, avoids the problem of labelling, and refers to them less picturesquely as Groups 1, 2 and 3. They do, however, have similar characteristics to Wagley's since the ethnic contribution to culture is the main element (Beals 1969). Beals's typology, however, refers only to Indian-*mestizo*-white relations and, therefore, excludes plantation Latin America. He sub-divides Wagley's category of Indo-America into two, according to the strength of the Indian component. A classification of regions, according to their cultural heritage, and along the lines suggested by Wagley and Beals, provides a useful introduction to the analysis of ethnicity.

Beals's Group 1, corresponding to Wagley's Ibero-America, consists of Argentina, Chile, Costa Rica and Uruguay, where European culture predominates almost to the exclusion of others. One might, perhaps, include southern Brazil in this category though it is excluded from Beals's Group 1 list. The contemporary Indian population in the southern cone countries is very small, and it is often suggested that this has always been the case. In this area, there is a myth that there was never a substantial Indian population, slaves were not imported in any significant numbers and the people have always, therefore, been predominantly white. Beals, however, challenges this myth quite effectively by referring to the statistics of those studying the origins of the Argentine population. These suggest that, in 1700, Argentina had a population of 600,000 made up of 3,000 whites; 50,000 *mestizos*; 530,000 Indians; 7,000 Negroes and 10,000 mulattos. By 1852, the estimate is 810,000 for the total population: 22,000 whites; 563,000 *mestizos*; 100,000 Indians; 15,000 Negroes; 110,000 mulattos (Beals 1969: 242). After this, the situation changed because of the influx of European immigrants. These figures suggest that Argentina was far from strongly white European in the early days. Similarly, in 1803, 26 per cent of the Uruguayan population was coloured and, in 1843, the proportion in Montevideo was 19 per cent. Today, at most, 2.3 per cent of the population in Uruguay is coloured (Hoetink 1973).

Chile, unlike the other countries of this region, does have an identifiable indigenous population, though it is extremely small. The Mapuche Indians have their own communities in the south of Chile, though many of them now are migrating to the towns and becoming involved in a national way of life.

In terms of Wagley's human ecology, the main socio-economic institution of the southern cone countries is the cattle ranch. This is the region of the pampa, the home of the gaucho, the Argentine cowboy, who became almost a national symbol for Argentina and an important theme in its national literature.

Regardless of racial composition, these countries have a way of life that is distinctly European. The most decisive influence came in the form of the European immigration that took place in the late nineteenth and early twentieth century. During that period vast numbers of Spaniards, Italians, Germans, Portuguese, Poles and other Europeans flocked to Chile, Brazil, Uruguay and Argentina, often attracted by the rich lands of the pampa and its semi-temperate climate, that was appropriate for a European style of mixed farming. They brought with them the knowledge and understanding of the institutions of the industrialised countries, which was to contribute to the economic growth of the New World. Although Italians were the most numerous in Argentina, and Germans in Brazil, many Latin American cities received a variety of immigrants from different parts of Europe.

Although, in general, their descendants have become acculturated and consider themselves Argentine, Chilean or Brazilian, there still exist a number of ethnic communities, maintaining many of the traditional customs of the mother country. In Santiago and Buenos Aires, there are bilingual Anglo-Chileans and Anglo-Argentines, who send their children to English schools, speak English at home and continue traditional English customs, such as afternoon tea. These groups support their own ethnic associations, usually sports or social clubs.

One of these is the *bomberos*, or firemen, who make up a town's fire brigade. In Santiago, the fire brigade is run on an entirely voluntary basis, for each company is recruited from a different ethnic group and is responsible for extinguishing fires in a particular district. Originally, these were based on the various colonies – the English, German, Spanish, Italian and French. The voluntary membership requires periods of being on call to man the company's fire engine. The premises are also frequently used as a social club.

Indo-America refers to the countries of Central America and the Andean region where there is a distinct Indian population. Taking Wagley's category and Beals's Groups 2 and 3 together, this region would include Mexico, Panama, the Central American republics of Guatemala, El Salvador, Honduras and Nicaragua, Bolivia, Ecuador, Peru, Paraguay and most of Colombia and Venezuela.

Here, the Spaniards encountered the complex Indian civilisation of the Aztec, the Inca and the Maya. The Incas in the Andes were not only skilled craftsmen in gold and silver, but had also developed a highly structured social organisation focused on local communities. Although backward in some areas of technology – they had not discovered the wheel, for instance – they had built paved roads and constructed suspension bridges high in the Andes. The Spanish conquerors in the sixteenth century destroyed much of these civilisations in order to make fast the Hispanic imprint on Latin America. During and after the conquest, the Indian population was drastically reduced, often through massacres but sometimes as a result of association with their white masters, because of contact with new diseases. The small number that survived withdrew into peripheral areas, where the conquerors were reluctant to go, usually mountainous areas such as the Andean slopes, or else rural areas in Mexico and Guatemala that were very distant from the centres of activity, and where land was of poor quality. Here, they reconstructed their communities, not exactly as before, but as closed communities where traditional customs could be maintained. As long as these communities were prepared to pay their taxes to those in power, the Spanish conquerors allowed them to remain relatively untroubled by outsiders.

Many of these communities continued into the nineteenth century without much alteration, but then they became subject to new laws which exposed them to the forces of change and opened their doors to the wider society. This has, however, meant in the twentieth century a distinct Indian contribution to the culture of these countries. In this century the customs and traditions of these communities have become accessible to urban Mexicans and Peruvians.

The cultural heritage of the area of Afro-America, excluded from Beals's categories, encompasses all three racial stocks of Latin America. The indigenous population in this region, which refers to most of Brazil and lowland parts of Venezuela and Colombia as well as Cuba, Haiti and Santo Domingo, were very few in number and had a much simpler social and economic structure than the Aztecs and Incas. The Indians of Amazonia lived in hunting and gathering bands. They were easily defeated, mostly by the Portuguese, and drastically reduced like their fellow Indians in Central America and the Andean region. The very small number that survived were driven into the jungle where, despite sporadic harassment, they have continued with their tribal organisation.

The devastation of the Indians left the European conquerors without a subservient labour force and so, when the plantation economy began to take form, a demand for cheap docile labour was generated. To answer this, millions of Negroes were brought over from Africa to work as slaves. They provided a vital element of plantation society and economy and, after abolition, the slave culture, which had become a blend of traditional African customs with those emanating from slavery, became an integral part of Brazilian culture. Like the rest of Latin America, Hispanic customs and values are the most pronounced in the area, but the contribution of the Negro, in cultural terms, can be seen in music, especially the samba and the samba schools, the carnival, spirit-possession cults such as *mucumba* and *umbanda* and in food and cooking methods.

ETHNICITY

Although the Indian societies in Middle America and in the Andean region presented more of an opposition to the Hispanic intruders than did the hunting and gathering bands in Amazonia, they were soon defeated with very great losses. But their greatly diminished numbers were able to reorganise themselves in villages along the lines imposed by the Spanish rulers. Through the *encomienda* system, each village was granted a legal charter and communal lands, thus each community became a land-holding corporation. Every family was entitled to cultivate a plot of land in the village, but the title belonged to the community. In return for this, the villages paid dues to the Spanish conquerors, which often provided the only real contact with their rulers, so that each community was able to live relatively independently and regarded itself as a distinct entity.

The general Spanish attitude, that the Indian was a legitimate object of exploitation in the pursuit of wealth, was modified by two factors. The Spanish Crown and bureaucracy saw the conquest as a mechanism of expanding Spanish citizenship and the Roman Catholic church saw it as an opportunity for bringing more souls into the Christian community. At the same time the dearth of white women, which was an aspect of colonisation throughout the region, led to widespread miscegenation. When increasing numbers of European women did begin to arrive in the New World, attempts were made to inhibit legal marriage between Indian and white. Sexual contact between white men and Indian women had become established by then and, although unauthorised for a while, it continued. It was soon only a few aristocratic families who were concerned to maintain the purity of their European background, by upholding rigorous constraints on inter-racial marriage. In Central America and the Andean countries, there developed a situation of isolated, exclusively Indian communities, *mestizo* populations and small white aristocratic groups.

In the nineteenth century, the integration of the Indian into society moved a stage further. Under the guise of ideological liberalism, Latin American governments passed laws aimed at substituting private property for communal holdings. As they abolished laws protecting communal property, the Indian communities lost their titles to land, as a group. The Indian response to this was of various kinds. Many were too poor to buy land individually and so their territory was swallowed up by neighbouring *haciendas* and they became peons for the *hacendado*. Other communities who were greatly opposed to selling land to outsiders, divided up the land among the villagers, sometimes managing to keep a small piece of communal land. Some even managed, despite the new laws, to retain their communal holdings, allocating parcels to their members periodically.

Stavenhagen has described this process as one of internal colonialism, for many Indians again lost their lands; were forced to work for strangers, since they were *ladinos* (*mestizo*) and, therefore, ethnically distinct; they were compelled to participate in a new monetary economy and became subordinate to new forms of political domination, since they no longer had the relative political independence of the communities (Stavenhagen 1970).

The *hacienda*, which came to dominate the lives of so many Indians, is not just an economic unit of a large agricultural property, but also a social system. On the *haciendas* are cultivated the export crops of coffee, sugar, cotton, etc. Most of the peasants who work for the *hacendado* are landless but they have a hut and small plot for subsistence cultivation on the land and, in return, are obliged to perform certain services, such as agricultural labour for so many days of the week and domestic services by the peasant's wife in the landlord's house. In the past, many of the peasants were paid for their work in kind so that not having the independence that cash brings, they were dependent on their master. In Hualcán, Peru, the Indians would work three or four days a week, receiving a plot of land to farm or pasture sheep on, free firewood and coca to chew (Stein 1961). In some cases, the *hacendado* lent money for the purchase of seed or tools for the garden plot, but then he often charged exorbitant interest rates. Once tied by this debt, the peasant was never able to escape. This debt peonage reached extreme levels in Chile where *inquilinos* borrowing money to buy tools, animals and seeds were charged interest rates of 200–300 per cent. Though payment in kind is much less the norm now and debt peonage is mostly a thing of the past, nevertheless, most of the *hacienda* peons today live and work in poor conditions.

Not all the *hacienda* peasants are landless, some rent land from the *hacendado* and, across Latin America, there is a great variety of landlord-tenant arrangements. Most of these exist on the basis of some form of cash-renting or share-renting. In the case of the latter, landlord and tenant agree that the rent will be paid in the form of a share of the crops grown on that land. This sort of arrangement makes it possible for a peasant, with no available cash, to rent land, but it also means that he does not get the benefit of all of his crop.

The *hacienda* is a complete social system because an Indian's life is totally encompassed within it. Any goods purchased are done so at the *hacienda* store, children go to the *hacienda* school and all the family are employed in some form on the property. The power of the *hacendado* rests, therefore, not only on economic dominance through owning land but, also, in the control that he has over a large number or peasants. Resident estate workers who were allotted a piece of land for subsistence farming were called *colonos*.

The nineteenth-century changes exposed the Indian to the wider society, in which he was particularly vulnerable. Three possible forms of land tenure were open to him. There was ownership of property, but not many were able to buy land, so many farms remained in the hands of *mestizos*; cash-renting or share-renting was an option taken up by some; others remained in their Indian communities working on communal lands. Many, of course, became landless and worked as agricultural labourers. Stavenhagen demonstrates how, as contact between Indians and *mestizos* grows, there is a shift from a situation of internal colonialism to one of class relationships. Colonial relationships are characterised by superordination/subordination in terms of power, race and culture, as demonstrated by different languages. Class relationships are firmly grounded in economic factors such as the marketplace and the hire of labour. For a while, there is an overlap of colonial and class relationships, when Indians participate in the market system, but demonstrate their vulnerability by maintaining Indian customs and language. Gradually they begin to speak Spanish and wear Western clothes but, although less obviously vulnerable in cultural terms, exploitation through class relationships increases.

In Guatemala, for instance, Indian workers are paid less than *ladino* and, usually, hired by *ladinos* on most exploitative terms. In San Cristobal de las Casas, in Mexico, large numbers of Indians compete with each other to sell to a small number of middlemen, thus, reducing their own opportunities (Stavenhagen 1970). Beals, too, interprets the development of race relations in these countries in terms of a shift from race to class (Beals 1969).

The changes described also represent a process of acculturation. Indians throughout Latin America are gradually adopting more *mestizo* cultural elements, such as the use of Spanish rather than an indigenous language, Western-style dress rather than Indian and the substitution of folk medicine by scientific medicine. The disinvolvement with the isolated community, based on communal land ownership, and increasing participation in the capitalist market economy, means the gradual replacement of Indian cultural traits by *ladino* ones. However, the most important aspect of this is the occupational change from subsistence farmer to wage labourer or cultivator of cash crops because this integrates the Indian into the class structure of national society and incorporates him in the lowest levels of that hierarchical structure.

These changes have been interpreted in different ways by the various academic schools of thought that have been very active in a country like Mexico, with its rich anthropological tradition. The *Indigenistas*, stressing the cultural distinctiveness of the Indian communities, felt this to be an impediment to modernisation and incorporation in the wider society. Since they believed in a benevolent national society, they considered integration in the form of a move from Indian to *mestizo* to be upward social mobility. Stavenhagen, whose ideas on internal colonialism are closely linked to the dependency school, saw this change in a much less favourable light. For him, acculturation meant the process of becoming marginalised or proletarianised in very poor conditions. (For a good discussion of these issues, see Hewitt de Alcántara 1984.)

Widespread miscegenation has made it extremely difficult to distinguish racial groups but, because of the historical development of Middle America and the Andean countries, Indian communities, defined in terms of ethnicity, continued for centuries. As these communities break up, the Indian cultural elements fade, in favour of *mestizo* elements, Indians becoming more *ladinised* in their behaviour patterns and lifestyle. At the same time, class factors become more important than ethnic in their relationship with others. This does not mean, however, racial terminology ceases to be important, far from it. Biological terminology is applied to culturally determined groups, since the isolated groups are called Indian, although distinguishable by cultural criteria – language, lifestyle, clothing, community identification, etc. In the same way, this terminology may be extended to socially defined groups outside the confines of the Indian community. Darker skinned poor rural workers may be referred to as Indians because of their socio-economic position in the rural social structure. Racial terminology is, therefore, often used in everyday life as a form of labelling to denote certain cultural or social significance.

INDIAN COMMUNITIES

There has been considerable debate about the nature of Indian communites if, indeed, they can be considered bounded entities at all. Early anthropologists concentrated on studying Indians within the framework of a community and so paid little attention to outside factors. This led to the application of the term 'closed community' to those corporate communities with communal land ownership and distinctive cultural traits that still exist, though infrequently found, in isolated parts of the region. The functionalists stressed the harmony and reciprocity of Indian life. But by emphasising the factors that held society together and contributed to its continuity, they neglected any explanation of the poverty and hardships of rural life (see, for example, Foster 1967). Since their research was bounded methodologically by the village under study, analysis stopped at its borders and they saw the external context as being of little importance.

Other anthropologists, whose connections with the dependency school had opened their eyes to wider societal implications, were less happy with the notion of a closed community. Eric Wolf, whose theoretical underpinnings, Alcántara describes as being a 'fusion of cultural ecology and Marxism' (Alcántara 1984: 74), recognised that some corporate communities remained in the twentieth century, but gave explanations for this in terms of external factors and pointed to the links these villages had with the rest of society. Wolf argued that the Indians had been compelled to set up their own forms of social organisation by the conquest and depression and as a form of protection against the Spanish conquerors and their descendants. Even from the beginning, the closed community had had some contact with the rest of society through church tithes, state taxes or labour provision for neighbouring *haciendas* (Wolf 1959). In this way, Wolf anticipated the modes of production approach.

Following Wolf's line of argument, we can see that today all communities are involved in the wider society, though to very differing degrees. This section of the chapter concentrates on areas where there is a predominance of Indian cultural traits, leaving a fuller discussion of rural society to Chapter 5.

Since these communities are so isolated, they have a subsistence economy based on the traditional Indian crops of maize, squash and beans in Middle America, and potatoes and quinoa in the Andes. Although there is often now individual land ownership, there are strong sanctions, still, on selling to outsiders. Members are encouraged to marry within the community, so that most people spend their lives within the one village. In Hualcán, for instance, William Stein found that in 1951, both parents of two-thirds of the children born there had also been born in the community and the remaining one-third had one parent who had come from elsewhere (Stein 1961).

Cultural patterns relate to areas, but may also be distinctive of particular communities. All the villagers in a region speak the same indigenous language, but they may have their own particular costumes, jewellery, dances or other customs. One community in Mexico is famous for its *voladores*, the flying men who, tied by a strap to a central pole, whirl dangerously around.

These communities do not have any recourse to doctors and clinics, but rely on folk medicine to solve illnesses and ailments. The curers use a mixture of herbal remedies, many of which come from plants that have been tested over time and may well have properties of a soothing or pain-numbing kind, and magical rites. Some have picked up, from the experience and accumulated knowledge of previous generations, skills such as bone-setting.

Reliance on these methods and the element of superstition that they involve, is part of a set of attitudes, which have been referred to as fatalist, passive, conservative and distrustful, in sum, making up a 'peasant mentality'.

Failure of rural development projects has often been attributed to this mentality, which would make the peasant hostile to change and suspicious of any innovation from outside. Any attempts to bring changes in the local economy, schools, roads, etc., to a rural area must, therefore, take into account the way the peasantry will respond.

In many ways, a fear of the unknown and reluctance to try out the new, is very understandable, given the insecurities of Indian peasant life. Life in an Indian community, over the generations, is characterised by a lack of control over the essentials. The subsistence farmer relies on his produce to feed his family, but he has no control over the weather and the conditions of the soil, which are so critical, he does not have recourse to fertilisers, pesticides and equipment to counteract the malevolent side of nature. The reasons for illness and death are unknown to him so he can do nothing to alleviate the high rates of infant mortality. A genuine lack of control contributes to feelings of fatalism and passivity, after all, what can he do to improve the situation? He is dependent on fate. If hunger prevails, all he can do is to kill a few chickens which, with luck, he has kept for such an occasion, to ease the situation temporarily, but he has no long-term solution at his fingertips. Long-term planning is, therefore, alien to the Indians living in these conditions. Moreover, since accident and misfortune are not fully understood, this is often attributed to witch-craft or magic, which is brought about by the hostile feelings of others. In such a situation, it is important not to make enemies, so peasants are reluctant to become too involved with others and are particularly suspicious and wary of newcomers. General insecurity, the inability to direct one's life in a positive way and a general fear of the unknown and, therefore strangers, all contrive to produce a disposition that does not favour the activities of planners and developers. In these ways, the attitudes of Indians in isolated communities are very similar to those of peasants living in the same sorts of conditions throughout the world (Bailey 1971).

In Latin America, this insecurity and the uneven distribution of scarce resources leads to an exaggerated concern to establish warm and useful relationships with others. For the mass of the people, jobs are badly paid and irregular, good quality land is in short supply, and the mechanisms of power in society totally beyond their comprehension, so, few can be sure of the resources they need to support themselves and their families.

Even the fortunes of the rich can oscillate significantly, due to unstable political and economic situations and changing local administrations. In such an environment of uncertainty, people need something they can rely on and they turn to people they can trust. In a situation where inflation can rocket to over 100 per cent, investing in personal relationships, by establishing good friends who can help in a crisis, may be more useful than putting all one's savings into cash. For the peasant, whose crop may he hit by blight or drought at any time, the only source of help and support often lies in those close to him. 'In Latin America, people invest much of their effort in consolidating their personal fields. They increase security in a narrow orbit to counteract insecurity in the wider orbit.' (Wolf and Hansen 1972: 200)

Explanations of fatalistic and passive attitudes in terms of a culture of repression (Huizer 1973) and image of limited good (Foster 1967) are rarely referred to now as many sociologists and anthropologists have come to challenge the view that the peasantry is conservative and reluctant to change. Peasants in the 1980s have shown that they are quite willing to experiment with what are for them new forms of technology. Huizer points out that the distrust of the peasantry can be overcome, if a genuine attempt is made to understand the peasants' situation and to explain fully the aims and methods of the development project. As part of a project sponsored by the United Nations World Food Program and the Chilean government to develop the agricultural potential of sixteen Chilean communities, Huizer and the rest of the team encountered initial resistance on the part of the local peasantry, who had in the past lost land to large landowners in the area and, as a result, were reluctant to trust strangers. Huizer encouraged the peasants to discuss their problems and, having learned that their main grievance was loss of land, he won their confidence by supporting them in this issue against vested interests. Then management of the World Food Program facilities at community level was transferred to the elected representatives of the peasant community, thus involving them positively in the project. An attempt to see the situation from the point of view of the peasantry, and to deliberately alleviate their fears, had turned hostility into participation. The consequence was that, in the following few months, 'seven roads were improved or repaired, eight schools were built, five irrigation canals were constructed or repaired, 2,000 lemon trees were planted and steps towards the formation of multi-purpose peasant co-operatives were made' (Huizer 1973: 28).

Various Indian communities have demonstrated a flair for entre-preneurship from within their own ranks, which shows that conservatism is by no means universal. The Ecuadorian Otavalo, renowned for their weaving, sell their ponchos not only in other Latin American countries but even as far afield as Europe.

The world view of the peasantry, as is the case for any social group, involves religious beliefs and the general philosophical attitudes of the society. In the more isolated Indian communities of Latin America, religion and, in particular, religious ritual, forms the pivot of society, since the ritual cycle provides the social organisation of the community, forms the basis of its political structure and has a profound influence on its economy.

The ritual cycle refers to a series of ceremonies held throughout the year, which involve a mass and social celebrations. Each ritual is sponsored by a member of the community, which means that he is responsible for all the finance and organisation necessary and, in return, he earns the respect of the rest of the community.

Zinacantan, a Maya community in Chiapas, southern Mexico, is a good example of a community which has a flourishing ritual cycle (Cancian 1965). Every year, fifty-five ceremonies are sponsored by Zinacantecos. The syncretic nature of the rituals is revealed in the calendar, which is a mixture of orthodox Catholic saints' days, and traditional ceremonies, originally dedicated to Maya gods. The ranking of the rituals, in the case of Zinacantan, involving four levels, requires the participant to sponsor one on the lowest level before he can go on to the next and so on to the top. The higher the level, the smaller the number of ceremonies and the larger they are so an incomplete career is the rule. The sponsor holds this position for one

year before the ritual, during which time he can save and make prep-
arations. Sponsorship involves a number of activities: organising the
church service, providing candles and flowers for the church, keeping
it swept and tidy; arranging the procession, in which a picture of a
saint is often carried; and preparing the food, drink, fireworks and
music for the fiesta afterwards. In the case of some ceremonies, such
as that of San Sebastian which lasts nine days, this can entail
considerable work. For this, the sponsor needs the help of others,
so he calls on relatives and friends to assist. To be successful in the
ritual cycle it is necessary to have a wide network of associates to
provide assistance, so the ceremonies have the effect of reinforcing
ties of kinship and friendship in the community.

These activities require not only work, but also finance, which is
not easily obtainable in a peasant community. The sponsor must save,
but he is also expected to be in debt as a result, and his skill in hand-
ling these debts is important. If he spends too much, he has difficulty
recovering it, which will make it hard for him to participate further
in the ritual cycle, but if he does not spend enough he is criticised
by the community for being mean.

Why, then, do poor Indians involve themselves in this time-
consuming and expensive activity? Villagers express their motives in
terms of serving the community, by keeping the rituals, they are
demonstrating their allegiance to God and the saints and securing
their support for the community through the difficulties of peasant
life. In this way, they are winning the respect of the community for
undertaking a task seen to be important for all and, therefore, winning
local prestige. Those who complete the ritual cycle are admired and
revered in the village. In a poor, small community where prestige from
wealth or power is impossible, people earn a good name through
distributing the little wealth available for the believed benefit of all
and, in so doing, demonstrate they have that wealth, albeit so small.
Moreover, local political offices are linked to these ceremonial
positions. The village mayor and his assistants are those who have
reached the top level of the cycle, so that the local political hierarchy
overlaps with the religious.

Many sociologists have pointed to the fact that this is a mechanism
by which surplus wealth is distributed through the community. The
'threat' of one man having greater wealth than the others and thus
causing jealousy and competition is removed and, in return, he
receives honour from his neighbours. A potentially disruptive force
is defused. It is therefore a valuable way of preserving harmony and
giving people self-respect in a relatively closed community where
there is little opportunity to spend the wealth on other things.
Through the ritual cycle people invest in community and social
relationships rather than material goods because the respected man

knows he can turn to others in times of need. In these communities, the opportunity for investment in material things is very limited for, although subsistence crops can be amassed, they deteriorate in a short time, unlike relationships secured through the cycle.

The functionalists emphasised the reciprocity involved and the contribution made by the cycle to the balance of the community. Wolf saw it as a levelling mechanism which reduced the threat of disruption to the community, therefore protecting it from internal friction and strengthening it against outsiders (Wolf 1959).

Once a community becomes involved in a market system, more opportunities for surplus wealth arise. It can be used for investment purposes in the form of fertilisers, ploughs and even land which will, in time, contribute to a greater surplus. In this situation, the ritual cycle appears to offer an economic penalty. However, in some areas, the ritual cycle acts as a stimulus for production. In some villages that specialise in pottery, production peaks tend to follow the ritual cycle rather than the market price system. People produce more in the period before an important fiesta in order to earn more from sales to finance the event.

The ritual cycle is closely identified with the Indian community and, as the latter becomes more involved in the wider society, the ritual cycle declines. The ceremonies reinforce community solidarity because they involve participation, co-operation and reciprocity and they define its boundaries, for anyone who refuses to participate is viewed as an outsider.

GOVERNMENT ATTEMPTS AT INTEGRATION

The process of integration of the Indian into national society is difficult, not for racial reasons but for cultural ones. Organisations set up by the Mexican government see the issue as a cultural problem, because the values and social organisation of the Indian communities are so different from those of national society. While the Indians stress equality, personal relationships and mutual aid, capitalist ideology encourages competition, individuality and the subordination of personal feelings to rational self-interest and, since the different features of Indian society are so interrelated through the ritual cycle, a change in one has far-reaching repercussions throughout society. Is it possible for them to join national society and retain some of their own values? Integration has invariably meant, as it did with the privatisation of land laws of the nineteenth century and involvement in the market today, losing the protection of the community and exposure to a competitive society in which the Indian is so vulnerable.

Attempts have been made at national level to encourage and ease this process of integration, with varying degrees of success. The Mexican revolution, which began in 1910, was aimed at reducing inequalities throughout Mexican society. Since the peasantry played such an important role in the revolutionary fighting, if not in the leadership, agrarian reform was stressed as one of the basic principles of the revolution. Land redistribution did take place, reaching its peak in the late 1930s, when education was extended to rural communities, and yet today the Indian appears to have benefited little from these reforms. What makes the plight of the Indian particularly dramatic is the rhetoric of the revolution which has mythologised the Indian as heroic and the true Mexican. Many of the world-famous murals painted by revolutionary artists, depict the Indian in a revered pose, with the Spaniards cast as outsiders. This symbolic representation contrasts vividly with the poverty and hardship of Indian life. Since attempts to integrate the Indian, through land reform and education programs, had failed, the Mexican government in 1948 set up the INI (National Institute for Indigenous Peoples) to produce programs of Indian acculturation. This was a body, independent of government and made up of anthropologists, who were to study the culture of the Indian communities and the problems facing them, and form a plan which would incorporate them into the wider economy, with the least disruption of the Indian culture. Various co-ordinating centres, staffed by specialists under the supervision of anthropologists, were set up in different regions. These gave agricultural advice, initiated bilingual schools and defended the Indians from outside exploitation, achieving a certain measure of success in terms of integration. A greater proportion of the Mexican population is now literate, wears shoes (going barefoot is a cultural aspect of Indian life) and eats bread (Indian communities eat *tortillas* rather than bread). But, because of the tremendous population explosion, these achievements are not so apparent in absolute numbers. Between 1930 and 1960 the absolute figure of those not participating in the national culture increased from two to three million (Unwin 1982).

There are other very real problems with the process of integration. The contradictions of changing an economic system and maintaining a culture have never been resolved, as witnessed by INI's initial emphasis on learning Spanish and then its move to protect indigenous languages. Is language a tool for economic advancement or a cultural symbol?

But most of all, INI has not solved the problem of the vulnerability of the Indian in the capitalist economy and has, indeed, been criticised for using integration as a mechanism for providing cheap labour for capitalism (Unwin 1982). Indians usually work as seasonal labourers, with no security and for extremely low wages but, in so doing, contribute to greater profits for their employers and, therefore, increasing capital accumulation. Others migrate to the towns where they are also often unable to find employment and so find themselves living in shanty towns and working as street sellers or shoe-shine boys. By drawing the Indian out of the traditional community, policies of regional development, often encouraged by INI, involve him in semi-proletarianisation or the informal sector, forms of production which articulate with, but are subordinate to, the capitalist mode, to the benefit of the latter. It is invariably the large firms who have benefited most from the integration of the Indian. Pemex, the nationally owned oil company, is permitted by law to expropriate the land it requires for drilling. Recently, it has forced Indians off their land in Chicóntepec, giving them quite inadequate compensation. They had no choice but to work as poorly paid labourers for Pemex or migrate.

In response to some of the perceived failures of INI, Indian groups quite independent of government organisation have been forming and a network linking these across the country has been set up. This displays a growing indigenous consciousness, which springs from the grass-roots of society and, though at an early stage of development, may form the basis for significant socio-political action.

Indian consciousness in the region is particularly apparent in Ecuador, with its large indigenous population. Federations have been formed, based on tribal groupings, which have a political role in defending their people's interests. They have also been energetic in setting up a widespread administrative network which, in the case of the Shuar, involves operating their own radio station.

RACE RELATIONS IN AFRO-AMERICA

The intermixing of the three different stocks in Brazil has led to a complex racial situation, often referred to as a colour class system. The implication is that generations of miscegenation make it difficult to define racial boundaries but, nevertheless, there is a clear correlation between skin colour and racial features on the one hand, and class structure on the other. One attempt to estimate the racial composition of Brazil puts the origins of the people as follows – European 54.8 per cent, African 5.9 per cent, Japanese 0.6 per cent, Mixed 38.5 per cent, and Indigenous 200,000 (too small a group to really quantify in percentages) (LAB 1980).

This composition derives from the social organisation of the plantation system and the social changes that followed abolition. The early economic development of Brazil relied heavily on the plantation, with sugar being important, virtually to the exclusion of all other crops, in the north, and coffee in the south. The *fazenda*, as the plantation was called, was not just an economic system, but also a social and political structure. This has been clearly identified by the famous Brazilian sociologist, Gilberto Freyre, who points out that it was at the same time a system of production; a system of labour (slavery); a system of transport (e.g. the ox-cart, the horse); a system of religion (family Catholicism, with a chaplain subordinate to the master of the house); a system of sexual and family life (patriarchal); a system of bodily and household hygiene; and a system of politics (nepotism and patronage) (Freyre 1946). The *fazenda* represented a total way of life and at its focus was the patriarchal family. The white landowner, living in the Big House with his white family, was very much the head of the system. Also living in the house were a small number of Negro slaves, but the majority lived with their families on the *fazenda*.

Freyre has suggested that relations between the white and coloured races in Brazil were conditioned by two factors: the system of economic production – monoculture and *latifundia* – and the scarcity of white women among the conquerors (Freyre 1946). The plantation economy, especially sugar-raising, required a large labour force and, given the dearth of a suitable indigenous population, this led to a great demand for slaves. Through the nineteenth century until the 1850s the slave trade expanded steadily, bringing increasing numbers of Negroes from West Africa to work on the plantations of the New World. The small number of white women migrating from Portugal to Brazil was exacerbated by low levels of life expectancy due to the harshness of life. Women usually married very young and, once married, one pregnancy succeeded another, so that wives, worn out by continual child-bearing and general ill-health, rarely lived as long as their husbands. The landowners turned to their female slaves for sexual gratification, with the result that in the *fazenda* often resided the coloured mistresses of the patriarch and their mulatto children. The status of these women varied, some became domestics, others concubines and a very small number lawful wives. At first, the racial intermixture of people was clearly denoted, with special terms for those with one-quarter 'white blood' and those with one-eighth, but soon the racial picture became too complex to validate the use of such terms. Many illegitimate sons inherited portions of the estate, a small number becoming legitimised first.

The same slave trade that fed the *fazendas* also supplied the plantations of the USA and yet racial intermingling did not take place there. One reason for this was that the basic unit of settlement in the southern states of North America was the single-family farm, unlike the feudal-type estate of South America. The North American homesteader settled with his wife and family, having little contact with his slaves except in their capacity as workers. Differences may have been reinforced by the role of the church in each area. It became the custom for slaves in South America to become baptised and, once a member of the Catholic community, they came under the guidance of the clergy, who saw them all as members of God's family on earth. For the Protestants of the north, the souls of the slaves had little appeal, so they remained completely outside the white community. It has also been suggested that the Spanish and Portuguese, accustomed to mingling with the Moors on an equal basis, felt no repugnance to darker skins as did the plantation owners of the northern hemisphere and, therefore, to sexual relations with Negresses and mulattos.

This difference in the way race relations have developed in the USA and Brazil has led to the suggestion that slavery was a gentler institution in the southern hemisphere. This originated from Freyre's analysis, in which he emphasised intimate links between slaves and masters, though he himself did not claim that, as a result, slavery in Brazil was less harsh than elsewhere (Freyre 1946). Other historians have developed and given body to this idea (see, for example, Nelson 1945, Tannenbaum 1946). They argue that, although the slaves worked very hard, a series of features tended to mitigate the worst features of slavery. The clergy, having brought the slaves into the Catholic community, defended them against harsh treatment. The coloured mistresses and offspring of the patriarch received special treatment, which led to a lifestyle considerably more comfortable than that of the average slave. But perhaps the most persuasive argument is that of the extent and ease of manumission, as it was encouraged in Brazil in various ways. The patriarch, on his deathbed might, as an act of piety or out of kindness, offer freedom to faithful slaves. Happy family occasions, such as the birth of a first son or the marriage of one of the landowner's children, provided opportunities for slaves to be manumitted. According to Tannenbaum, law and custom made possible various forms of obtaining manumission. Freedom could be purchased, a Negro could be freed if unduly punished by his master, a slave was free to marry a non-slave and, by law, the children of a non-slave mother would be free, and a slave appointed guardian of a free man's children became free (Tannenbaum 1946). Not only did the law make it relatively easy for slaves to buy their freedom, but syndicates of slaves were formed to help buy each other out. By the nineteenth century, manumission was widespread though evidence suggests that, in the majority of cases, it was free fathers emancipating their own children by slave mothers. By the time of abolition it is estimated that there were three times as many Negro freemen as Negro slaves and then abolition was achieved in Latin America, unlike the USA, without violence, bloodshed or civil war.

This line of interpretation has been attacked from two different perspectives. From the moral point of view, it is argued that whether or not slavery was better or worse than in the United States is not really relevant, for it was still slavery and slavery is, by definition, an evil institution which has a damaging psychological effect on both master and slave (Elkins 1976).

It is, however, more effective to document the suffering and exploitation that the slaves endured. Life expectancy was desperately short. In the eighteenth century, the average life of a Negro slave in the mines or on the plantations has been estimated at 7–10 years (Banton 1967). According to Stein, it was common for only twenty-five out of every one hundred slaves to acclimatize successfully because of hard labour, poor feeding, poor clothing and the variable climate (Stein 1957). Disease was widespread during the nineteenth century, *fazendas* often registered from 19 per cent to 25 per cent of the slaves sick, with diseases such as typhoid, tuberculosis and those resulting from dietary deficiencies.

Infant mortality in the 1870s/80s was not less than 30 per cent and some planters managed to raise to manhood one-quarter of the slaves born on the *fazendas* (Stein 1957). The slaves that did survive were very strictly supervised, any misdemeanours were instantly and severely punished by the overseers. Hostility to the system, and especially their superordinates, is witnessed by the number of lynchings and assassinations of overseers, the flight of some slaves and the insurrections that took place, such as the slave revolts in Bahia in the 1830s and in the coffee regions in the 1840s.

It is clear that, as elsewhere in the world, slavery was extremely cruel. What is distinct about the Brazilian situation is the extent of miscegenation that took place and the mixed racial population that has resulted.

Slavery was finally abolished in Brazil in 1888, although the moral reasons were probably not as important as the economic. Certainly, the way had been paved by the work of liberal abolitionists, but slavery was becoming out of keeping with the new forms of production. The short life expectancy of the slaves and their debilitating existence was making them less remunerative than free labour. The modernisation of agriculture meant a desire for more capital which could be got from freeing that frozen in the buying and administration of slaves. Moreover, geographical mobility of labour was seen to be an advantage because of the seasonal nature of agricultural activities. Slavery had articulated with the dominant capitalist mode of production but, once it ceased to be beneficial to that mode, it was abolished.

As long as slavery was the major form of labour, Brazil held little attraction for immigrants but, once free labour replaced slave labour, the flow of immigration gained great momentum. The total number of immigrants arriving in São Paulo during the last five years of the nineteenth century amounted to more than four-and-a-half times the number of immigrants who entered between 1827 and 1884 (Mörner 1970). These immigrants, with their experience and knowledge of European society, were able to take advantage of the jobs now available.

Generations of slavery had not prepared the Negro for participation in the competitive market system. The slave had been compelled to work at the master's bidding, there was certainly no encouragement of initiative, entrepreneurship or individuality. He had never had the experience of finding lodgings, food or jobs. Moreover, for the better jobs of skilled manual labour or craftsmanship, the foreigner of European descent was given preference to the ex-slave. As a result, abolition provided the Negro with freedom, but little else for it did not equip him to use that freedom in his best interests. As a result, he was pushed to the social and economic periphery of society, finding himself, if he was lucky, in the poorest jobs and often living in makeshift huts on the outskirts of the town. The Brazilian population, in general, suffered from the competition of immigrants, but Negroes and mulattos especially so. By 1983, immigrants constituted 79 per cent of those employed in manufacturing, 85.5 per cent of those as craftsmen, 81 per cent of those in transport, and 71.6 per cent of those in commercial activities (Mörner 1970).

As post-1935 saw an acceleration of economic growth which provided an expansion of job opportunities, it became easier for Brazil's coloured population to find work, but the immigrants had established themselves in the more highly paid posts, so coloureds entered the labour force in the lowest income categories. Further industrialisation after 1940 expanded the number of job opportunities, thus encouraging the integration into the labour force of the coloured population, but their involvement was still confined to the low-income sector. This process is reflected in a survey done in 1951, which showed that, from a sample of coloureds, 29.39 per cent were craftsmen, 20.76 per cent were in domestic work, 9.18 per cent were government employees, 8.13 per cent were in industry as either skilled or semi-skilled workers, 7.08 per cent were office workers, 4.46 per cent were in the retail business (salesmen, etc.), 3.93 per cent were seasonal workers, 2.33 per cent were horticulturalists and gardeners and 14.69 per cent were in other occupations (Mörner 1970).

Changing occupations for the coloured population was accompanied by changing attitudes of society to the ex-slaves. Most of the immigrants had had no experience of Negroes and, therefore, wanted to maintain social distance, believing them to be both socially and psychologically inferior. Rather than risk involving themselves in either discriminatory or friendly behaviour, they avoided contact with them. This differed from the relationships the Negroes and mulattos were used to which had entailed greater involvement, whether it be paternalistic or of the master/slave type. The frequent reaction to this was resentment which, at times, led to behaviour that gave support to stereotype racial images.

COLOUR CLASS

The distinct characteristics of slavery in the northern and southern hemispheres of the Americas, and ensuing events after abolition, have led to different patterns of contemporary race relations;

> two decisive features are now said to distinguish the Brazilian model of Negro-white relations: (1) the absence of a rule of hypo-descent of the type which, in the United States, requires that any individual who has a known Negro ancestor be regarded as a Negro and hence as a member of a single subordinate group or 'caste'; and (2) the presence of a system of racial typing based on gradations of *physical appearance* on a continuum of pure Caucasoid (valued positively) to pure Negroid (valued negatively). One effect of these two characteristics – neither of which, it must be stressed, implies an absence of discrimination or freedom from prejudice – is that there are in Brazil no sharply defined racial groups which may be said to interact with one another. By their very attention to minute variations in the external appearance of their fellows, Brazilians inhibit the formation of specifically racial groupings. (Booth 1976: 113)

In Brazil, there is a public ideology of racial equality. The internationally renowned footballer, Pele, is often considered a symbol of equal opportunity for, despite being black and coming from a humble background, he has been socially mobile enough to reach the pinnacle of a world prestige system. Many commentators have pointed to the fallacy of this notion of equality in reality. Although it is impossible to distinguish clear-cut racial categories, and actual physical segregation according to racial type is absent, discrimination still exists, based on social distance related to physical characteristics, such as skin colour and facial features. 'A public ideology of racial equality could exist with the private practice of discrimination, because colour was compounded with other forms of differentiation,' (Banton 1967: 262). What has resulted is a colour class system where colour has been integrated into the general social order, as one of the various criteria which identify people in a status system. Wagley lists the criteria he considers important for membership of the local upper class in the four communities he studied – income, occupation, education, family background and, finally, physical appearance (Wagley 1969). The majority of Negroes and mulattos, because of their experience of slavery and resulting integration into the labour force in the lowest paid jobs, have been unable to achieve any significant social mobility. Thus, socio-economic factors and discrimination combine to keep darker skinned people in the lower ranks of society. Nevertheless, social mobility is possible for, as the Brazilians say, 'money whitens the skin'. Proletarianisation of the Negro and mulatto has meant steady work with regular wages and, therefore, improved standards of living and now both groups are beginning to move into the middle classes. Wagley found, in his study of Itá in rural Brazil, the major obstacle to social mobility was not physical appearance but social position at birth and lack of economic opportunity or educational chances (Wagley 1953).

Racial attitudes vary across Brazil and may appear to be contradictory within the same group of people. In the south of Brazil, slavery was more akin to the USA, so that when the Negro appeared in competition with the whites, traditional prejudices were adjusted to keeping the Negro in an inferior position. In the poor rural areas of Bahia, the superiority of the white man over the Negro is considered to be a scientific fact and stereotypes of Negroes as being less than human are well developed, but everyday behaviour differs from this. A poor white addressing a coloured, who is in a superior status, such as shopkeeper or doctor, will use the same terms of deference as if he were a white. The criterion of race can be counterbalanced by prestigious occupations, education or wealth (Harris 1971).

Although some writers, such as Wagley, while accepting that 'a mild form of racial prejudice exists on all levels of society in rural Brazil' (Wagley 1969: 55), are hopeful that economic development is opening up opportunities for blacks and so encouraging social mobility, others are critical of this optimistic view. Ianni attacks 'the intolerable contradiction between the myth of racial democracy and the actual prevalence of discrimination against Negroes and mulattos' (Ianni 1970: 267) and the way that this continues to act as an obstacle to research in some aspects of race relations. Ianni sees the dependence relationship influencing Brazil at all levels – in terms of ideology, the integration of the Negro into the capitalist mode of production in a subordinate role and the problems which Brazilian social scientists face when studying their own society. Fernandes points out that the myth of racial equality is seriously challenged by the existence of early and outspoken black consciousness movements. These movements unmasked the myth on three different levels. Liberty and equality in terms of the law were, in reality, useless because: the Negro was unable to participate on equal terms in the new competitive order; racial prejudice existed informally if not overtly; the whites remained in the dominant socio-economic positions in society (Fernandes 1974).

Although a colour class system condones a situation where physical appearance is one of the factors determining life chances, it is clearly less unjust in racial terms than any form of apartheid, as exists in South Africa. One consequence, however, of a colour class system seems to be an absence of continuing and numerically significant black protest movements, which have played such a major role in restructuring relationships between different ethnic groups and redressing the wrongs done to blacks. The very factors which give coloureds greater access to life chances in Brazil than in South Africa, detract from any growing consciousness on the basis of race or colour. The very few Negro protest groups that have appeared in Brazil have been short-lived and the same can be said for pre-revolutionary Cuba which then had a very similar colour class system. It is in the USA and South Africa that black nationalism has developed a sophisticated ideology and flourished. Because of this, David Booth argues that 'it may very well turn out less easy in the long run to bring about the definite suppression of the heritage of slavery in countries like Brazil and Cuba than in more obviously racist societies such as the US'. (Booth 1976: 172)

Booth's work on Cuba suggests that, despite the anti-racist policy of the Cuban revolution, discrimination still exists. The revolution has clearly abolished excesses in this area and eliminated its overt manifestation, but the Cuban government has been more concerned with the general redistribution of goods and services than the singling out of colour for particular attention. It is possible for personal racial attitudes to have remained relatively untouched. The political leadership, although providing the right ideological framework, has not developed measures much further, leaving innovations to a small group of black intellectuals and artists. It may be that the Cuban revolutionaries' aim, of totally eliminating colour prejudice, would have been easier had any black protest movements, armed with a clear and sophisticated ideology, been present.

INTEGRATION OF INDIANS IN AMAZONIA

The Indians who had, before the Hispanic conquest, not established complex civilisations, such as the Aztecs and Incas had done, fared even worse than them after the conquerors had arrived. The land their tiny numbers were compelled to inhabit was the inaccessible region of Amazonia in Brazil and Venezuela, for it was only in these jungles and plains that they felt safe from land-hungry Europeans. There they have remained, retaining their own tribal organisation and maintaining no real links with Brazilian society. The only contact is usually in the form of conflict with land speculators invariably ending in the death of one of the parties.

The decline of the Indian, and the way it has come about, has been so drastic that it has reached the international press and prompted pamphlets by liberal organisations. In this century, in Brazil, forty indigenous groups have disappeared and numerous others are in the process of extinction (LAB 1980).

Recent massacres have resulted from the opening up of the Amazon area by the Brazilian government for land colonisation schemes, which have brought Brazilians and Indians into clashes over land. In some cases, there have been atrocities, such as the gift of sugar that was seasoned with arsenic and given to a community, with the result that the Tapiuna Indians were wiped out. Another Mato Grosso tribe was shot up and bombed from the air with sticks of dynamite by a band of gunmen (Brain 1972). Sometimes contact with outsiders has brought fatal illnesses to the Indians, who do not have the body's defences to fight off the cold and other diseases unknown to them.

In this situation, where the government is opening up the interior, some form of organised integration is essential, for the Indians can no longer remain completely separate and, yet, the kind of contact that is developing can only be detrimental to them. One of the most successful attempts is Xingu Park, the brainchild of two anthropologists, the Boas brothers. During the 1950s, the tribes of the upper Xingu were being very hard-pressed by surveyors and prospectors, so the Boas brothers came to their aid. The jungle was cleared and in 1961 the area declared a national park under the authority of the two anthropologists. Tribes were encouraged to come into the park, where they received the benefits of modern society, such as medicines but, at the same time, their lives and their culture were protected. It clearly has been very successful in saving the Indians in this territory from further destruction. 'Some, like the Txikao, who were on the point of extinction are now increasing.' (Brain 1972: 46). It also attacked the issue that the Mexican government faced, that of assimilating the Indian into the contemporary society and economy but, at the same time, preserving his/her culture. Indians were taught skills which they could use to earn a living outside the park, but they were given the opportunity to learn these at their own speed and in their own way. At the same time, they kept up their dances and ceremonies but, although the various tribes spoke different languages and had their own myths, the cultures have become much more like each other through contact. It was often difficult to attract the Indian into the park, given the nature of his previous contacts with the white man and, in some cases, it took up to two years to bring in a group. But, despite numerous problems, Xingu proved a great success, about 1,500 Indians from fifteen different tribes benefited from its protection (Brain 1972).

The Brazilian government has approached the problem of integration by setting up an agency – FUNAI, the National Foundation for the Indian. FUNAI has been mostly concerned with land, attempting to integrate the Indians by offering protection if they inhabit the areas designated by FUNAI. Preservation of the Indian, therefore, means control as well as protection by FUNAI. Land, however, has value to others and even when FUNAI has had well-intentioned leaders they have not been able to fend off the strength of economic interests. In 1980, FUNAI, convinced by anthropologists that the physical and cultural survival of Brazil's last large group of primitive Indians, the Yanomami, required considerable space, put forward a plan to develop a 6.4 million hectare reserve for these Indians. The opposition, however, was powerful. Politicians objected because they said it would impede economic development of the area and sectors within the armed forces did not wish it to be along the Venezuelan border, which was vital to the plan since it would then facilitate contact with the Yanomami in Venezuela. But the strongest opposition came from the state-owned mining company, who had discovered large deposits of high-quality natural tin oxide in the area. They proposed that the Indians should be catered for by twelve small separated reservations, which would have had the result of disrupting their hunting patterns and social organisation. The President of FUNAI resigned for, again, the survival of the Indian was sacrificed to powerful economic interests (LARR Brazil 4 Jan. 1980).

A degree of integration for a small number of Indians, and the ineffectiveness of government in assisting the Indians, has led to some political action on their part. In 1980, a union of Indian nations was launched with various aims: to represent their communities; offer mutual aid; recover their lost territories and organise legal and economic assistance for their projects. Although FUNAI refused to recognise this, it was followed by meetings and assemblies through the first few years of the eighties. One of the successes of this political movement has been the election of an Indian congressman, the only one so far, but as an Indian leader, Juruna is able to campaign for their rights within his party. His sometimes controversial appearances have sparked off public debate about the integration of Indian communities into Brazilian society (LARR Brazil Oct. 1983). The Brazilian experience has been marked by violence and bloodshed but now, for the first time, the Brazilian Indians are getting organised, taking a stand and showing signs of indigenous consciousness.

This chapter has suggested that, although ethnicity plays a crucial role in the determining of life chances of Latin Americans, race does not operate in such a way as to demarcate distinct groups. Ethnic labelling is used to set boundaries, in some cases as a form of exclusion, but in others in order to minimise the exploitation that certain types of socio-economic contact bring about. Since group identity has been on the basis of culture, often linked to rather isolated Indian communities, it has not led to the emergence of a consciousness of race or ethnicity in any political form. Black protest movements have been minimal and Indian organisation in Amazonia and Indian political mobilisation through national organisations such as INI, are at the very earliest stage of development.

The pattern of colonial and post-colonial development, with its intermixing of racial groups, was quite different in Latin America from other parts of the Third World, such as Africa, where strict divisions between the white colonial power and the black indigenous population were maintained. There, these distinctions have remained, leading to conflict between very distinct and racially bounded groups with their own ideology and awareness. It may well be the case that class systems have developed within these sectors of society, so that we find a black middle class has emerged in the USA and South Africa but, especially in South Africa, it has not managed to compete successfully with whites for the benefits of society. In this case, class factors operate as a stratifying principle within colour boundaries, unlike Latin America, where physical appearance is one of a number of criteria which contribute towards class definition.

Minority nationalism has not flourished in any political sense and only ambiguously in a cultural one because historical trends, and the lines of social and economic division, have not favoured its emergence. The grossly disproportionate distribution of wealth and power has meant that lines of conflict have not been drawn between racial, which would have been virtually impossible, or ethnic groups but that oppression has been suffered by one class at the hands of another. Where class and race have overlapped, such as in the Indian communities of Mexico and Peru, resistance has taken the form of affirming distinctive cultural traits rather than forming dissident racial or political movements (Cubitt and Cubitt 1980).

There are, however, some signs that this situation might be changing with the growing ethnic consciousness and growth of social movements with their basis in ethnicity.

FURTHER READING

For a particularly good discussion of the different approaches used to analyse rural society, see:

Hewitt de Alcántara, C. (1984) *Anthropological perspectives on rural Mexico*. Routledge and Kegan Paul, London

Booth, D. (1976) Cuba, colour and the revolution. *Science and society* XL, no. 2, summer

Freyre, G. (1946) *The masters and the slaves. (Casa-Grande e Senzala): a study in the development of Brazilian civilisation* trans. S Putnam, A A Knopf , New York

Mörner, M. (1970) *Race and class in Latin America.* Colombia University Press, New York and London

Wolf, E. Hansen, E. (1972) *The human condition in Latin America.* Oxford University Press, New York

Values and social relations

The previous chapter suggested that the Hispanic heritage was the major element contributing to the cultural formation of Latin America and, since values constitute a vital component of culture, the Hispanic influence has been considerable in shaping norms. At the heart of these have been the institutions of church and family and a code of behaviour based on personal honour. Commentators on Spanish culture through the centuries have pointed to its emphasis on dignity and the corresponding fear of shame which leads to behaviour that is continually concerned to respect others and, above all, their individuality (Pitt-Rivers 1977). The resulting emphasis on personalism and personalised relationships has become very much a feature of social life in the New World, too.

CHURCH

Durkheim's investigations into religion, with their historic results, were prompted by the fact that he saw religion as the major source of values and, despite increasing secularisation, religion still plays an influential role in society's moral codes. With the exception of the indigenous groups of Plantation America and some small groups who have been evangelised by Protestant missionaries, Latin Americans are Roman Catholic. The conquest brought not only soldiers to Latin America but also priests and missionaries, for the christianising mission of the Spaniards and Portuguese was vital to their cause.

These priests were instructed to, if possible, incorporate and then translate pagan religion and culture into the Catholic orthodoxy, rather than destroying completely these alien beliefs. This proved more feasible for the Incas than the Aztecs but eventually, with varying degrees of repression, the indigenous people were brought into the Catholic fold. Some historians have argued that, once the Indians had become part of the Christian community, their cause was championed by the church who protected them from some of the worst excesses of colonial power (Poblete 1970). Like the argument concerning the church and slavery, however, it must be remembered that, although priests may have alleviated the lot of a small number, the colonial epoch still retains a place in history which is notorious for the brutality shown to the Indians.

During the colonial period, the church was closely aligned with the state, giving full support to the dominant power and, in return, receiving special privileges. The church for its part acted as an administrative agency of colonial expansion and a major institution of social control. After political independence, however, many Latin American countries became involved in conservative-liberal struggles, forcing the church to make a choice between the elite groups. In general it allied itself with the conservative sector, knowing it could then rely on the wealth and status of this group and, in return, offering a value system that supported their regimes. It was in this role that the Catholic church entered the twentieth century. 'In the main, the church and its leaders drew their importance from the support they gave to the existing powers and from their multiple involvements in education, social welfare and administration.' (Vallier 1967: 193).

The church, having survived independence movements, inter-elite struggles and, in the case of Mexico, the virulent anti-clericalism of the revolution, continues to be an important institution in twentieth-century Latin America. Its strength lies partly in its scope, for Roman Catholics make up about 90 per cent of the population; for instance, the figure is 89.1 per cent for Brazil (LAB 1982) and 88.7 per cent for Mexico (1980 Census); and also in its institutional links with other aspects of life, such as education, health, leisure and community activities. But the power and attitudes of the church vary considerably with different Latin American countries. Colombia, often considered the most traditional of the Latin American republics, is a clerical country. The church has a strong hold on education, the clergy command great respect from the population and the church leaders, like other Colombian elites, have not favoured social change. The Chilean church, however, has often been referred to as 'the most progressive Catholic system in Latin America'. (Vallier 1966: 220). The hierarchy, often in the hands of the liberals, has promoted reform programmes, such as technical training for peasants and the forming of cooperatives in the shanty towns, become involved in politics through the reformist Christian Democrat party and opposed the brutalities of the military regime since 1973, by speaking out openly against their excesses and providing soup kitchens for the needy. Mexico is a country where the church does not have a strong grip on the population because of the force with which the revolutionaries opposed the clergy, believing them to be partly responsible for the backwardness of rural areas. The revolution made education secular and reduced the wealth of the church by confiscating some of its land. Today although church schools have emerged again and crucifixes and images of the Virgin Mary and the saints are to be found adorning many homes, especially in rural areas, the church's influence on the dominant groups in society is not great. The question, then, relates not so much to the continuing vigour of the church, but as to which direction it will take. Will it continue to uphold the conservative values of those in power, or will it offer a more radical alternative?

In this century, differences have emerged between leading churchmen in the region and, especially since the 1960s, the differences have developed into significant splits within the church. Prior to the middle of this century, the Catholic Church had concerned itself predominantly with spiritual matters. The Second Vatican Council (1962–65), however, redirected the church's interests towards the temporal world and especially issues such as justice, human rights and freedom. Not only was the traditional ideal of union between church and state relinquished but also the Council stressed the responsibility of the church to pass moral judgements, even on matters touching the political order, whenever basic personal rights or the salvation of souls make such judgements necessary. 'Many bishops in Latin America, Asia, and Africa, since the end of the Council, have exercised this prophetic role vigorously, denouncing political disappearances, torture, economic exploitation, and racism perpetrated by authoritarian regimes in their countries.' (Smith 1982: 5) This shift in official church policy has made possible a greater integration of religious and secular values and also the move from legitimisation of the existing social structures towards the promotion of greater equality.

In Latin America, the Second Vatican Council was followed up by a meeting of bishops from all over the continent in Medellín, Colombia. The message to emerge from this conference was one of liberation, from both spiritual and material bondage, and this liberation was to be achieved by the participation in the whole life of the church, not just church services. The conference also stressed the development of Christian Base Communities – CEBs. This is an aspect of pastoral development in which small groups meet together principally for Bible study but, in many cases, they may be devoted to promoting other activities as well, such as literacy classes or agricultural cooperatives. The CEBs represent a radical move for the church for various reasons. They are, for a start, a product of the local community, not the church hierarchy. They are organised and led by the people and, although a religious leader is present to offer assistance, the nature and activities of the group are decided by the members. The organisation is highly democratic, for lay readers are elected and then must consult their members in decision-making. Many nuns and priests who have worked with the CEBs have found that members become much more self-confident, they no longer feel cowed by fate (Montgomery 1983).

Accompanying these changes in the policy and organisation of the church was the growth of new developments in theology, which have come to be known as the Theology of Liberation. This is a truly radical development for the church, because it takes much of its thinking from Marxism. Liberation Theology explicitly links society, politics and religion and in so doing, bases much of its social analysis on dependency theory. Poverty, injustice and other secular problems are, therefore, seen as being the result of exploitation by world capitalist powers. Any sort of improvement for the masses must involve a reordering of the social structure. This change can not take place without the involvement of the people themselves and, therefore, they must be moved from their traditional passivity towards an active role in shaping their own lives. In line with the movement towards participation in temporal affairs, liberationalists believe that they must demonstrate genuine Christian love by committing the church to creating a more egalitarian society through religiously inspired political action. Liberation Theology, therefore, advocates action and exhorts the clergy to emerge from the cloisters to help the people to help themselves.

The call for action has been put into practice in some parts of Latin America, especially in Central America. After the successful Sandinista revolution in Nicaragua, two priests were included in the Marxist government. This was going too far for the established church in both Rome and Nicaragua, with the result that the Pope called for their resignation. In 1983, the Pope, concerned by the spread of Liberation Theology, visited Central America, ostensibly in order to promote church unity. The Nicaraguan part of the tour was marked by a well-publicised clash between the Pope and Sandinistas, which was prompted by a briefing-paper presented to the Pope by church right-wingers.

The same split between conservatives and progressives can also be found in Guatemala, Honduras and El Salvador, In the latter, the progressives have been active in the top echelons of the church hierarchy. Archbishop Romero, although thought to be a moderate when he took up the Archbishopric, proved himself to be a zealous proponent of Liberation Theology, broadcasting his masses, which included political messages, to the people throughout the country, by radio. Romero linked his readings with the reality of life in El Salvador and each week his sermon was followed by 'a reading of every documented case of persons who had been killed, assaulted, tortured or disappeared by any group on the left or the right'. (Montgomery 1983: 78) Since far more attacks were brought about by the government's death squads than the left, Romero's vast audience soon became aware of what was happening in their country. Romero's beliefs and bravery, however, cost him his life for on 24 March 1980 he, too, was assassinated by a professional hit-man hired by the extreme right.

These events in Central America demonstrate the church at its most radical. Many churchmen, however, have not been happy with these developments, which have given rise to schisms threatening enough to warrant the Pope's visit. Some church leaders fear that a political commitment on the part of the church would undermine the value of the spiritual dimensions of the Christian faith, for it threatens their mission of salvation. For many, the whole idea of using Marxist concepts of analysis is out of the question for a Christian and the spectre of communism has been one of the most divisive aspects. Another fear of the critics of Liberation Theology is that the logic of the argument leads to violence, since violence may be the only means available to overthrow corrupt regimes and this, they feel, no Christian should condone.

In many areas, the split is not into a clear cut one of those for and against, but often includes middle groups who are sympathetic to some of the ideas of Liberation Theology but can not go all the way with it. In Central America, three groupings can be identified. The institutional church, preoccupied with orthodoxy and fundamentally opposed to Marxism because it is viewed as materialistic and aetheistic, is made up of bishops, priests, laity and religious movements who, though not very numerous, are powerful, partly because the laity of the group belong to the wealthier classes. The centrist sector, who favour a middle way, is opposed to repression and violence whether it is from right or left. This group, which does not ally itself with either American intervention or with Marxists, represents the greater part of the church in Central America. The popular church, with its base in the CEBs and animated by Liberation Theology, feels that risks must be taken to right the social and political evils of the world and so is sympathetic to revolutionary movements. Though not large, this sector of the church is qualitatively important.

Weber suggested that the Protestant ethic produced the value orientations and attitudes in which capitalism could prosper and that Catholicism, like most other religions, hinders social progress. It could be argued that Latin America offers a good example of this. Catholicism, for centuries, allied itself with conservative forces opposed to progress but now that elements within the church have come out in favour of change, they appear to be opting for a more socialist, rather than capitalist, line. 'Traditional Catholic principles, once an obstacle to change in emerging capitalist economies, when they were identified with corporatist ideologies, now appear to be more compatible with various socialist models of development.' (Smith 1982: 4).

EDUCATION

Other institutions have come to challenge the church's traditional dominance of the value system. As mentioned in Chapter 1, education has an important part to play in development, in both its contribution to structural change and to changing values. In the former, education can provide more people with the skills and information to secure them good jobs and, thus, produce an increase in the number of people prepared for fulfilling and materially rewarding occupations. This can open up new opportunities and create social mobility. Values are maintained or altered because education is one of society's mechanisms of socialisation. Education, too, can be directed to encourage certain ideals.

Education is a sector which has expanded greatly in Latin America. There can be no doubt that it is a growth area, which has had distinct achievements in many countries. Traditionally, the prerogative of the elite, education is now available to most Latin Americans. Have these developments brought about social mobility? The difficulty with the argument, that more and better education leads to mobility, is that better-trained people do not, on their own, lead to an increase in the number of better-paid jobs. As Kahl has said, education 'reinforces the existing status system and provides for movement within it' (Kahl 1970: 137), but this suggests that it does not change the system. It is industrial growth, the expansion of bureaucracies and services, and social and economic policies of governments, that shape a society's occupational profile. Education can equip people to fill these positions, but it does not control the expansion or contraction of the job market. Some sociologists claim that low levels of social mobility only provide movement within the system but that, on a bigger scale, this mobility can change the system (Kahl 1970). This, however, still overlooks the fact that the larger numbers of better educated have no power base from which to bring about change, if there are no jobs or positions in society for them.

What has been happening in Latin America is that the growth of education has been much faster than structural change in society, with the result that some of the potential value of education for social mobility is lost. Some Latin American educationalists predict that the ensuing frustration of an educated population that can not find appropriate work, will lead to social conflict.

In quantitative and qualitative terms, how extensive have the changes in education been? Literacy rates, a good indicator of educational achievement, have improved very considerably during the century. In 1895, the illiteracy rate for the population aged fourteen years and over was 53 per cent in Argentina, and 68 per cent in Chile. Even by the second decade of this century, the illiteracy rate for the Brazilian population was about 80 per cent. By 1950, there had been improvements but they were slow in taking place. In that year, with the exception of Argentina, Chile, Costa Rica, Cuba and Uruguay, the illiteracy rate of populations aged over fifteen years, exceeded 30 per cent in all Latin American countries, 50 per cent being recorded in Brazil and higher percentages in Central America (Rama 1983: 16). It is since the 1950s that the expansion in education has really accelerated, with a resulting boost to literacy rates. Now, in Argentina, Chile and Uruguay, they have topped the 90 per cent mark, with 94.2 per cent (1982), 95.6 per cent and 96.3 per cent (1983) respectively. Mexico is not far off, with 87.9 per cent (1983). Apart from Haiti, with illiteracy as much as 63.1 per cent in 1982, even the poorer countries record relatively high literacy rates – 87.9 per cent in Nicaragua in 1981 and 92.0 per cent in Paraguay in 1984 (Inter-American Development Bank 1985).

These improved rates have been brought about by increasing school enrolment. In the period from 1950–80, the school-age population (under twenty-four-years-old and over five) attending school, doubled. By 1980 in Argentina six out of every ten individuals of school age were incorporated in the educational system. This growth has accelerated in recent years, much of it taking place in the 1970s and it has been concentrated more in the higher levels of the education system. Between 1950 and 1980, participation in higher education rose from 5 to 16 per cent, in secondary from 15 to 25 per cent, and in primary education from 50 to 90 per cent (Filgueira 1983: 69). Education, in recent years, has been characterised by less rigidity, less concentration and greater opportunities for mobility, but all these features become more apparent higher up the educational pyramid. These changes have brought about a reduction of inequality in education throughout the region.

This expansion of education has not brought about a similar

increase in social mobility. Class background is an important factor in the level of schooling achieved, partly because the higher the level the greater the cost (if only in terms of opportunity costs) and partly because educational facilities are best in the well-to-do residential areas. Eckstein found in Mexico that in over three generations, there had been little upward occupational mobility, especially into the white-collar class (Eckstein 1977).

But it is not just that access to the increased educational facilities is conditioned by social background, even where people achieve educational mobility, the economic structure has not provided a corresponding increase in jobs to match that mobility in occupational terms. Eckstein found that the best educated had access to the most rewarding jobs, 'but because such jobs are not expanding as rapidly as schooling, education in itself provides no guaranteed job'. (Eckstein 1977: 205). Filgueira points out that the reduction of inequality in education

> is in contrast to the behaviour of income distribution, where inequity has been but little reduced during the same periods, and which shows extreme relative rigidity and concentration in comparison with the greater equalizing capacity of the educational system. The figures for inequality in income distribution in the countries of the region (for example, Uruguay, 0.49; Brazil, 0.70; Chile, 0.50) are always higher than those for educational inequality, and dynamic trends suggest that the gap between them tends only to widen. (Filgueira 1983: 70)

Filgueira suggests that, since the major educational developments have taken place so recently, it may be too soon for them to have brought about greater reorganisation in society. He does add, however, that structural changes are also necessary to accommodate the benefits of educational expansion.

The growth of formal education systems could not have taken place without the incorporation of sectors in society, which had previously been excluded. The expansion of primary education has benefited the peasantry and the urban poor, in particular, since rural education has lagged behind urban. A United Nations study showed that most of the students completing secondary education, represented the first generation of their family to reach this level (Filgueira 1983: 71). Those who reap the benefits of higher education, however, are recruited predominantly from the middle and upper classes. A study of Uruguayan professionals who graduated in 1970, revealed that barely 11 per cent came from families in which the father worked in skilled or unskilled manual occupations. Mobility, however, is greater if educational levels of fathers and graduates is measured. Eighteen per cent of the professionals had fathers with incomplete primary schooling, and 27 per cent came from families where the father had achieved no more than a primary level of education. The graduates had frequently been more successful than their fathers, in educational achievement but, in general, were entering occupations of similar status to those of their fathers (Filgueira 1983).

The proportion of students from poorer families who enter higher education is similar in other Latin American countries, though there are variations according to courses and institutions. Short and intermediate courses and those which do not involve the student in heavy costs tend to have a more democratic social composition. But the greater the prestige and reputation of an institution, the more it will recruit from the upper echelons of society.

Although biased towards the higher levels and urban areas, the quantitative development of education has been very significant. However, so far, it seems that this has had little influence on the redistribution of wealth and power in society. This suggests that either educational reform has just not gone far enough or that, although improved educational standards constitute an important development goal, they can only be effective when accompanied by structural changes in the rest of society. Perhaps both are the case.

In terms of values, education is the way in which young people experience socialisation. Traditionally, literacy campaigns in peripheral rural areas would rely on the Bible, which was not just a source of reading material but, also, a way of encouraging conformity. In the same way, the literacy campaigns of the Cubans and the Nicaraguans have used Marxist-Leninist tracts, and other material, in line with revolutionary ideas. In the years following the violence of the Mexican revolution, great attention was paid to the content of education, in an attempt to involve the young in the principles of the revolution, but this emphasis has declined in the second half of the century.

In general, education has reinforced society's values, but there have been some experimental attempts at providing education to radicalise values. One of the most famous was Freire's Movement of Popular Culture in Brazil's north-east, which was aimed at raising the consciousness of his students. Freire wanted to bring people to a critical awareness of their real situation in the socio-economic context, only then could they really learn and understand. He argued that the lack of awareness of the needy in Brazil's poorest region only facilitated their exploitation. Education, he believed, should offer a means of escaping from the alienation and poverty that bedevils that area (Freire 1968). Freire's experiment was cut short by a military coup, so it is difficult to judge the results.

Many schools, colleges and universities in Latin America are part of the church's empire and so values, inculcated here, are in line with the dominant Catholic Hispanic mores. Dissent has occurred at times among university students in attempts to radicalise dominant ideas. One of the most famous occasions was the student movement in Mexico in 1968, when student marches, demonstrations and general opposition to the government of the day prompted the intervention of the army. In the final analysis students, although able to generate new ideas and disseminate them within a limited circle of people, do not have power and are no match for the military.

MASS MEDIA

One of the visible contradictions of the Third World that is apparent in Latin America is the spread of sophisticated and technological forms of mass media in poverty-stricken areas. The recently arrived visitor in Mexico City is quick to notice the mass of television aerials that rise from the shacks in the poorest districts of the city. The stereotype of the Mexican peasant, dwarfed by his sombrero and sitting by a cactus should, perhaps, be more realistically presented as listening to his radio set. A study of peasant families in the Cochabamba area of Bolivia revealed that 90 per cent of them owned radios (Ortega 1982). The contradiction is probably most apparent in Mexico, where cheap radios, televisions and films can so easily be imported from the USA, but the media is also very much a feature of contemporary life in other Latin American countries.

In terms of statistics, Argentina ranks 5th and Uruguay 19th in radio set ownership in the world, Argentines owning more radio sets per 1,000 of the population than the British. When it comes to television sets, Latin Americans are not so well endowed. Out of 138 countries, Argentina is ranked 42nd, Uruguay 53rd, Panama 58th, Venezuela 59th, Mexico 65th, Brazil 66th, Chile and Costa Rica 68th, Colombia 70th and Cuba 71st for television set ownership per 1,000 of the population. In comparison with other peoples of the world, Latin Americans read newspapers more than watching television, but less than listening to the radio. Uruguay, this time, outranks Argentina, coming 22nd in world figures for newspaper circulation. Out of 134 countries, several Latin American republics appear in ranks between 37 and 53 (*The World in Figures* – figures for 1975–76, newspapers 1970–75).

The debate over the role of the media is similar to the master/servant debate over bureaucracy. Is the media merely a tool that can be used by the dominant group in society to bring about whatever change or lack of change they require or does it, by its nature, shape the influence it has on the population? The discussion is closely linked to the different approaches of modernisation and dependency theories.

The modernisation school sees the media as, on the one hand, an aspect of modern society and, on the other, a means by which elites can modernise further. Joseph Kahl, in his attempt to measure modernism, picks out participation in the mass media as one of his key criteria of the modern. For him, modern man reads newspapers, listens to the radio, watches television and follows national and international events. In his research on Mexico and Brazil, he found that a good proportion of his samples were interested in following national and international news on the radio and in the newspapers (Kahl 1970).

The power of the media, as a mechanism for change, lies in the scope and breadth of the population it reaches. Often referred to as a means by which a nation, or even the world, can become a community, it makes possible the transmitting of messages from a small group of people to a vast number. Television and radio can be used for educational purposes, to spread modern values and inform people. In Mexico and El Salvador, television has been used experimentally as an educational medium and, in Brazil, classic novels have been serialised to give people a knowledge of their own culture. In theory, the media can be used to promote certain policies though, in practice, this is not often the case, partly because broadcasting, the obvious channel, needs to attract advertising to finance itself and, since educational programmes do not often have mass appeal, they are unlikely to draw in the necessary funding. The Cubans, however, with the help of state resources, have used television and film to encourage the development of the values of the revolution, especially where these are at variance with traditional and deeply held views. Television has been used to promote equality between the sexes by showing short features suggesting that sons and daughters should be brought up equally at home and girls not expected to wait on their brothers.

Taking the perspective of the dependency school, mass media in the LDCs is an aspect of cultural imperialism. The technology necessary to produce films, and television and radio programs, is so much more advanced in the industrialised countries than in the LDCs, that it is frequently much simpler and cheaper to import material than to produce it in the Third World. Although countries like Mexico, Chile and Brazil have budding film industries, the products of which are now reaching the industrialised world, it is still North American and European films that predominate in the cinemas of Mexico City, Santiago and São Paulo. Brazilian cinema has expanded particularly rapidly, for its share of the domestic market has risen from 14 per cent in 1970 to 38 per cent today (LAWR Brazil 25 Nov. 1983) but, nevertheless, this still leaves nearly two-thirds to films from abroad. Television and radio in the region have several channels so, while some are devoted to local issues and productions, others are packed with imported serials, films and games. Not only are foreign programmes often better made, but they also have the allure, real or imagined, of being sophisticated or trendy. The point about imported material is that it contains the values of the society where it was made and, so, through modern techniques of diffusion, all social levels of a Third World society are exposed to the product of a small group of people in the industrialised world. The world becomes a community, which is influenced by the small elite who control the media. 'In a dependent society the media demonstrate the imperialist system's concept of change – a conception which in fact ends up being the denial of change.' (Mattelart 1978: 23).

The implicit values in drama are made more explicit in the advertising that sponsors and accompanies the fiction. In promoting consumer products, in competition with each other, the advertisements promote the values of capitalism – the stress laid on wealth and working hard in conventional modes to try and achieve it, competition and the importance of consumer goods as an expression of self and status. According to Mattelart, North American advertising agencies in Latin America have gone one step further by explicitly promoting models of political development (Mattelart 1978).

Although it is clear that the potential for considerable influence is there, how effective is the mass media in changing or maintaining values and behaviour patterns? A study of drinking patterns in Mexico reveals the strength of advertising. Mexico has one of the highest rates of alcoholism in the world, which appears to be the result of the coincidence of traditional and modern advertisement-inspired modes of behaviour. Mexicans have always been known for heavy drinking because traditional forms of alcohol are cheap, peasants often making their own, and this is a classic way of forgetting the drudgery of poverty. But, in recent years, alcoholism has become a greater and nationally recognised social problem. The figures show that beer and spirits together constitute the industry with the greatest publicity in Mexico (Harvey 1983). Those with a little cash to spend, who want to be modern and sophisticated, as advertisements suggest, buy imported whiskey and brandy. As a result, alcoholism affects all levels of society and all age groups.

Not only visual representation, but the written word, too, is not free of imperialism. Latin American newspapers, unable to afford their own reporters in different parts of the world, often use syndicated news from North America or other foreign sources. This bears the imperialist nation's view of world events and is then reproduced for the mass of Latin Americans to read. As well as newspapers, and for those whose literacy level is not up to the language of a newspaper, comics for adults are widely available. An aspect of popular culture that is not found much in the industrialised world, comics are read by all levels of society and all age-groups.

Changes within the institutions which influence values are taking place and, in general, reflect a gradual shift towards the values of contemporary capitalist societies, corresponding to the process outlined in the previous chapter of incorporating peripheral groups into society. The ideas that the media purveys are certainly both modern and an aspect of cultural imperialism, for they emanate from the core countries of the capitalist world. Education has expanded very significantly, thus giving a much greater number of people information and skills to assist them in improving their living standards. The church, however, seems to be out of step for, having opposed change for so long by supporting the status quo, it is now demonstrating an element of true radicalism since a minority of its clergy wish to take change beyond capitalism towards socialism.

However, as with education, the impact of change has been limited by a lack of a corresponding expansion of the job market. This suggests that economic and political factors are vital in shaping the nature and extent of the effects of changes within these institutions, an argument that will be examined more closely in later chapters. For the moment, it is important to relate these changes to one of the themes of the book and see whether they have brought about less inequality. This chapter looks, in particular, at the realm of social relations.

PERSONALISM

Despite the spread of values emphasising achievement and competition, personalism remains an essential feature of social relations in Latin America, probably because of the continuance of uncertainty and insecurity. Relationships between two people anywhere in the world can be expressed in terms of a dyadic contract (Foster 1967). The formal institutions in society provide the individual with a framework and, within this, he/she can choose with whom to interact, thus setting up a dyadic contract, that is, an informal relationship that binds two people. Although informal, this relationship can be recognised through reciprocity. Whether it be through the exchange of goods, services, esteem or confidence, all relationships are marked by some sort of reciprocity. The exchange of food and drink through dinner parties, coffee mornings, pub evenings, etc., is a universal means of establishing and maintaining social relations. In Latin America, relationships are built up in this way not just for personal support but, also, to promote commercial and political ends.

The Brazilian *panelinhas* are informal groups made up of a number of dyadic contracts, that is, people linked by personal ties – family, kin, friends – but the members are selected according to their occupation. Each *panelinha* tries to represent a range of occupations, such as doctor, lawyer, banker, engineer, architect and a variety of different businesses. Members of one group will try and do business with each other, rather than outsiders, knowing they have the advantage of the personal contact and can, therefore, trust the person concerned (Leeds 1974). It is not just in professional and business circles that personal contacts help people obtain jobs. From her Mexican study, Eckstein reports that about 38 per cent of the men with factory and white-collar jobs said they obtained their work through a personal acquaintance (Eckstein 1977).

Dyadic contracts can be divided into colleague contracts referring to relationships between those of equal status and patron-client contracts, where the status of those involved is different. Colleague contracts, such as most friendships, involve an exchange of similar kinds of things whereas, in the patron-client relationship, the different status is reflected in the fact that the patron offers something quite different to the relationship from the contribution of the client. One of the most widespread expressions of the colleague contract is *compadrazgo*.

Compadrazgo, as Latin Americans call ritual or pseudo-kinship, is a means by which people imbue relationships of friendship with the lasting and obligatory character of kinship. Friendship has the advantage of choice, friends are chosen by the individual concerned but it is, also, flexible and not necessarily lasting. Kinship is binding and permanent but permits no choice of personnel, the individual must accept the relatives he has. *Compadrazgo* is a compromise which attempts to combine the best of friendship with the advantages of kinship (Foster 1967).

Compadrazgo relations are set up through the ritual sponsorship of the church system of appointing godparents for children. On at least four ritual occasions in the life of a young person – baptism, confirmation, first communion and marriage – the parents have the opportunity of asking friends to sponsor them, thus becoming their godparents. This establishes a set of permanent relationships between parents, godparents and child/godchild in which the most important social relationship excludes the child, for it is between parents and godparents. They become compadres or ritual kin. The godparent may have a ritual role to the child, such as participating in his wedding ceremony, and taking on certain responsibilities regarding his religious education, but the relationship that is strongest and requires respect, warmth and the obligation to help at all times, is the one between parents and godparents.

In the task of fortifying oneself with supportive personal relationships, *compadrazgo* offers extensive manipulative opportunities. Each ceremony for each child requires a new set of godparents so, as most Latin American couples have many children, there are numerous opportunities for establishing new sets of *compadres*. Moreover, one can extend secondary relationships to the kin and *compadres* of a *compadre*, with whom one has a primary relationship. In the early years of married life, a couple may try and establish as wide a social network as possible and, then, in later life if they feel that it is sufficient, they may ask relatives to be godparents, thus reaffirming existing kinship ties, rather than extending the network further. At the level of village life, this pattern provides stability and cohesion, for villagers are interlinked by the criss-crossing relationships of *compadrazgo*.

In urban areas, *compadrazgo* is more informal though, in some areas, just as effective. There is, however, considerable regional variation. In Mexico, especially in rural areas, it operates as an important principle of social organisation while, in Chile, it has lost a lot of its formal and obligatory nature and is not very meaningful for many people.

Clientelism, however, continues to be a firmly entrenched pattern of social relations throughout the region. The exchange of dissimilar things in the patron-client relationship occurs because the patron offers the qualities that accrue to his superior status, that is, power and influence to help the client while, in return, the latter contributes support and esteem. From this the client gains assistance which he needs in his weak position. The peasant, for instance, who wishes to sell his avocados or pots in the local market may need a licence to do so, something that is outside the realm of the usual activities of a peasant, especially an illiterate. His patron, usually the local landowner, can acquire the necessary application forms and show him what to do with them. For his part, the patron gains the personal support of the client and, when he has accumulated a number of these clients, he becomes a prestigious person in the area due to the cumulative honour from them. This support can be turned into power by an astute patron. The patron can call on his clients for active support, a facet which is important in local power struggles. Candidates in local elections can expect their followers not only to vote for them but to campaign for them as well. Political power can be built up in this way, with the result that many Latin American leaders owe their position to a network of clientelist relationships.

Although the status difference may be emphasised in the style of the relationship, with client addressing the patron as *usted*, but the latter using the more familiar *tu*, the whole relationship is imbued with a personal element. Patron and client may be *compadres*, in which case the patron is expected to take an interest in the child. The initiative to set up the relationship often comes from the client though, at times, this is difficult because he has to approach someone in a very different social position. In this case, he may resort to the use of a *palanca*. Literally meaning a lever, the *palanca* is a means of access to the patron, he/she is an intermediary between the two. While studying Tzintzuntzan, the anthropologist George Foster found that the female villagers would ask his wife to approach him for a favour (Foster 1967).

It may seem, so far, that in terms of clearly defined benefits, the client comes off best out of the deal. However, in the long term this is not the case, because of the extent of the power that can be gained by patrons. The client gets help for day-to-day problems, but the price he pays for this is to be the landlord's follower, to do his bidding and accept his view of the world. In this way, a small number of landowners can control the peasantry in rural areas. It is a way in which the dominant class of landowners manipulates a subordinate one. Through clientelism, the allegiance of the peasant is to his patron rather than to other peasants, so that it is more difficult for solidarity between those in the peasant class to develop. The structuring of loyalties vertically in this way inhibits the development of horizontal bonds and thus class identity among the poor. Moreover, clientelism prevents the peasant making contact with the wider society. As the landowner acts as intermediary, the peasant gains no experience of wider society and must depend on his patron for his interpretation of the world. The essence of clientelism requires class differences and, therefore, although it softens the harshness of status differences it also ensures their continuation.

Far from declining with industrialisation and urbanisation, clientelism has flourished. Many businesses, including large and successful ones, are based on the personal relations of clientelism. SIAM is a large Argentine industrial-commercial complex which was run, by Torcuato Di Tella, as a family business. Those at the top level had Di Tella's confidence through a relationship of kinship or friendship and links between middle and upper management levels were based on personal relationships. Di Tella took a personal interest in the lives of his workers, giving gifts at weddings and on the birth of children and taking responsibility for the health and welfare of the workers and their families. In return, he could count on their loyalty and support for him and the firm. There was little delegation of authority, but Di Tella's personal participation enhanced his authority and gave him considerable control. This style of management continued after his death (Wolf and Hansen 1972).

Rothstein argues that patron-client relationships are well suited to the peripheral capitalist development that has taken place in Latin America because they are a way of paring down the number of recipients of industrial gains, when these gains are few in number. Economic growth in Latin America has accumulated benefits in the hands of a few, rather than distributing them as predicted by the modernists. The small surplus that is distributed is so limited that it can not be shared by all, but patronage is a mechanism of selecting a few workers to benefit. Clientelism is a strategy used by capitalists and workers to adapt to a situation where there is limited mobility. For the worker, patronage yields access to some of the benefits of industrialisation and, for the manager, it is a way of distributing a small number of benefits, at the same time assuring support and a disciplined labour force (Rothstein 1979).

FAMILY AND GENDER

The most obvious place to turn to for close ties is the family. The family offers the potential for a large number of links and is a source of permanent relationships, even if conditions around one are changing. Large families and the recognition of a wide network of kinship ties is a feature of Latin American life. Expansion of this network is greatest among the rich, where people may retain contact with one hundred to two hundred relatives. In this connection, family names are important. Latin Americans maintain the Spanish custom of adding the mother's surname after the father's, thus denoting both families of origin. In some countries, names demonstrate aristocratic status and the elite may be referred to, as it is in Peru, as the forty families. But the family among the rich is not only a source of prestige, it has a very instrumental aspect, family networks are manipulated in the course of politics and business.

Some of the most modern industrial companies in Latin America are family businesses, whose boards of directors are made up of relatives and close friends who can be trusted. Businesses are sometimes seen as a source of employment for family members. The owner of a large concern may well feel an obligation to find a position in his firm for a hard-up cousin. Above all, the family is a property-owning unit, whether the property is a business, estates, land or houses, so that these resources are controlled and acquired by succeeding generations through the family.

For the poor, the family is not a mechanism to control resources, but an institution to turn to because of the scarcity of resources. The scope of their kinship networks is smaller, but just as significant because they provide help in times of hardship. It is usually to relatives that the peasant migrating to the city turns for help in the new and frightening environment. It is kin, often, who provide shelter during the first days in the town and who help the migrant build his/her own home. It is they, too, who lend him/her money for the journey and help him/her look for a job in the urban environment. The migration process frequently involves a chain of relatives from rural village to urban neighbourhood.

Traditionally, the family was patriarchal and authoritarian. The head of the family frequently had under his control a large number of people, both relatives and servants, and considerable resources. The best documented examples come from Brazil, where the patriarchal family appeared after the Portuguese colonisation with the agrarian families. The patriarch's power over his wife and offspring was absolute and often rigorously exercised. The strength of the institution can be seen in the fact that it lasted for generations in the sugar estates, despite social changes taking place around it.

The strongly authoritarian role of the head of the family has been undermined by the opportunities created by urbanisation for young people to be independent and earn a living outside the family, and by conceptions of the North American family as portrayed by the media. Nevertheless, the family remains patriarchal and a key institution in society. Much of its strength can be attributed to the vigorous support of the church, which has always placed the family at the centre of Christian living. The church's view, that marriages sanctioned by religious ritual should not be broken, is reflected in divorce laws. In several Latin American countries there is no legal concept of divorce. In Mexico, however, where the state broke with the church quite violently during the revolution, divorce is possible (and, indeed, in some places very easy). The church's opposition to mechanical and chemical contraception and to abortion, greatly encourages the large families that are so characteristic of the region.

The population explosion has been one of the major phenomena in Latin America this century. Since 1950, the population has been steadily increasing from 164 million to 382 million in 1982. This is very much a Third World phenomenon for, throughout these areas, the rate of population increase is considerably higher than in the industrialised world. For the period from 1975–82, the annual rate of population increase was 2.9 for Africa, 1.4 for East Asia, 2.2 for South Asia, 1.5 for Oceania and 2.5 for Latin America. Europe, however, during this period had an annual rate of only 0.4. Even for LDCs, the Latin American rate is high. Apart from West Africa, with a rate of 3.1, Middle America is the sub-region with the highest annual rate of population increase (3.0) in the world (Demographic Yearbook 1982).

Although, as suggested in Chapter 1, not a major development problem, rapid population increase is a cause for concern in the region. It has meant that in Mexico, for instance, although the proportion of illiterates nationally has decreased every decade, in recent years absolute numbers have been increasing. Birth control, however, is a very controversial issue. Some programmes, set up by North American and international development agencies in order to alleviate the population pressure on food and thus reduce poverty, were aimed at direct population control rather than giving the woman the right and freedom to control her own fertility. These have gained the reputation for testing unsafe contraceptives on poor Latin American women and enforced sterilisation. The Peace Corps, the United States volunteer programme, has been expelled from both Bolivia and Peru for its activities in sterilising peasant women without their knowledge (Bronstein 1982).

Fear, partly due to rumours about these sterilisation programs, and ignorance, prevent the majority of Latin American women from using contraceptives. The attitude of the church has made it difficult for governments to openly promote birth-control programs, that do anything more than advocate natural methods. In Mexico, the government has encouraged the spread of contraceptive methods through television advertisements, advocating the advantages of small families, but it has been forced, because of the influence of the church, to take a low profile and operate very discreetly.

Throughout Latin America, except for Cuba, abortion is illegal but, nevertheless, a considerable number of women do resort to abortion, which is often carried out in unhygienic and inadequate conditions. Their numbers are estimated at 800,000 per year in Mexico and 280,000 in Colombia, even though in both countries women experiencing abortion can be punished by imprisonment. For Latin America as a whole, Bronstein suggests that 30 per cent to 50 per cent of all maternal deaths are from improperly performed abortions (Bronstein 1982).

Undoubtedly, rapid population expansion in Latin America can be traced, in part, to *machismo*. Taken from the Spanish word, *macho*, meaning male, *machismo* refers to an ideology of behaviour in which distinctly different lifestyles are deemed proper for men and women. *Machismo* is an exaggerated cult of virility which expresses itself in male assertions of superiority over females, and competition between men. To fulfil *macho* behaviour patterns, a man must show no fear, demonstrate sexual prowess, father many children and exercise tight control over female kin. Adultery is seen as natural for a man, but a serious offence for a woman. *Machismo* is a New World phenomenon with roots in old world cultures. Concepts of honour and shame associated with manliness can be found in many of the cultures of southern Europe but, while this behaviour pattern seems to have declined in Spain, it has flourished in Latin America. Since its early expression was in the form of sexual relations between conquering white soldiers and dominated Indian women, it has taken on a distinctly aggressive element which can emerge in the form of violence. It is a characteristic of *mestizo* Latin America, for studies of Indian communities often reveal a relative absence of *machismo*. Its counterpart is *marianismo*, the submissive female role. The ideal woman is gentle, kind, long-suffering, loving and submits to the demands of men, whether they be husbands, fathers, sons or brothers. She has an infinite capacity for humility and sacrifice and an abundant store of patience. In one area, however, she does come into her own, since she has spiritual strength and moral superiority. This strength makes her the centre of the family and the one responsible for keeping members together. The role model for women is the Virgin Mary, hence the term *marianismo*.

Gender roles in Latin America are conditioned by these cultural factors embodying the notions of *machismo* and *marianismo* and, also, by structural factors, which relate to the peripheral capitalist nature of development in the region. *Machismo* is receiving some challenge from women's movements and organisations, but these are only supported by a very small number of women. Most women's groups are primarily concerned with political aims, they work often for the right to fight equally alongside their men to achieve political liberation, rather than fighting for women to replace men in superior positions. Women's movements as responses to economic and social problems are increasing rapidly in the region. In Chile, they provide a source of protest against the military government; in Bolivia, the miners' wives fought alongside their husbands to get better working conditions and pay; Nicaraguan women have formed a distinct group within the Sandinista revolutionary movement; and in Brazil, women's groups have formed to protest at price rises in food and other essentials.

WOMEN'S ROLES AND SOCIAL STRUCTURE

Changes in structural factors have taken place in the form of peripheral capitalist industrialisation, which has had a considerable impact on the participation of women in the labour market. Extent of labour force participation is an important indicator of the position of women because, on the one hand, it is a way in which women contribute to the economic development of their countries and, on the other, because work is a major source of income which gives access to education, culture, power and other factors influencing social status.

Many modernisation theorists argued that industrialisation would open up opportunities for women, providing them with a greater variety of possible roles and increasing chances of social mobility and a less subservient existence. There is a good deal of evidence to show, however, that industrial capitalism places women on the periphery of the economy, and for women in a Third World country which is itself on the periphery of a world economy, the situation is even more difficult. In a pre-industrial society women may have important occupations in handicrafts or in garden agriculture, jobs which can be done in the home. But industrial development takes remunerative work out of the home, making it more difficult for wives and mothers to participate. Women participate in poorer jobs and in the tertiary sectors, areas which have suffered the most from peripheral capitalist development.

The high rates of unemployment so characteristic of underdeveloped countries make women especially vulnerable. For example, in Brazil, peripheral capitalist development is responsible not only for a lower level of participation of women in agriculture but also a lower level of integration of women in urban development. In 1872, 45.5 per cent of the workforce of the nation were women, but by 1920 this proportion had dropped to 15.3 per cent and by 1950, it had fallen even further to 11.3 per cent (Saffioti 1978). 'It is not industrialisation *per se* that creates underemployment and marginalisation, but an industrial finance capitalism and advanced technology (intensive in capital) which does not permit fundamental changes in the economic structure.' (Vasquez de Miranda 1977: 273)

In the stage of early capitalist development the demand for labour in a previously agricultural economy is high. But in a situation where industrial growth is conditioned by the needs of monopoly capitalism, as happened in many underdeveloped countries, this stage may be virtually omitted. Because of multinationals, industrial production means little improvement in levels of employment. Therefore, opportunities for men and women, though especially the latter, are limited to traditional and backward sectors such as subsistence agriculture and domestic service. The latter has become the major occupation for women, for about one-fifth of Latin America's female workforce are maids – 19.8 per cent of the Mexican female labour force are servants in private houses (Gonzalez Salazar 1976) and 32 per cent of the total Brazilian female workforce are live-in maids (Filet-Abreu Souza 1980).

Nash argues that the position of women has deteriorated despite development activities because of the concentration on production for profit rather than for the welfare of the population in many Third World countries. This leads to a so-called rationalisation of economic activity which implies the increasing use of technology at the expense of human labour (Nash 1977).

One of the reasons why women are more vulnerable than men with the introduction of highly technologised industry is that female workers are considered inappropriate for mechanised industry. In

Guatemala, for instance, changes in the character of the manufacturing sector influenced the participation rates of women in the labour market. The industrial censuses of 1946 and 1965 showed a decline in female workers from 22 per cent to 18 per cent. The largest declines were in textiles, tobacco, chemicals, rubber, paper and food. For male workers, however, employment was rapidly increasing in the areas of electrical appliances, transportation and furniture which first appear in the 1965 census as well as metal products and some of the areas traditionally open to women – chemicals, paper and rubber (Chinchilla 1977).

Similarly, Bolivian women lost out to men in the mechanisation of the mines. From the early period of tin mining to the 1940s women were often concentrators of minerals. When the new methods of concentrating minerals were introduced, large numbers of female workers were replaced by male in the sink and float plants. Since 1960, with the complete mechanisation of the mines, no women have worked as metal concentrators (Nash 1977).

The result is that the present rate of labour-force participation by women in Latin America hovers around 20 per cent and has remained fairly stable for over twenty years (ECLA 1975). Table 4.1 shows that

Table 4.1 Participation of women in the workforce in the principal geographic zones of the world, 1960 and projections for 1975

Geographic zone	Rate of female activity (a)		Rate of female participation (b)	
	1960 %	1975 %	1960 %	1975 %
Universal	29.8	27.9	35.0	34.3
Africa	25.4	23.0	31.5	30.9
Latin America	12.6	12.0	19.2	196
North America	24.2	27.6	31.4	35.0
Far East	37.1	35.8	40.1	38.0
Middle East	25.4	22.4	30.6	29.7
Europe	29.3	29.3	33.6	34.4
USSR	48.5	48.0	51.6	30.4
Oceania	22.7	25.4	27.2	30.4

Source: Jiménez 1979
(a) Economically active women as a proportion of the total female population
(b) Economically active women as a proportion of the total workforce

Latin America has the lowest female participation rate of any region in the world, including the Middle East, despite their stringent constraints on women's activities. The table also shows that, in the fifteen years from 1960–75, there was a tendency for female labour force participation to increase in the industrialised world and decline elsewhere, except Oceania. In Latin America the percentage of the total female population who worked, decreased during this period showing that, as in other LDCs (with the exception of Oceania), the proportion of women in the labour force was smaller in 1975 than previously in 1960.

It must be remembered, however, that participation rates of women in the workforce are notoriously inaccurate. Women are often statistically 'invisible' because they work in areas that are not recorded as full-time occupations. Much of women's rural work, such as caring for poultry, milking and craftwork within the home is not included, as men are registered as the family breadwinners, as farmers, and women as housewives. So, too, similar 'home industries' of women in the towns do not find their way into occupation statistics. The official statistics, therefore, can only be used as indicators, rather than accurate statements, but they do offer some guides to the occupational picture.

There are some exceptions to this general trend. Some large firms have demonstrated a preference for female workers, often on the grounds of their supposed nimble fingers though, in reality, usually because they can be paid less and are less likely to unionise and form any opposition to management. Firms that have employed women in this way are, for example, the American concerns, the *maquiladoras*, that have been set up in northern Mexico near the US border. These receive tax concessions for operating in Mexico but their location is so close to North America that they are near their distribution networks and markets, and other North American facilities. They employ women for long hours and often in poor conditions in the production of textiles, pharmaceuticals and a variety of other items.

There has been some expansion, too, of opportunities for women in the white-collar categories of employment;

> The rapidly rising number of girls receiving middle and higher
> education, coinciding with the growth of urban bureaucratic and
> commercial activities, has led to a corresponding increase in the number
> entering clerical and professional or semi-professional employment,
> generally prior to marriage and temporary or permanent withdrawal from
> the labour force. The very expansion of the school systems has by itself
> created an enormous job market for teachers, with women in the
> majority. In the sluggishly expanding industrial labour market women
> have lost ground relative to men, and an important proportion of the
> women who must seek work because of inadequate earnings of the
> husband or because the family lacks a male breadwinner continue to be
> restricted to domestic service, street vending, and other marginal low-
> income occupations. (ECLA 1975: 13)

The growth of large corporations and banks with international involvements has expanded commercial activity which requires clerks and salespeople. In Guatemala, the proportion of women in clerical work rose from 20.4 per cent in 1950 to 34.1 per cent in 1973, and those in sales from 30.2 per cent to 35.1 per cent (Chinchilla 1973). In Brazil the rates of participation in the workforce of women with university education are 66 per cent for married and 77 per cent for single women (Filet-Arbreu Souza 1980).

There are various reasons for this. Although, generally, women lag behind men in educational achievement, at higher levels the proportion of female students is not very different from that of male, with the result that a small number of highly educated women enter the labour market each year. Despite the general lack of opportunities for women, sex-typing of occupations reserves some areas of work mainly for them. Jobs which represent an extension of the wife-mother role, such as nursing and teaching, and those which require an attractive image, such as secretaries, are predominantly filled by women. In Venezuela, women represent 74.6 per cent of teachers and 59.5 per cent of those in the medical professions (Schmink 1977). It seems, too, that traditional values that prescribe a life of domesticity are weakening. According to Safa, 'the ideology that equates female confinement within the home to higher class status has begun to influence working-class women at the same time that its influence has begun to wane among women of the elite'. (Safa 1977: 134). But the crucial factor which makes it possible for middle-class women to enter the labour force and, at the same time, maintain traditional values in the home, is the existence of the domestic servant. The presence of maids obviates any need for husbands to undertake traditionally female tasks and so, while a woman following her career does challenge a husband's *machismo* in the sense that it gives her some independence (both economically and socially), it does not do so in the sense of changing his role in the home.

In general, women have not benefited much in the job market from capitalist industrialisation nor have they gained much influence in society outside the family through political channels. The political activity of women is limited and, in the few cases where they do achieve positions of some power, these positions are often linked to the traditional female role. Elsa Chaney found, in her study of women active in government in Peru and Chile in the late 1960s, that they were overwhelmingly engaged in feminine stereotyped tasks related to education, health, social welfare and cultural fields. Out of the 167 women interviewed, nearly 70 per cent did stereotyped female work and/or held appointments in agencies carrying out tasks considered of particular concern to women. As a result, she epitomised the successful political woman's role as that of a 'supermother' (Chaney 1979).

If capitalist industrialisation has done little to improve the position of women, is there any evidence to suggest that they have fared better with alternative paths of development? Both Nicaragua and Cuba have seen significant changes for women, but the Cuban example is particularly instructive, since there has been time for new gender roles to develop.

As the Cuban revolution was dedicated to reducing inequalities of all kinds, it was only a year before the Federation of Cuban Women (FMC) was set up to tackle the problems facing women. Since previous to the revolution the majority of women had very low levels of education and, therefore, few opportunities open to them, the FMC embarked on an educational program and a rehabilitation scheme for the many women who found themselves in degrading and unrewarding situations. To this end, schools were set up for peasant women and for prostitutes, who were numerous since Havana had previously been a notorious entertainment centre for North Americans, to give them an education and to provide them with some skills and training ready for the job market. It must be remembered, too, that the early years of the revolution saw a great demand for labour in order to rebuild the economy and, also, to fill the immense gap left by the departing middle class. As industrialisation takes work out of the home, women, if they are to be encouraged to join the labour force, must be assisted in child and home care. The state, prompted by the FMC, has taken numerous measures to encourage women in this way and has set up nursery schools, crèches, workers' canteens, automatic laundries, the provision of medical facilities and a system of grants. Laws were passed to make it easier for women to participate fully in the development of their country as well as maintaining their family life. Perhaps the most radical of these is the Family Code, adopted in February 1975. This is one of the most progressive pieces of legislation in the world in attempting to establish equality between men and women as the rule in marriage. According to this law, both partners in a marriage have a duty to help each other, must share the housework and have the same obligations and duties concerning the raising and education of their children. The Code particularly guarantees the participation of both men and women in the economic, cultural and political order of the country (Latin America and Caribbean Women's Collective 1980). Nor is the law an arid statement of ideals, for defaulters may be taken to court by their partners.

There is no doubt that the FMC which, by 1980, represented over 80 per cent of Cuban women, has done much to improve opportunities for women and, above all, to give them dignity and respect in society. They provide a very active participation in the many voluntary groups supporting the revolution and contribute much more than previously to development through participation in the labour force.

The main area of weakness lies in the political arena. When it comes to the obvious sources of power, gender differences seem to be similar in socialist Cuba to capitalist Latin America. Most full-time political representatives in Cuba are men, with very few women standing for election and even fewer succeeding. This problem became one of national concern when Fidel Castro commented on the elections to the Popular Power Assembly in Matanzas Province. In this case, women represented 7.6 per cent of the candidates proposed and only 3 per cent of those elected. Investigations followed which revealed various reasons. Lack of time was one factor, for many women now had work outside the home as well as family responsibilities. Some felt that women lacked the cultural and political training necessary. *Machismo* was still very evident, for many people felt that men were better suited than women to lead and, in some cases, women had been forbidden by male relatives from entering politics.

Cuba has gone a long way to reducing gender inequalities, though power relations still clearly favour men, a fact of which all Cubans, including their leaders, are very aware. In 1974, Fidel Castro said, in his closing speech to the Second Congress of the FMC, 'We live in a socialist country, we made our revolution sixteen years ago, but can we really say that Cuban women have in practice gained equal rights with men and that they are fully integrated into Cuban society?' (Latin American and Caribbean Women's Collective 1977: 96)

CONCLUSION

The manipulation of the web of personal relations has an ambiguous role for, on the one hand, it serves to ease difficulties and build bridges across social divides but, on the other, it helps to maintain the status quo and, therefore, the inequalities in the social structure. Resorting to personal ties to survive or advance is a mechanism which has been used to some effect over the generations, but which prevents people turning to organisations or political activity which might, in the long run, prove more effective in solving their problems. Inequalities between patron and client, peasant families and landowning families and men and women, therefore, continue.

Where modern values have been incorporated they have often not reduced inequality. Because the elite, through their superior wealth, are better able to live up to the so-called modern values, which are all the more costly to support because of their external source, they are further differentiated from the poor. The latter, through mass media and education, are made aware of the 'new' but are unable to attain this. As Kahl found during his research in Mexico and Brazil, the higher the social status the greater the likelihood of modernism

(Kahl 1970). New values thus have the effect of reinforcing traditional differences. For example, managers of large companies have usually reached their positions through the traditional channels of manipulating the personal ties of kinship, *compadrazgo*, clientelism and friendship and also through the modern channels of merit, that is, acquiring qualifications and skills. To obtain the appropriate qualifications, however, is a costly business, for the most desired are earned through attendance at expensive North American business schools. As we have seen, higher education in Latin America is predominantly the prerogative of the rich and, so, to have the opportunity to display merit, the Latin American businessman must come from a wealthy background.

The so-called modern values bring about a convergence of culture through improved mass communications, the elites of Third World countries come to share the same culture as those in the industrialised world. This reinforces the social inequality and regional disparities encouraged by the concentration of wealth and capital in the big cities and in the hands of the dominant classes.

FURTHER READING

Bronstein, A. (1982) *The triple struggle*. War on Want Campaigns, London

CEPAL review 1983 no. 21, December

Levine, D. H. (1981) *Religion and politics in Latin America: the Catholic Church in Venezuela and Colombia*. Princeton University Press, Princeton, Guildford, Surrey

Smith B. H. (1982) *The church and politics in Chile. Challenges to modern Catholicism*. Princeton University Press, Guildford, Surrey

Strickon, A, Greenfield, S. (eds) (1972) *Structure and process in Latin America: patronage, clientage, and power systems*. University of New Mexico Press, Albuquerque

Wellesley Editorial Committee (1977) *Women and national development. The complexities of change*. University of Chicago Press, Chicago and London

Wolf, E, Hansen, E. (1972) *The human condition in Latin America*. Oxford University Press, London

5

Changing rural society

Although Latin America is becoming increasingly urban, rural society still represents a very sizable sector. At the beginning of the 1980s, about a third of the total labour force was employed in agriculture. The farmers of the region are predominantly peasants, who depend mainly on family labour, as nearly four-fifths of the agricultural sector are smallholders, cultivating one-fifth of all farmland.

The characteristic feature of this sector is its heterogeneity, brought about by the changes of the last few decades. Some countries such as Mexico, Brazil, Argentina and Colombia, are at the forefront of agricultural development. The vast irrigated areas of Mexico's north-west have produced a highly modernised fruit and vegetable industry. In the south of Brazil there are multi-million-dollar soybean processing plants owned by multinationals and surrounded by large-scale mechanised farms. In other areas, like the Peruvian and Bolivian Andes, traditional farming techniques, such as the digging stick, machete and hoe, are used. Countries vary as to the proportion of the farm labour force taken up by the peasantry. In Bolivia, the proportion is 90 per cent; in Brazil, Ecuador, Panama, Peru and Venezuela it fluctuates between 70 per cent and 80 per cent; in Guatemala it is 60 per cent; in Colombia, El Salvador and Mexico 50 per cent; and in Argentina, Costa Rica, Chile and Uruguay less than 50 per cent (López Cordovez 1982).

This chapter examines the way that change has taken place, in particular in relation to social structure in terms of changing social relations of production, and the contribution to this process of change made by different social groups, such as political elites and the peasantry. The changes that take place vary and result from three different kinds of processes.

Firstly, the penetration of capitalism into rural areas brings about the spread of the commercial nexus, usually through the market system. This generates a number of economic changes which because of the overlap of social, economic, political and religious systems in rural communities, have extensive social repercussions. Secondly, some change may be organised from above in order to encourage agricultural productivity and curb social injustice. These are agrarian reform programs, planned at government level to alter land distribution and modernise traditional agricultural methods, and also policies concerning food production and distribution. Thirdly, peasant mobilisation may be a source of change. Although the peasantry have not often been prompted to rebellion, they have played a major role in a national revolution in two Latin American countries, Mexico and Cuba.

The peasant economy, which is affected by these processes, can best be defined in Stavenhagen's words:

> The peasant economy can be defined quite simply as that form of farm production (and associated activities) in which the producer and his family till the land themselves, generally utilising their own means of production (tools and instruments), with the object of directly satisfying their basic needs, although for a number of reasons they may find themselves required to sell a part of their produce on the market in order to obtain goods which they do not produce. (Stavenhagen 1978: 31)

PENETRATION OF CAPITALISM INTO RURAL AREAS

Andrew Pearse describes this process as the incorporative drive of national market systems and he argues that it is the major cause of rural change (Pearse 1975). He does not deny internally generated change, which might occur from natural factors, such as drought or population growth, but suggests that the latter forces are more important in pre-industrial conditions. The incorporative drive refers to national level forces which emanate from an urban centre and gradually involve more peripheral areas in a national way of life. It includes three main elements: the spread of the market system; the spread of a communications system; and the penetration of national institutions.

The spread of the market system brings the peasant into contact with a nation-wide network of distribution. Business is now done through a middleman, an outsider with whom he, initially at any rate, does not have a personal long-standing relationship. The market makes it possible for the peasant to grow and sell cash crops, rather than just maintaining a subsistence economy and therefore to produce a surplus. The penetration of the national capitalist system also makes available the consumer goods, which can be purchased with the income from the surplus. The market system holds out opportunities for the peasant, but it also makes his situation more precarious. As the peasant moves from subsistence agriculture to the production of cash crops, he loses the security that a subsistence plot provides, that is a basic food supply. If the cash crops fail for any reason, he has nothing to fall back on. The peasant is also vulnerable in the market for he has to operate within a new system of values, one that emphasises competition, astuteness and individuality. He is unfamiliar with national levels of price-fixing and laws of supply and demand.

At the same time, improvements in communications raise aspirations and hopes. Radio, television and films project images of sophisticated living that are often presented as being available to all who work hard enough. Consumer goals which were never contemplated by the peasantry in the past, now appear on the screen in their own homes and villages. Better roads and more efficient and cheaper forms of transport have facilitated contact between town and country.

The penetration of national institutions seeks to incorporate the peasantry into a variety of local segments of national organisations, such as schools, church groups, political parties, peasant unions and cooperatives. These are often sponsored by the urban middle class, with the result that there may be some incongruence between these programs and the needs of country people.

Lenin contrasted two types of development that can result from the penetration of capitalism in agriculture: the Kulak or American path and the Junker path. With the Kulak path, some members of the peasantry adapt successfully to the market system, thus becoming relatively wealthy, while other peasants only become impoverished, so creating internal social differentiation within the peasantry. The wealthy become capitalist farmers, often employing the poor whose impoverishment leads to the loss of their land. The Junker path involves the increasing proletarianisation of the peasantry, who lose their plots to encroaching landlords (for a more detailed discussion of Kulak and Junker paths, see de Janvry 1981).

Pearse identifies the same process as the Kulak path when he shows how the incorporative drive draws out what he calls the progressive element among the peasantry (Pearse 1975). A small number are able to manipulate the new situation because they are able to get credit, to establish good terms of trade with middlemen and to generally come to terms with the different conditions. The majority of the peasantry, however, have neither the resources nor the social advantages necessary to become entrepreneurs. Because of debts, they are often forced to sell their land and therefore lose the means of livelihood that their family has known and understood over the generations. Security is lost and the traditional social networks have broken up in favour of the commercial nexus.

The Kulak path has occurred in many different parts of Latin America. Changes that have taken place in the Highland Zapotec region of Oaxaca, Mexico, are a good example. Kate Young's data from the two villages of Copa Bitoo and Telana reveal how social differentiation can take place (Young 1978). In the nineteenth century, both villages were self-sufficient, mostly in maize, the land was owned communally and there was no internal stratification. Prestige was allotted according to the principles of the ritual cycle. The little money that was needed to pay state taxes and church tithes and to fund festivals, was obtained from the sale of cotton lengths, which were made by the women. In the 1860s, the supply of cotton dried up because the Mexican cotton growers had started replacing North Americans, who had become involved in their civil war, as suppliers of cotton for England. As Oaxacan peasants needed some source of cash, the men started seasonal migration, which was disliked because the plantations had a reputation for malaria and poor living and working conditions in general.

At this point the two villages started on different paths. In Telana, coffee cultivation was introduced by the local *cacique*. Coffee could be grown quickly, cheaply and easily and sold for cash. Gradually coffee came to replace maize as the main agricultural produce of the community and foodstuffs were bought with surplus cash. Specialisation was underway and, since households were now in competition with each other, reciprocal labour agreements disappeared and each household became more dependent on its own resources. During the turbulent years of the revolution, coffee production declined, but in the 1930s, new coffee wholesalers entered the area and began to buy for cash. Telana now became involved in not only the national market economy, but also an international one, as these wholesalers were buying for export. During the period from 1938 to 1954, the world market price of coffee rose twenty-two-fold, so Telana prospered from these boom years. The community was now devoted to coffee growing, subsistence plots had disappeared and internal differentiation was taking place. Those who did well out of coffee growing started employing labourers and consolidated their control over the best land. The women, who had lost their craft specialisation, had few opportunities to develop any new specialisms and so lost the independence and prestige they had had from making cotton lengths. After 1957, coffee prices fell drastically, with the result that all the villagers suffered. They had no subsistence plots to fall back on, some tried reviving traditional handicrafts but these could not compete with the manufactured goods that had been made available by the market system. The wealthier survived because they had control of tracts of good land, but the poorer villagers had to sell the little land they had, to pay off debts and were compelled to work as landless labourers for the rich. The 1970s saw considerable migration from Telana, as desperate peasants went in search of work.

The peasantry of Telana had become involved in international trade, with the result that they were affected by world booms and slumps. Some had fared considerably better than others, leading to a differentiated society. Kate Young found that three classes had developed on the basis of wealth, land ownership and relation to the means of production. Firstly, there were the rich, who owned farms and employed labour in both agriculture and the home and who made up 20 per cent of the population. The middle 30 per cent owned land but did not employ labour, as they relied on family members. The poor were the landless who provided labour for the rich.

Copa Bitoo, although internally differentiated, had not developed such a marked stratification system. Copa Bitoo had moved away from a subsistence economy, but was producing fruit and nuts for the local market, not for export. Here, similar classes were emerging but only about 10 per cent were able to employ wage labour regularly and only 20 per cent provided it regularly. The bulk of the villagers fell into the middle category.

Both communities demonstrate the way that involvement in the market system creates differentiation, though this is greater where bigger fluctuations take place. Participation in local markets and national capitalism generates differences, but insertion in the international system accentuates the peaks and troughs of economic cycles, which means a greater gap between rich and poor in peasant communities.

The categorisation of rural change into the two alternative paths of Kulak and Junker is schematically useful, but does not exhaust the possible forms of agricultural development. Roxborough demonstrates how both paths have been combined in the agricultural history of Chile (Roxborough 1979). The process of proletarianisation itself is a more complex issue than might at first be supposed. Proletarianis-ation implies an increase in the number of wage labourers, which can be demonstrated by statistics, but figures also show that in some parts of Latin America, the numbers of the peasantry are increasing. Between 1970 and 1981, the agricultural population of Latin America increased by 8 million persons, of whom 4 million are described as producers, 5 million as peasant farmers and 1 million as landless workers, who must therefore seek work in wage-earning occupations

(ECLAC/FAO 1985). At the same time, as the next chapter shows, many of the rural population have been migrating to urban areas in the hope of joining the labour force there. Is it the case that the rural sector is undergoing a process of proletarianisation or peasantisation? (See Goodman and Redclift 1981 for a good discussion of this debate).

PROLETARIANISATION OR PEASANTISATION?

Marx originally argued that the growth of large-scale industry led to the demise of the peasantry and the development of the proletariat. His argument is that the penetration of capitalism into the countryside leads to the articulation of the capitalist mode with the subsistence economy, which in turn leads to the diversification of the village economy, with wage migration becoming an increasing part of rural life. Small peasant farmers can not compete with capitalist concerns, with the result that they often lose their land to them and end up working for them or migrating to the towns in search of wage labour. Modernisation theorists too thought that the peasantry, through the diffusion of modern ideas and consumer goods, would develop out of existence. Some Latin American social scientists working on the topic have suggested a two-stage process, in which the penetration of capitalism initially leads to an increase in wage-earning workers, but this is followed by a stage of the intensification of capitalism, characterised by deproletarianisation and semi-proletarianisation (Miró and Rodríguez 1982). It is the argument of this section of the chapter that the deepening of capitalism in the countryside has led to a heterogeneous pattern of labour relations, according to area and nature of commercial expansion.

Proletarianisation has occurred in Latin America because the peasantry have been dispossessed of their land or because their land has become insufficient to support a family. Dispossession has been encouraged by the transformation of the estate to a modern commercial farm. Traditionally the landowner need not cultivate the land intensively to provide sufficient to maintain prestige and a very good life-style. Today, with greater opportunities for profits from export and the advantages of modern transport and mechanisation, the landowner exploits his property to the full to maximise production and profits. In this situation, it is often cheaper to hire labour on the open market when needed than to maintain workers and their families permanently on the estate. For this reason, many landowners have followed the Junker path, taking over the land of sharecroppers and *colonos* and compelling them to sell their labour on the open market. Small peasant farmers, who own their own plots have often been compelled to sell land through poverty and debts. As land is passed on over the generations, it gradually ceases to be a viable unit.

The process of proletarianisation has also received some impetus from the spread of agribusiness in the region. Agribusiness refers not just to large-scale rural enterprises, but to concerns which have an integrated system of production and distribution. Agricultural produce is grown, processed and distributed within the one company, although these activities may, and usually do, take place in different parts of the world. The influence of agribusiness is felt throughout the Third World, though North American firms have found a major outlet in Latin America. The areas of agro-industry in which transnational corporations and other private foreign investors in Latin America are most active are branches of milling, oils and fats, chocolates and sweets, and meats and dairy products. This gives them a distinct influence on the development of agriculture and the food economy of the region.

Large-scale commercialised farming, that is agribusiness and domestic agricultural enterprises, have to compete with other big corporations for investment capital and markets and must therefore make profits as efficiently as possible. To this end, commercialised farming emphasises different forms of labour utilisation according to the needs of the company in different areas. In some cases, firms, such as Nestlé in regions of Brazil, having purchased *haciendas*, are now running them with modern agricultural techniques. In other parts of Brazil, giant corporations exist alongside small peasant producers, with whom they have developed a complex inter-dependence, based on the supply of goods rather than labour. In several countries the second stage of the Miró and Rodríguez thesis is in operation. For example, the Banana Company of Costa Rica, a subsidiary of United Brands, has been converting plantations to African palm production, an enterprise which has a guaranteed internal market, as Costa Rica imports nearly all its vegetable oil. This economic activity requires less than half the labour needed in banana cultivation and therefore must result in the loss of a number of jobs (LAWR 1983). In some areas, mechanisation is replacing labour although in the countryside this has not gone as far as on North American farms. Some harvesting machines are now being used in Brazilian sugar plantations and Mexican sugar and cotton fields. The shift from labour intensive coffee growing to capital-intensive soybean production in Brazil created unemployment for tens of thousands of workers in the early sixties (Burbach and Flynn 1980).

The form of social relations of production which is on the increase in the region is semi-proletarianisation. This is due to the seasonal nature of so much agricultural work, which makes it cheaper for the company to employ labourers during the planting or harvesting rather than maintain a labour force throughout the year. Seasonal workers do not have the security of full-time employment, since they must seek other means of support for part of the year. The pay is very low, as cheap labour is part of the incentive for entrepreneurial farmers, nor do they receive even the minimum security benefits of full-time work. Agribusiness that operates in sectors marked by seasonal fluctuations has been prone to this sort of employment. Del Monte employed in 1976 about 1,750 workers in Irapuato, Mexico, but only 120 were permanently employed. Ninety per cent of the remaining seasonal workers worked for four to six months a year for a low wage. (Burbach and Flynn 1980).

Semi-proletarianisation takes a variety of forms. A rather unusual example are the *boias-frías* in Brazil. These labourers, who have no access to land ownership, live in urban areas but are unable to find work there. They therefore travel daily from town to country to do seasonal work as agricultural labourers. Their name is derived from their food, which they are obliged to take with them and eat cold. Semi-proletarianisation is closely linked to temporary intra-rural migration, as numbers of peasants move to a particular area for seasonal work and then move back to their small plots of land or on to another area, where a different crop has reached the planting or harvesting stage. This is particularly apparent in Central America, where it is estimated that seasonal migrants make up 70 per cent of the labour force employed in agriculture. In El Salvador, about half the active agricultural population are employed for less than six months of the year (Miró and Rodríguez 1982). Guatemala's large seasonal migrant population, who work on the coffee and cotton plantations for part of the year, sometimes migrate over the border to the plantations in southern Mexico. Intra-rural migration is also evident in South America. On the Bolivian altiplano 1.2 persons per peasant family migrate temporarily to seek work (Ortega 1982). In areas such as northern Argentina, central Chile, Peru, various regions of Brazil and Mexico, this is becoming a basic element in the subsistence of the economy.

The intensification of capitalist farming has not meant the disintegration of the peasantry, for there is evidence to show increasing numbers of peasant farmers in many regions. Census data for a group of seven countries, Brazil, Chile, Colombia, El Salvador, Honduras, Peru and Venezuela, for the 1960s and 1970s, show that the number of agricultural units of less than 20 hectares in these countries rose from 4.7 million to 6.5 million, that is by 38.5 per cent (Ortega 1982). This expansion is the result of several factors. Firstly, subdivision, because inheritance is shared between siblings, takes place throughout the region. Secondly, agrarian reform has in some areas such as Peru and Chile (in the early 1970s) had the effect of dividing large expropriated landholdings among the peasantry. Thirdly, new territories have been cultivated, thus extending the agricultural land available, as for example the colonisation of new lands in Amazonia. Between the 1950s and early 1970s, 140 million hectares in the region were brought under cultivation for the first time (Ortega 1982).

How can the existence of these two apparently contradictory trends, proletarianisation and peasantisation, be explained? There is an obvious demographic point that has to be made first. The population has been increasing so fast in most Latin American countries that despite out-migration, the numbers of the peasantry are still on the increase. But there are more fundamental factors, to which attention must be drawn. Industries in the LDCs have demonstrated a structural incapacity to absorb all the migrants and all those in search of work. Neither industry nor farming can absorb the population of working age. As a result, many of the peasantry maintain a subsistence plot but, since this is usually insufficient to support a family, the male members of the family have to seek seasonal labouring work, leaving the women to maintain the family farm. In Mexico, where 51 per cent of farm units are infra-subsistence, that is, not big enough to support a peasant family, the peasant must find other forms of income (Stavenhagen 1974). The small farmer can combine the seasonal work offered by agribusiness and urban enterprises with his family farm and must do this to survive. For the employer, a part-time workforce means a cheap labour supply which contributes to capital accumulation.

In some cases, the link between the peasant sector and commercial farming may rest on the sale of goods rather than labour, as in the following example taken from the state of São Paulo.

> The almost absolute dependence of the small and medium-sized landholders on large-scale capitalist enterprise is illustrated by the case of tea, where the agro-industries possess their own *haciendas* and the organisation of labour is completely of the wage-earner type. However, these agro-industries also deal with family or independent units of production, to which they supply fertilisers and other production inputs. These same enterprises send their trucks for transporting merchandise during the harvest periods, and the classification of tea leaves for quality is also done by the enterprise, without the participation of the small producers, who are paid in accordance with this classification. These small farmers may be tenant farmers, sharecroppers or owners of small farms. (Miró and Rodríguez 1982: 57).

This continuation of the peasant sector alongside the development of industrialisation is a distinct aspect of capitalist development in the periphery and characterises much of rural development in the LDCs. Capitalist industrialisation in the periphery, often because of transnationals which can import sophisticated technology, has not been able fully to absorb all the labour available. Commercialised farms that do rely on labour frequently use seasonal labour. The subsistence economy, however, provides security for irregular workers. The peasant economy, therefore, reproduces the labour force for capitalism at a low cost because, due to the subsistence sector, men can be employed on an irregular basis. The peasant economy provides a reserve of cheap labour for capitalism and so contributes to capital accumulation. Moreover, subsistence plots produce goods at competitive prices by the working of long hours, using unpaid household labour and accepting low standards of subsistence. The conclusion of this is that 'the constant recreation of the peasant economy is functional for the capitalist system' (Stavenhagen 1978: 35). Thus the capitalist mode articulates with the peasant mode, with the latter playing a subordinate role and the former benefiting. The capitalist economy, while ensuring the continuance of the peasant sector, does not allow it to develop sufficiently to extricate itself from its subordinate role, for this would destroy its value for capitalism.

This articulation, however, does generate its own contradictions. The resulting poverty of the peasantry, who must find work in two different sectors to survive, limits their spending power and therefore discourages the purchase of consumer goods. This inhibits the growth of a market which would stimulate local economic development and so promote the expansion of manufacturing firms.

AGRARIAN REFORM

Both international politics and the philosophy of the day gave rise to a number of agrarian reform programmes in the 1960s and 1970s. Prompted by the fear of another Cuba in the region and desires for economic growth, Latin American political elites came to an agreement with the United States over aid for reforms. Thus, the Alliance for Progress, which gave rise to many agrarian reform programmes, was set up in the early 1960s. At the same time, modernisation theory, still influential in the 1960s, suggested that the removal of obstacles to change was necessary for development and a major obstacle in Latin America was the *hacienda*. Modernisation implied the elimination of these feudal-like institutions and the modernising of agriculture, both socially and economically.

In social terms, the *hacienda* system represents a very unequal distribution of land, with a small number of people monopolising the bulk of cultivable land. In 1960, before agrarian reform got underway, there were 111 million rural inhabitants of whom some 100,000 owned 65 per cent of total agricultural land (*International Labour Review* July-August 1961). This pattern of land distribution reflects such great disparities and brings about so much poverty that it represents one of the major problems that agrarian reform has addressed.

The other problem is economic. The large estate system leads to an inefficient use of the two most abundant factors of production in Latin America, the land and the labour force. Traditionally, the large estates have concentrated on one crop, often for export. This leads to an underemployment of land and labour, because neither is being fully utilised throughout the year. Cattle-ranching requires only a small number of cowboys and large tracts of land, which could alternatively be intensively cultivated, with the result that there is underemployment of labour and a low physical and economic return per unit of surface area. Not only does this mean that the rural population is not being fully utilised in terms of labour power, it also means they are too poor to provide a substantial market for industry. Agrarian reform was needed to release the peasantry from traditional forms and low levels of remuneration in order to increase their purchasing power to provide a stimulus for the growth and expansion of local manufacturing firms.

Agrarian reform programmes have two basic aims, one of which is redistributive, to provide a juster pattern of landholding and alleviate poverty by giving the peasants more substantial plots of land. The other is productive, to provide more agricultural produce by more economic and efficient means of farming. In order to achieve these goals, an agrarian reform programme should have three main elements. Firstly, a broader distribution of the ownership and control of land is necessary, but this on its own is not sufficient. Secondly, in order to make redistribution successful, both in economic terms and for the beneficiary, the implementation of modern, efficient and productive techniques is needed. It is not enough to enlarge a peasant's piece of land, he must have the wherewithal to cultivate it. Finally, to be successful, an agrarian reform program should include the development of comprehensive and realistic programs of community development including schools, health programmes, services for the protection of life and property, the construction of local roads and bridges, agricultural extension activities and farm credit facilities. A supportive infrastructure is needed to make the best use of the land.

Most Latin American countries have embarked on some sort of land reform programme, though these have varied considerably across the region in scope and depth. In countries like Colombia and Venezuela, there has been some tinkering with the traditional agrarian system, but on the other hand, Cuba has experienced a complete restructuring of the agrarian sector. Some countries, such as Mexico and Chile, have gone through periods of quite radical change, only to be followed by changing political conditions, which have led to a reversal of policy.

In order to see what can be achieved by a successful agrarian reform policy and yet how these achievements can subsequently be reversed, it is worth examining Chilean agrarian changes. Agrarian reform was put into practice in the second half of the 1960s with the passing of a law, which made it possible to expropriate estates of over 80 hectares and they began by taking over the most economically inefficient. The basic criteria of the reform programme were: firstly, the peasants should gain ownership of the land they worked; secondly, they should be encouraged to become full and active citizens of the nation; and thirdly, productivity should be improved at all levels of agriculture. Embodied in these are the two elements of social justice and increased productivity.

Once the land had been expropriated, it was to be turned into cooperatives but, because the government felt it would be difficult for peasants, who had had no previous experience of administering a large farm, to move straight to a cooperative, there was an intermediary stage. This, referred to as the land settlement, was run by the peasants but with the supervision of officials from the agrarian reform agency. The peasants, therefore, had the chance to get experience of administration and problem-solving but, at the same time, had experts to assist and prevent mistakes of any magnitude. The intermediary stage was intended to last for three to five years. From 1964 to July 1970, agrarian reform involved the expropriation of 1,408 properties, with about 30,000 beneficiaries (Kay 1978). Towards the end of the decade, with elections looming, land distribution decreased in favour of greater emphasis on raising agricultural yields.

The 1970 elections were won by a coalition of left-wing parties, led by a Marxist, Salvador Allende, with a radical programme which included a pledge for a total and speedy programme of agrarian reform. The new government decided to use the existing legal framework to save the time and possible difficulties that new laws might bring about, but with certain modifications. Expropriations were to be speeded up and the land settlements were to become new reform units, with wider criteria for membership, thus increasing the number of beneficiaries. Different types of reform unit emerged, but the most common, known as Peasant Committees, were not very different in their organisation from the previous land settlements. All the reform units offered their members security in the form of assured employment and access to a plot of land and full voting rights in the unit. The wider implications of agrarian reform were tackled in this period, for there was a redistribution of credit in favour of smallholders and the state took over some marketing networks, though this was primarily to get supplies to the urban consumer at low prices, rather than to assist agriculture (Castillo and Lehmann 1982).

Within two years, the Popular Unity government had expropriated 3,278 farms, that is, over twice as many estates as the previous government had done in six years (Castillo and Lehmann 1982). The main losers were the *hacendados* and those who gained were the permanent workers, who benefited from increases in the minimum rural wage and from secure employment. This meant a redistribution of income in the rural sector from the wealthy to the permanent workers, though it may be the case that there was a widening differential in incomes between permanent and temporary workers. The great achievement of this period was the eradication of the very large *hacienda* from the countryside. In 1973, according to official statistics, there were no privately owned properties of over 80 hectares in Chile. The economic results of the reforms are very difficult to judge because the period was too short for any economic stability to be achieved.

In 1973, Chile experienced a military coup in which Allende and thousands of his followers were killed, others fleeing into exile. The new government set about reversing previous policies, not least of which was agrarian reform. The agrarian reform units were dismantled, either by returning land to previous owners or distributing it to others. By 1979, just under 30 per cent of the land in the reformed sector had been restored to its former owners (Castillo and Lehmann 1982). The remaining land was to be given out in family units, in line with the government's ideology of private ownership. Since the remaining land was not sufficient to accommodate all the 75,000 beneficiaries of Chilean agrarian reform, the military regime started a selection process. A point system was introduced in which participation in the management of the agrarian reform units and in unions tended to count against people, whereas qualifications such as holding a degree in agronomy gained points. The average size of each plot of land available rose, with the result that fewer people could benefit. The effect of this was that, of the 75,000 original beneficiaries, 51 per cent did not receive any land. The military's policy brought about a greater disparity in landholdings and by 1977, the large estate was back, since there were 1,512 estates of over 80 hectares that year (Castillo and Lehmann 1982).

In economic terms, many of those who still had land in the years following 1973 were not able to farm it successfully. The institutions which had previously been set up to aid small farmers had their lending capacity cut considerably, making it difficult for many of the beneficiaries to find sufficient capital. Although until April 1980 it was illegal for beneficiaries to sell land, researchers found evidence of land being sold and also of farms that had been turned over to sharecropping. This suggests that many small farmers, unable to cultivate successfully, turned to the sale or renting of land. The farmers who are successful are those with medium-sized farms, who are growing for export. Agricultural and fishing exports increased four-fold in value from 1974–77. The produce is mainly fruit and luxury vegetables for upper income groups. Export requires resources for capital investment, which excludes the small farmer, but the growing of fruit and vegetables does not necessitate very large tracts of land and, therefore, the medium-sized farmer can accommodate this. Chilean apples were on sale in British supermarkets in the early 1980s, despite the vast quantities of apples grown in Britain. The result in Chile is that poor, small farmers exist alongside medium-sized farms which are capital intensive and produce for export, and a large number of the rural population have become landless and are poverty-stricken.

The difficulty with many agrarian reform programmes has been achieving both social justice and economic growth. In Cuba, the former has been emphasised with marked success, while economic growth has been subject to fluctuations. Development there has been described by Lehmann as 'modernisation with fitful growth', because the expansion of the state apparatus has meant modernisation in terms of growing bureaucracy and an increase in formal, at the expense of clientelist and personal, relationships at work but at the same time agricultural productivity has been erratic (Lehmann 1982).

The predominant unit of production in rural Cuba is the state farm, although there exists, despite the nationalisation of privately owned businesses in the 1960s, a distinct private sector in the countryside, half of which lies in Oriente province the home of the peasants who supported Castro in his bid for power. What the development of state farms has meant is the demise of the peasant plot based on unpaid family labour, the reduction of seasonal employment and a growth in proletarianisation. It is worth pointing out that before the revolution, Cuba, due to its sugar-based economy, had relatively fewer small-holders and relatively more agricultural labourers than most Latin American countries. The revolution, through state control, has given agricultural labourers greater security and better wages by turning them into state employees. The success of collectivisation is revealed by the increasing number of cooperatives in the private sector. This mushrooming of the producers' cooperatives, often through the amalgamation of small farms has been welcomed by Cuban leaders because the cooperatives are generally well integrated into the revolutionary process.

Nicaragua, which has also had a socialist revolution, has a greater emphasis on the private sector in its agrarian policy. This sector plays a leading role, not only in controlling the greatest share of land, but also in producing three-fifths of the volume of agricultural production (Curtis 1983). Because of Nicaragua's dependence on agricultural produce and agro-exports, it has been important not to let production levels fall. As a result, because the properties that were expropriated were modern commercial farms, the government has maintained the structure of production, but, unlike the organisation prior to the revolution, the workforce now has a say in administration. Small farms in the public sector have been grouped together in cooperatives to gain all the benefits possible from size and concentration. At the same time, the social benefits in the few years since 1979 have been significant. Unemployment fell due to agrarian reform from about 32 per cent in 1979 to 20 per cent in 1980 and unionisation has got well underway (Petras 1981).

Agrarian reform programmes have differed in their emphasis, whether it be on land distribution or agricultural production. Often it seems that although there is in theory a clear commitment to land reform, in practice programmes concentrating on higher levels of production are preferred. The first agrarian reform in the region took place in Mexico after the revolution and went through its most radical phase in the 1930s, when much good land was turned over to the *ejidos*, the public sector. During the 1940s, the government, having decided that sufficient redistribution of land had taken place, began to concentrate on increasing agricultural productivity. Today the major part of the public sector operates below subsistence level, while production is concentrated in a small number of large, efficient private enterprises.

In other countries, despite the rhetoric of the Alliance for Progress that stressed social justice, the officials, bureaucrats, agronomists and administrators frequently implemented and supported programmes that could demonstrate that they could bring about higher levels of production. It is the large farm, with its abundant land and capital and modern machinery, that has invariably been perceived as capable of greater yields. Indeed the commitment to size for greater productivity is demonstrated by the socialist countries, who own large modern farms, but replace the private owner with the state.

This assumption that big means better can be questioned. Many commentators have noted the fact that the small plot of land may produce more per acre than the large, because of necessity it is cultivated more intensively (see *CEPAL review* 1982 for example). The Ecuadorian peasantry seem to be particularly productive. A study of the Ecuadorian censuses for 1954 and 1974 estimated that production on the smaller units had grown by an average of 2.7 per cent per year during the period, but on the larger units, growth was at the rate of 1.2 per cent. The Bolivian peasantry have also demonstrated impressive rates of output. Between 1950 and the mid 1970s in the Bolivian Andes, the production of cold and temperate-climate crops, grown by the peasantry, expanded at an average annual rate of 4.4 per cent, particularly high levels being recorded in the 1950s after agrarian reform (Ortega 1982).

FOOD POLICIES

Agrarian policies have come to be focused less on land tenure arrangements and more on the growth and distribution of food. If there are problems of malnutrition and hunger, these can be tackled at source by attempts to produce more food. Greater food production also means improved incomes for farmers. To understand government policies concerning food, we need to look at nutritional levels and the quantity and nature of food production.

Statistics for calorie consumption in the region show that despite considerable variation between different areas, nearly all the countries raised their calorie requirement satisfaction rates during the 1970s, the greatest progress being made by the countries with initially the lowest levels. According to these rates the best-fed people of the region live in Argentina, Costa Rica, Cuba, Mexico, Paraguay and Uruguay, while Bolivia and Haiti still maintain low levels of calorie intake. Dietary changes also reveal improvements in food consumption patterns, since there has been an increase in the consumption of oils, chicken meat, eggs and milk, which in the past have been beyond the reach of many of the poor. Sugar contributes more to calorie intake than in the past, mainly due to the increased consumption of processed beverages and foods, which may bode ill for the population's teeth, but also reveals increased purchasing power. The declining contribution made by cereals and pulses to calorie intake affects the low income groups (López Cordovez 1982). It could be interpreted as a shift towards other foodstuffs or as a worrying decline in the basic calorie consumption of the poor.

Latin America's nutritional levels are higher than in many other parts of the Third World, and yet it is estimated that 15 per cent of the region's children suffer from medium to high-level malnutrition, which means, given the differences within the region, high levels in some areas (López Cordovez 1982). One of the major factors inhibiting greater improvements in consumption levels is inflation, to which food prices become very vulnerable. Because of inflation, real food prices in the great majority of Latin American countries were higher at the end of the 1970s than the beginning. It is estimated that 60 per cent of the rural population of Latin America lives in conditions of poverty (ECLAC/FAO 1985).

When it comes to the level of food production, it needs to be pointed out that food production rates for the region are not unimpressive. FAO statistics show that in the period from 1971–80, Latin

America had the highest growth rate (3.9 per cent) in food production of the various world regions (Figueroa 1985). Increased yields were made possible by mechanisation and the expansion of the cultivated area. With the recession of the 1980s, however, agricultural production grew by only 1.6 per cent from 1981 to 1984 (ECLAC/FAO 1985). Part of the problem lies in the fact that much of this produce is exported and therefore land which could have been utilised to feed a domestic market is supplying an overseas population. In the early 1980s, 80 per cent of agricultural exports were made up of the following items, in order of importance: coffee, sugar, soya beans, oil seed meal and oil-cake, cotton, cocoa, bananas, beef and live cattle, maize and wheat (López Cordovez 1982). Governments argue that they need these exports to obtain the foreign currency wanted to finance the region's debts.

Agribusiness, which has been moving into the luxury end of the market, with the growth of carnations in Colombia and strawberries in Mexico for sale in the United States, has contributed to the high level of exports. Agribusiness has also found a profitable outlet in the production of animal feed. Much of the Colombian countryside has been turned over to the growing of soya and sorghum to feed chickens, thus depriving the Colombian peasants in the area of a food supply and contributing to the increased protein deficit in Colombia. Similarly, most of the Peruvian anchovy catch is turned into fishmeal to feed chickens.

At the same time, the volume of agricultural products being imported to the region is increasing. This increase was at an annual rate of 10 per cent between 1975 and 1980, due to increased purchases of wheat, maize, sorghum, vegetable oils, dairy products, beans and sugar, all basic foodstuffs. A third of these imports came from the region itself, but over 60 per cent came from the industrialised countries (López Cordovez 1982). Wheat has come to be an important imported product which reflects the increasing consumption of bread as a staple, rather than maize-based food products such as *tortillas*. Armstrong and McGee make a more explicit connection between the growth of agribusiness and commercial farming on the one hand and increase in agricultural imports on the other. Between 1960 and 1978, 'Food imports rose in a number of countries where agribusiness and local commercial farmers have been most active in modernising the sector (Argentina, Colombia, Guatemala and Mexico)' (Armstrong and McGee 1985: 77).

What is required in Latin America is a policy that will stimulate food production for the domestic market and the raising of income levels of the rural poor. Given a situation where land is being used to provide agricultural produce for export, one solution to the problem of food shortages, would be to make the land that supplies the domestic market more productive. Scientific breakthroughs made this seem possible and gave rise to the Green Revolution.

This international campaign, aimed at increasing the productivity of land by means of the introduction of science-based technology had, as its goals, freedom from hunger for the populations of LDCs and also a freedom from food dependence. Latin America is not alone in the world in being an agricultural producer and at the same time dependent on imported foodstuffs. The aims were to be implemented through accelerated increases in food production, which were made possible by the discovery of high-yielding grain at two international research centres in Mexico and the Philippines. Between 1953 and 1970, the high-yielding seeds, which were introduced in a number of LDCs, such as Mexico, Colombia, India, The Philippines, Sri Lanka and Indonesia, often led to more abundant harvests of rice or wheat. In Mexico, entrepreneurs in wheat production achieved quite a high level of profitability.

In order to get the best results from the new seeds, technology in the form of machinery, chemical products and fertilisers, was necessary and therefore capital was required to purchase these. The new cereals were capable of doubling or trebling the produce of a cultivated hectare but this could only be done by investing in a package of changes. Therefore only those who could afford this, either on the basis of capital or loans and those who could master the changes and new technology were able to benefit. In Asia, the miracle rice was wiped out in many areas because it had not been treated with the necessary chemicals.

The Green Revolution in Latin America has led to a Kulak path of development. Some have done well, but they are those who have more land, have access to capital, have higher levels of education and are generally more socially advantaged. It encouraged the incorporation of the peasant community into the wider society, because it operated through the market. Peasants were enticed away from subsistence agriculture because of the potential profits and, in order to buy the necessary equipment and fertilisers and to sell the final produce, they had to work through the market. In Mexico, the private sector was able to take advantage of the new seeds, but the peasants on *ejido* land, often unable to get credit and farming for the first three years without fertilisers were not so productive. From 1953–65, the period when the Green Revolution was underway, the wheat yields of the *ejido* sector lagged behind those of the private sector (Pearse 1980).

The technology that was needed to cultivate the high-yield grains successfully often had to be imported, which led to the suggestion that food dependency was being exchanged for technological dependency. Moreover, the necessity for greater capital and technological inputs and the move away from a subsistence agriculture involved the peasant in greater risks. In Colombia, many of the peasants were persuaded to give up their coffee and cocoa trees, which though not highly productive, could be relied on to produce and, instead, to take up seasonal crops such as corn, soybeans and tomatoes. Cultivation of the new crops required tractors, fertilisers and pesticides, and plants, such as tomatoes, need constant care and spraying. This implies capital investment and, although credit was available for the Colombian peasants, interest rates were high. Rubbo cites the example of a farmer, who borrowed the equivalent of $800 to plant tomatoes. A month before harvesting, the plants were washed away by some unusually heavy rains, leaving the farmer with a loan and interest that he was unable to pay (Rubbo 1975).

The new seeds were a scientific success but in their introduction to the LDCs, too little attention was paid to the social and political context. The programmes were implemented by governments through existing political channels, thus allowing dominant groups to take advantage of the situation. Many countries who received aid to introduce the Green Revolution had repressive regimes, whose policies had in the first place brought about the poverty.

The Green Revolution did bring about an increase in the production of food, which is needed for both urban and rural populations. Those who benefited from improved earnings, however, were not the rural poor, but the farmers who were able to take advantage of the opportunites the Green Revolution had to offer. The main problem was that the socio-political implications of scientific and technological change were not thought through thoroughly.

A growing urban demand for food has tended to stimulate production in the larger and more commercialised enterprises, but this is not of necessity nor is it always the case. The potential for developing a peasant economy can be seen in the Ecuadorian situation. In the 1970s, Ecuador enjoyed an oil boom, which for a few years gave a boost to the economy as a whole, though the gains were felt mostly in the urban sector. This led to an increase in urban employment opportunities and the expanding workforce gave rise to a greater demand for food. Rural-urban migrants were able to take advantage of the former, often sending financial assistance back to their relatives in the countryside and so contributing to increased income levels there. Urban consumer demand was met by an expansion in food production by the farmers in the Sierra, who, although still the poorest members of Ecuadorian society, had benefited from agrarian reform. The consequence was a real, though small, rise in the incomes of this peasantry (Commander and Peek 1986).

The circumstances of this case are unusual because of the oil boom, and the following economic crisis of the 1980s, which has now eroded the income gains of those small farmers, has demonstrated the inability of the economy to sustain the development that had taken place. The fact that economic growth had been externally generated meant that when the outside impetus, rising world oil prices, receded, there was no continuing growth. Nevertheless the Ecuadorian case shows that the peasantry can respond to and benefit from the food demands of the urban population.

With the problem of hunger still in evidence in LDCs, some Third World governments have turned to other strategies to make the best use of resources and organise distribution, the onus being on distri- bution as much as production. Mexico, as the world's fifth largest oil producer in 1980, was able to take advantage of its large revenues to finance a new development strategy known as SAM, the Mexican Food System. The aim was to use the wealth from one natural resource, to fund a system that would return Mexico to self-sufficiency in basic foods. The policies had three main objectives: to increase home production of strategically important food crops (maize, beans, rice and sugar); to organise the distribution of food to the benefit of the rural and urban poor; and to improve the nutrition of particularly vulnerable groups (Redclift 1984b). Peasants were encouraged to cultivate basic food crops such as beans and corn by the raising of their prices and by assistance in the form of free, improved seeds, cheap fertiliser and credit facilities being made avail- able. The government organisation concerned with food distribution was improved and expanded, so that its subsidised outlets could be found in many poor areas, both urban and rural. The nutritional elements were especially innovative. At the time about 35 million Mexicans, over half the country's population, failed to reach per capita daily food intakes of 2,750 calories and 80 g of protein, the most vulnerable of these being women and children. To attack this problem, a Recommended Basic Food Basket was introduced, which meant the subsidising of essential foodstuffs.

Despite what would seem admirable objectives and a sound finan- cial backing, SAM was short-lived. One of the problems was political, for a change in government, accompanied by the repercussions throughout national and local-level bureaucracy that this entails, occurred in 1982 and altered the commitment of organisations to SAM. Even before the change, many of the policies, by the time they had been through the rather over-bureaucratic structures, became distorted and did not benefit the peasants to the extent that they should have done. In common with many other Latin American coun- tries, it was the weakness of technical and administrative institutions in charge of peasant agriculture that was partly to blame for the failure of a rural development policy. The peasants themselves were, at times, reluctant to trust government officials and resisted inter-

ference from the state. SAM did nothing to reduce the investment
of American-owned companies in Mexican food production, which
dominate the fertile irrigated areas (Redclift 1984b). The national
economic crisis led to the removal of many of the subsidies on foodstuffs. The National Foodstuffs Commission, replacing SAM, has
been set up to implement government strategy that consists of price
supports for basic food production, special incentives to producers
of priority foodstuffs, the phasing out of subsidies for non-priority
foodstuffs and a plan to tie retail prices of basic foods to increases
in the national minimum wage.

National level plans to bring change to the countryside have varied
across the region and changed in emphasis. Initially the stress was
on land tenure arrangements with the agrarian reform programs, but
in many areas the focus then moved to the production of food and
some governments are now concerned with distribution and access
to food.

PEASANT MOBILISATION

It has been suggested that agrarian reform is a reformist strategy for
undermining the revolutionary potential of the peasantry by providing
rural populations with sufficient reforms to prevent any outright
opposition to the system. The peasant, who receives a plot of land
through redistribution becomes a member of the petty bourgeoisie,
identifying his interests with those of the farmer. This view is well
expressed by de Janvry and Ground when they say 'the primary role
of the reform sector is political. Its function is to stimulate the development of a conservative agrarian petty bourgeoisie and thus reduce
the threat of social instability in the countryside' (de Janvry and
Ground 1978: 106).

Others have disagreed with this, but from different perspectives.
Petras and Laporte suggest that agrarian reform brings about revolutionary attitudes through the frustration felt by those who have
failed to benefit (Petras and LaPorte 1971). Other studies have
showed that profiting from agrarian reform can be combined with a
more radical political commitment. Bossert found that the peasants in
Chile's central valley with the highest levels of political consciousness
were precisely those who benefited from agrarian reform. He
concludes that agrarian reform can, therefore, play a part in raising
the revolutionary potential of the peasantry (Bossert 1980).

The debate over the radical or conservative nature of the peasantry
is a long-lasting one which still continues with some vigour. 'The
peasants are conservative' view combines early anthropologists and
Marxists in its supporters. The anthropologists saw the rural small-

Plate 1 Spice traders, Mexico. (Copyright Hamish Wallace).

Plate 2 Children with dolls, Mexico. (Copyright Hamish Wallace).

Plate 4 On the steps of the cathedral, Guatemala. (Copyright Hamish Wallace).

Plate 3 Tortilla and coke, Mexico. (Copyright Hamish Wallace).

Plate 6 Market women, Guatemala. (Copyright Hamish Wallace).

Plate 5 Carrying thatch, Guatemala, (Copyright Hamish Wallace).

Plate 8 Market day, Guatemala. (Copyright Hamish Wallace).

Plate 7 Religious procession, Virgin and Sun, Guatemala. (Copyright Hamish Wallace).

holder as the bearer of tradition and wedded to the same way of life as the generations before him. For Marx, the peasant represented a conservative force because of his structural position in society, which separates him from those who might share his class interests. Low levels of class consciousness are exacerbated by clientelism, which links the peasant through personal relationships to someone in another class.

In some cases where peasant movements have taken place, they are said to be clientelist-based. Galjart argues that, despite the successes of the Brazilian peasant leagues and rural syndicates, these were not class movements, but 'followings' of an innovative patron. He shows that the organisers of those leagues were not local peasants, but outsiders, often Catholic priests or members of the communist party. Their achievements, such as wage rises and the setting of minimum wage levels, were not won through class struggle, but received as favours from local government in the expectation of their political support in return. In some instances, the followings of different leaders competed with each other for different favours. In this way, they operated in a patron-client manner rather than as a united class opposing another and winning reforms through class struggle (Galjart 1964).

Contrasting views of the peasantry point to their radical participation in the Mexican and Cuban revolutions, peasant movements such as that of La Convención in Peru and the high levels of political consciousness of some sectors of the Chilean peasantry. These views stress different factors that encourage peasant mobilisation.

The now famous middle peasant thesis suggests that certain sectors of the peasantry, precisely those which the anthropologists and Marxists labelled as conservative, have the potential for political mobilisation (Wolf 1969). According to this thesis, the wealthy peasant has no reason to rebel and the poor landless peasant is limited in his actions by his dependence on a landowner. Any sign of political activity would cost him his livelihood. The middle peasant, the small freeholder, has the tactical leverage of independence. He is in a better position than others to initiate confrontation and he has some resources at his disposal. Wolf suggests that it is this sector that provides the catalyst for rebellion and he shows how, in six major revolutions in the world, it is the middle peasantry who have formed the pivotal group for peasant action. In Mexico, the peasants from Morelos, led by Zapata, were middle peasants fighting to prevent the loss of their land. In Cuba, although Castro did not receive the support of the *colonos* as a class before 1959, half his fighting force was made up of peasants from the Sierra. These Wolf calls middle peasants because, although they were squatting illegally on the land, in practice they owned and worked their small plots.

The debate over the middle peasantry can only be resolved by referring to concrete situations. Kay suggests that the action of a particular peasant group varies according to the nature of the dominant mode of production. 'The middle peasantry may be a revolutionary force during the transition from feudalism to capitalism, a conservative force in capitalism, a facist force under the threat of socialism (or capitalism in crisis), and a reactionary force under socialism' (Kay 1978: 119). The mode of production is, as always, important and, as Kay suggests, the transition from feudalism to capitalism may well stimulate peasant action. Wolf shows how the areas in Mexico where there was considerable peasant agitation during the revolution, were those where farms were modernising and becoming more capitalist. In Morelos, the landowners, compelled by increased competition and encouraged by improved communications, were expanding their sugar estates and, in so doing, encroaching on peasant lands. Capitalist agriculture was also expanding in the cotton areas of Durango and sugar plantations of Sinaloa, which were other areas of peasant revolt. In the south of the country, in places like Chiapas, where most peasants were landless and there was little modernisation, the countryside was relatively quiet (Wolf 1969).

It can be argued that the peasantry in LDCs today have revolutionary potential because their situation is so similar to that of the urban proletariat in Marx's day. Marx's argument that the proletariat becomes a revolutionary force because: machinery reduces differences thus homogenising the labour force; the nature of work in a modern factory requires organisation; and the exploitation of the industrial system leads to poverty and alienation, can be applied to rural society in Latin America. Imperialism focused on one or two natural resources, thus creating a homogeneous agricultural proletariat, all doing the same labouring job. The *colono* system and rural proletarianisation, encouraged by agribusiness, led to a factory-like situation. Domination, first by a foreign power and then by an elite, leads to poverty and alienation. This argument puts forward the notion that the peasantry working in these conditions would provide revolutionary potential.

According to Shanin, the peasantry, in general, have a low level of class consciousness, but in times of crisis this rises (Shanin 1971). This would certainly explain the frequently found apathy towards radical politics but, at the same time, the revolutionary potential, when provoked. There is clear evidence that the peasantry have risen in rebellion on historic occasions, but how much likelihood is there of their political mobilisation in the changing context of rural Latin America?

In the Southern cone countries, the peasantry represent a small sector and one that is diminishing. But in Central America and the

Andean countries, they constitute one of the major groups in society. Reactions here vary according to different situations. Peruvian agrarian reform has had the effect of raising the consciousness of the peasantry. In Ecuador there has been little unionisation, but organisations based on ethnicity have given the indigenous rural population an effective foundation for action. In Guatemala, the Indian population has opposed attempts to seize their land by wealthy landowners and the army. Nicaraguan peasants, having played a vital part in the Sandinista revolution, are participating actively in agrarian reform. Peasant federations in Costa Rica, a country with a reputation for democratic institutions and relative equality, have been protesting at the surprisingly skewed distribution of land, by seizing unused land belonging to multinationals.

The peasant movement in El Salvador has developed through the peasants' own ability to organise and form a union in the face of growing landlessness and poverty. Pearce argues that two catalysts, the church and the revolutionary organisations, encouraged the movement to rebel and support the guerillas in the civil war, but she stresses that these acted as catalysts rather than agents. In the guerilla areas of El Salvador, the peasants for the first time have the chance to administer their own lives and here they have set up elected councils, along with health and education programs and they organise production (Pearce 1986).

CONCLUSION

Changes in the countryside have had different implications for the rural population depending on: nature of the terrain; extent and type of capitalist penetration; existence and extent of agrarian reform; access to government assistance; and levels of peasant organisation. The result is a varied picture with interlocking modes of production, but in general these changes have promoted economic and social differentiation. The two aims of increasing productivity and redistribution that have permeated agrarian thinking have often been seen as competing rather than complementary. In response to the multiplicity of factors affecting their lives, the peasantry have shown that they can act positively, making the most of opportunity when it presents itself. In the face of repressive regimes, the peasantry have shown a capacity and willingness to organise and mobilise.

FURTHER READING

Castillo, L., Lehmann, D. (1982) Chile's three agrarian reforms:

the inheritors. *Bulletin of Latin American Research* vol. 1 no. 2

de Janvry A (1981) *The agrarian question and reformism in Latin America*. The John Hopkins university press, Baltimore and London

Goodman, D., Redclift, M. (1981) *From peasant to proletarian: capitalist development and agrarian transitions*. Basil Blackwell, Oxford

Pearce, J. (1986) *Promised Land: peasant rebellion in Chalatenango El Salvador*. LAB, London

Pearse, A. (1975) *The Latin American peasant*. Frank Cass, London

Redclift, M. (1984) *Development and the environmental crisis: red or green alternatives?* Methuen, London

Stavenhagen, R. (1978) Capitalism and the peasantry in Mexico. *Latin American Perspectives* Issue 18 vol. 5 no. 3

Chapter

6

Urbanisation

One of the major social phenomena in Latin America since the
Second World War and one that has had a profound effect on the
social transformation of the continent, is the urban explosion. In the
1950s, Latin America was predominantly rural, now the majority of
its population live in towns and cities. Table 6.1 shows how urban
Latin America has become since 1960. The rapidly rising birth rate
is only part of the explanation, since the birth rate has not risen as
fast as urban populations have increased. Urban population figures
have been rising at a much greater rate than rural. Roberts, using
statistics for 1960, 1970 and projected for 1980, shows how in six
of the largest Latin American countries, Argentina, Brazil, Chile,
Mexico, Peru and Venezuela, the urban population has grown at a
faster rate than has the total population (Roberts 1978). This
suggests that the expansion is largely due to rural-urban migration,
which is estimated to account for 40–70 per cent of urban growth
in the post-war period up to 1970 (Morse 1971), and about 50 per
cent since then. These statistics are well supported by local studies
of rural areas demonstrating out-migration and urban studies showing
an influx of peasants. Though Latin America is more urbanised than
most other parts of the Third World, the process of urbanisation is
very much a feature of LDCs in general. 'In the space of one
generation, two hundred million people have moved from the countryside to the cities of Asia, Africa and Latin America' (Hellman 1986:
216). From 1950 to 1980 in Latin America, 27 million people migrated
from rural to urban areas (Hurtado 1986).

Table 6.1 Urban and rural population, by country, 1960 and 1984 (Thousands of persons)

	1960			1984			Growth rates of urban population 1960–84 (percentages)
	Urban	Rural	% Urban	Urban	Rural	% Urban	
Argentina	15 172	5 439	73.6	25 071	5 026	83.3	2.1
Bolivia	887	2 407	26.9	2 943	3 310	47.1	5.1
Brazil	33 068	39 257	45.7	95 896	35 289	73.1	4.5
Chile	5 018	2 578	66.1	9 873	2 005	83.1	2.9
Colombia	8 256	8 957	48.0	21 269	7 204	74.7	4.0
Costa Rica	410	910	31.1	1 198	1 262	48.7	4.6
Dominican Republic	1 138	2 303	33.1	3 172	2 930	52.0	4.4
Ecuador	1 515	2 914	34.2	4 618	4 497	50.7	4.8
El Salvador	935	1 726	35.1	1 940	2 816	40.8	3.1
Guatemala	1 347	2 574	34.4	2 531	5 209	32.7	2.7
Haiti	388	3 187	10.9	1 479	3 879	27.6	5.7
Honduras	438	1 550	22.0	1 649	2 583	39.0	5.7
Mexico	18 815	18 258	50.8	53 237	23 806	69.1	4.4
Nicaragua	622	881	41.4	1 790	1 373	56.6	4.5
Panama	441	779	36.1	1 195	939	56.0	4.2
Paraguay	605	1 354	30.9	1 570	2 006	43.9	4.1
Peru	4 630	5 755	44.6	12 780	6 418	66.6	4.3
Uruguay	2 006	611	76.7	2 530	460	84.6	0.9
Venezuela	5 104	2 859	64.1	14 362	2 495	85.2	4.4

Source: Adapted from IADB Report 1985

This rapid growth of urban areas reflects a process of concentration. Capital, very often originating from abroad, is being concentrated more in the industrial centres, not just towns but big cities where it can prosper. People follow in search of work, adding population concentration to capital accumulation. Armstrong and McGee see this as contributing to the growth of countries with more industrialised centres and the decline of the smaller republics, thus intensifying regional disparities (Armstrong and McGee 1985).

Industrialisation has clearly led to economic growth. Expansion in output was fuelled by growing external demand and generally expansive domestic economic policies. Although consumption grew faster than output leading to a rapid expansion of imports, the generally improving terms of trade rendered the trade gap small. The very impressive rates of growth reached, especially in Brazil, can be seen in Table 6.2. In the early 1980s these rates were greatly influenced by the economic crises prompted by debt problems, with negative rates being recorded for most countries. By 1984, however, economic growth had begun to pick up again.

RURAL-URBAN MIGRATION

Before looking any further at the process of migration, it is necessary to ask why it is taking place and, therefore, to examine the motivations of migrants. These are often described in terms of 'push-pull' factors, the 'push' being those that drive migrants from their villages, while the 'pull' attract them to the city. 'Push' factors refer to the difficulties of earning a living that were described in the previous chapter. It follows that one of the major 'pulls' of urban life is the opportunity of employment, though this is often not borne out by reality. The city also holds out the hope of a better education for the migrants' children, urban facilities, modern consumer goods and a variety of cheap diversions. The emphasis is very much on the hope of betterment and opportunity, the town offers a fluid situation, where the chance of improvement may arise, unlike the countryside, where opportunities are far more limited. Though conditions are poor in the towns, poverty is not as great as in rural areas.

Who are the migrants? With regard to age, they are mostly young adults, who have fewer ties and are therefore more mobile and who are also more likely to be attracted by the 'pull' factors. The highest rates are to be found among the population between the ages of 15 and 30 (Ortega 1982). A similar situation exists with African migration where especially with the early stages of migration, out-migrants are mostly young adults (Roberts 1978).

In virtually all migration statistics, females outnumber males (Gilbert

Table 6.2 Growth of gross domestic product and GDP per capita, by country, 1961–84 (Percentages)

Country	Gross Domestic Product						Gross Domestic Product Per Capita					
	Average annual growth rate			Annual variations			Average annual growth rate			Annual variations		
	1961–70	1971–80	1981	1982	1983	1984	1961–70	1971–80	1981	1982	1983	1984
Argentina	4.2	2.4	-6.2	-5.1	2.9	2.0	2.8	0.8	-7.8	-6.6	0.3	0.4
Bolivia	5.0	4.5	-0.9	-8.7	-7.6	-3.0	2.3	1.8	-3.6	-11.2	-10.1	-5.7
Brazil	6.2	8.6	-1.6	0.9	-3.2	4.5	3.6	5.9	-4.0	-1.6	-5.5	2.1
Chile	4.3	2.8	5.7	-14.3	-0.6	5.9	2.1	1.0	4.1	-15.9	-2.3	4.2
Colombia	5.2	5.5	2.3	0.9	1.0	3.0	3.1	3.3	0.1	-0.8	-1.5	0.9
Costa Rica	6.0	5.7	-2.3	-7.3	2.3	6.6	3.3	3.0	-4.5	-9.4	0.0	3.1
Dominican Republic	5.4	7.0	4.0	1.7	4.0	0.6	3.1	4.4	0.8	-2.5	1.8	-0.8
Ecuador	4.9	9.1	3.9	1.8	-3.3	3.0	1.8	5.8	0.8	-1.3	-6.3	-0.1
El Salvador	5.7	3.3	-8.3	-5.6	-0.7	1.5	2.7	0.8	-9.0	-6.4	-1.5	-1.3
Guatemala	5.5	5.7	0.7	-3.6	-2.7	0.1	2.6	2.7	-2.1	-6.3	-5.4	-2.6
Haiti	0.9	4.8	-2.7	-3.9	0.9	1.8	-0.8	3.0	-4.6	-5.7	-0.4	0.1
Honduras	5.0	4.8	1.2	-1.8	-0.5	2.8	1.8	1.6	-2.0	-5.1	-3.8	-0.6
Mexico	7.0	6.6	7.9	-0.5	-5.3	3.5	3.6	3.5	4.8	-3.4	-8.0	0.5
Nicaragua	7.0	1.5	5.3	-1.2	4.7	-1.4	4.1	-1.7	1.3	-4.8	0.9	-4.7
Panama	8.0	5.6	4.2	5.5	0.4	-1.2	5.8	3.1	1.8	3.0	-2.0	-5.9
Paraguay	3.8[1]	8.8	8.7	-1.0	-3.0	2.9	2.7[1]	5.3	5.4	-4.0	-5.8	-0.1
Peru	5.3	3.5	3.0	0.9	-11.8	3.5	2.6	0.9	0.4	-1.6	-14.0	0.9
Uruguay	1.6	3.1	1.9	-9.7	-4.7	-1.8	1.0	2.6	1.4	-10.8	-5.3	-2.8
Venezuela	6.1	4.2	-0.3	0.7	-5.6	-1.7	2.6	1.1	-3.3	-2.2	-8.2	-4.4

Source: Adapted from IADB Report 1985
[1] 1963–70

1974; Bossen 1984; Simmons, Diaz-Briquets and Laquia 1977). It is true that females predominate in most Latin American populations, but the difference between numbers of males and females in national populations is much smaller than the difference between them in migrant populations. As agricultural work is considered a male occupation, there is little employment available in rural areas for women. In one rural Argentine study, the contribution of the sons to the family productive unit was in the form of agricultural tasks, but that of the daughters took the form of monetary contributions, earned through migration (Miró and Rodríguez 1982). A Chilean study reveals that at the peak migration ages of 15–29, there were 62 males for every 100 females. For migrants aged 30–49 years, the ratio was 75 males for every 100 females (Simmons, Diaz-Briquets and Laquia 1977). This contrasts with Africa and Asia, where migration is predominantly male (ISS-PREALC 1983). There, men frequently migrate to the towns, leaving their families behind either to be visited at week-ends or to join them in the town at a later date. Women play a larger part in agricultural activities in the African and Asian contexts than the Latin American.

Generalisations about the education level and skills of the migrants are difficult to make for such a numerous and varied section of the population. Evidence from Peru, Chile and Mexico demonstrates that it is the more educated and more skilled who migrate (Roberts 1978). The census data on immigration to Lima since 1940 shows that, with the exception of Ancash, migrants come from departments with the highest literacy rates (Roberts 1978). Roberts goes on to link educational achievement with the level of economic development of the region of out-migration. He proposes a time perspective in the analysis of skill level and the pattern of movement. In the early stages of migration, the peasants come from the richer and more developed rural areas and so frequently have more skills to offer when they reach the town, than those in the less developed areas. With time, migrants begin to come from poorer parts. In the case of Peru, initially the departments that contributed the most migrants to Lima were Ancash, Junín, Ica, La Libertad and Arequipa. All these departments had experienced economic development by large-scale enterprises and often for the export economy. With the exception of Ancash, they also had the highest proportion of people living in urban places. Very few migrants came from poorer regions such as Puno in the south. Latterly, Lima has been receiving more migrants from the poorest and remotest departments. Roberts reports a similar trend in Mexico and Brazil, demonstrating that as capitalism penetrates further into peripheral regions, so these areas contribute more to the migratory process.

The migration process may involve more than one stage. Stage migration occurs when a peasant moves to a provincial town for some time and then on to the city. It has been suggested that stage migration is most likely to take place in countries where there is a significant network of small towns and villages, such as Chile, Brazil and Colombia. In countries where the non-metropolitan population is farm-based, such as Bolivia, migrants to the capital city are more likely to be rural (Simmons, Diaz-Briquets and Laquia 1977).

PROBLEMS OF SHELTER

The impact of the migrants has varied from country to country, but two areas which stand out as having been profoundly affected throughout the continent are housing and employment. Initially it was the basic problem of shelter that attracted social scientists, with the result that the main concern was for the home environment of the poor. The rapidly increasing urban population has placed an impossible strain on the provision of housing. The housing deficit in Mexico is about 4 million units, which means that about 30 per cent of the population is in need of housing (Hurtado 1986). Since the standard housing of towns and cities has been unable to provide shelter, urban populations have been compelled to take the situation into their own hands and put up their own homes.

These squatter settlements have sprung up in great abundance, generally in undesirable and inaccessible areas, which are unsuitable for standard building. The settlements are often found on steep slopes, such as those in Rio de Janeiro, which cover the hills behind the luxury tourist attractions of Ipanima and Copacabana beaches. Often referred to as shanty towns, these make-shift settlements now house one-third to one-half of the population of many cities. The self-built homes of Mexico City have increased from 14 per cent of the population and 23 per cent of the built-up area in 1952 to more than half the total population and built-up area today (Hurtado 1986). By 1982, at least 50 per cent of the total population of Guayaquil, Ecuador lived in poorly constructed and overcrowded homes (ISS-PREALC 1983).

Each country has a different name for them, often reflecting local attitudes, such as the graphic *villas miserias* in Argentina, highlighting the poverty of the communities. On the other hand, Peruvian squatter settlements were named young towns in 1968, in order to emphasise the youth of their inhabitants and to suggest a hopeful future for them. The Chileans use their local word for mushrooms, *callampas*, to imply that they spring up overnight.

The squatter settlements originally came into being through illegal land invasions. A group of urban poor, some of whom may be recent migrants, driven by the insanitary conditions, high rents and over-crowding of the slum areas, squat on a piece of unused land, and hastily erect a temporary shack. Since the invasion is illegal, it is often met with some sort of opposition but in general, the shanties remain, mostly because there is nowhere else for their inhabitants to live. The shacks are constructed out of any materials that are to hand, such as planks, cardboard, canvas, thatch, mud, corregated iron and often rubbish, but these are temporary and often improved upon at a later stage. At first, the settlement consists only of shacks, there are no roads, no water, no street lighting, though urban facilities may in time be extended to these areas. Once in existence, the settlement attracts new migrants, thus expanding quickly. The shanty town of Cuevas in Lima, founded by a group of 500 in 1960, had a population of 12,000 by 1970 (Turner 1970).

One of the issues that arises concerning the inhabitants of squatter settlements is integration into city life, since many of them are migrants and all of them are living in an area which is peripheral, in terms of city services and location. Patterns of adaptation to city life vary across the different countries.

The relationship of the squatters to urban populations has often been expressed in terms of marginality. This concept implies peripheralisation, an existence on the borders of society, where there is a lack of participation in the urban social structure. Marginality may occur on different levels. Cultural marginality refers to a different set of values, lifestyle and cultural patterns from the urban environment, thus suggesting that migrants may still have rural attitudes and traditions though living in the town. Bonilla argues that the lack of integration of Rio's *favelados* (the inhabitants of Brazilian shanty towns) into city life is due to their rural values and orientations which are different from those of the city-born and though modified to some extent by the new situation, still hinder a smooth adaptation (Bonilla 1970). Cultural marginality, which encompasses the culture of poverty concept (Lewis 1966), has been largely discredited because of the implication that traits such as apathy and passivity, which are the hallmarks of the culture of poverty, are very strongly imbedded in those who grow up in such a culture and therefore prevent them responding positively if opportunities arise. In many cases, the traits of resignation and the low aspirations that Lewis describes are merely responses to the situation in which the poor find themselves and will therefore change if the situation changes.

Many sociologists have been reluctant to employ the notion of cultural marginality because of the qualitative difference it implies between squatters and their urban counterparts living in the city centre, but have used structural marginality to assess the lack of participation in the urban system. Portes argues, from research in

Santiago, that marginal man is really one who is in a state of transition (Portes 1970). He found there was no real difference between Santiago marginals and those in higher strata in a cultural way, that is, they shared the same values and aspirations, but the squatters were unable to realise these because of structural features. Both urban and marginal men believed that education was the best means to achievement, but the former had better opportunities to actually benefit from schooling. The main difference between the integrated and the marginal man is not qualitative but a quantitative difference in the structure of occupational, educational and housing opportunities.

Although the terms marginal and marginality have frequently been used to address the situation of squatters, they have also been strongly criticised. The notion of marginality carries with it the sense of dualism, since it implies being on the boundaries of urban and rural society, but not integrated into either. Marginality can be criticised on the same grounds, that is to say a separation of rural and urban is not useful since many of the problems of rural areas stem from the integration of the two. Marginal implies that squatters are outside the system, rather than a part of it and, therefore, that they are outside the class structure. The research by Portes shows that the difference between the squatters and the urban population is one of degree rather than kind, the implication being that they are disadvantaged within the system, rather than being outside it. Perlman found the notion of marginality to be a myth in Brazilian *favelas*, because the inhabitants, far from being peripheralised, were involved in urban political activities and leisure clubs and were fully aware of what the city had to offer (Perlman 1976). Many of the squatter settlements exhibit high levels of social organisation and stability rather than marginal characteristics. Lomnitz has shown how squatters manipulate social networks to establish themselves in the city (Lomnitz 1977).

A rather different approach is taken by Turner, an architect who, for some time, worked in Lima (Turner 1965). In reaction to the many comments to the effect that shanty towns are full of poverty, misery and crime, he pointed out that these settlements were an improvement on the city centre slums. The Turner thesis stresses the self-help that is so fundamental to the squatter settlements. According to Turner, many migrants arrive in the city and, after spending a short time in the wretched conditions of the slums, decide to improve their living standards by moving to a squatter settlement. This represents an improvement in various ways. In terms of space, sunlight and unpolluted air, the squatters are better off than they were in the crowded, unventilated and noisy slum courts. Most important of all, there are no rents to pay and no fear of eviction.

Research in Mexico, Colombia and Venezuela, carried out several years after Turner's work, lends support to some aspects of the

Turner thesis, but not others (Gilbert and Ward 1985). Turner's view that migrants move into the city slums and then out to the shanty towns, is not so much the case now since the large number of spontaneous housing settlements and the widespread knowledge of their existence make this sort of housing immediately available. In Mexico city and Bogota for instance, most new migrants find accommodation in rooms in the squatter settlements.

The argument that these spontaneous housing settlements are a superior form of accommodation to the city slums is borne out by the consolidation that takes place in low-income settlements. In many Latin American countries, governments have realised that the cheapest way of attempting to solve the housing problem is to upgrade existing housing settlements and ease the development of new sites and services, rather than attempt the seemingly impossible task of constructing buildings sufficient to house the urban population. The kind of assistance that governments have offered has usually been through self-help schemes, the giving out of land titles to the inhabitants or offering loans. In 1974, there were 80 proposed or completed self-help schemes in 27 countries throughout the world, that were taken up by governments or the World Bank (Gilbert and Gugler 1982).

Successive governments in Peru since the 1950s have brought improvements to the settlements through a variety of measures. This reached a peak with the military regime (1968–80) which, in order to raise standards through self-help, improved many settlements by installing city services, handing out land titles and strengthening community organisations through the training of local leaders. Their policies culminated in attempts to turn the young towns into vast cooperative centres, by bringing industry to the settlements.

Self-help schemes have contributed to the consolidation and upgrading of housing in the settlements, so that in countries like Peru, Chile, Venezuela and Brazil, some of the accommodation is of two storeys and houses are constructed of brick and other regular building materials. Consolidation has been accompanied by an increase in renting, a phenomenon which existed for some time in African shanty towns, before it became common in Latin America. Gilbert and Ward found that renters made up 36.4 per cent of their sample of inhabitants of spontaneous housing settlements in Bogota, 12.7 per cent of those in Mexico City and 4.5 per cent in Valencia (Gilbert and Ward 1985). Although the proportion is still small in Valencia, in all three areas of their research (Bogota, Mexico City and Valencia), it is on the increase. Further research on renters and owners showed that the main difference between them was age. Renters were younger and at an earlier stage in the developmental cycle. Many of the owners had once been renters, thus, suggesting a pattern where young migrants, who cannot afford land or property, rent until they have sufficient savings to set up a home of their own. Renters are not 'down-and-outs', but those who do not yet have the opportunity to own a home, though they may well do so in later life.

Another reason why the increase in renting is likely to continue is its relationship to land prices and availability. Gilbert and Ward found the highest ownership levels in Valencia, where land is cheap and the highest levels of renting in Bogota, where land is expensive (Gilbert and Ward 1985). Since land prices, which are related to land availability, are, in general, rising it would seem likely that renting would increase.

The Turner thesis has been criticised by Marxists for over-emphasising the differences between the slum dwellers and the squatters. They argue that the differential in living standards between the two groups is minimal and to see this as social mobility is to detract attention from the important fact that they are all part of the large urban poor whose poverty is due to the wider social formation and, in particular, the capitalist mode of production. Self-help schemes relieve the state of the immediate necessity of providing housing and offer a cheap source of shelter, thus making it possible for the poor to survive on very low incomes (Burgess 1978).

The criticisms of both marginality and the Turner thesis have suggested that the problems of spontaneous housing cannot be fully understood without some reference to the wider society. The initial founding of a squatter settlement is, itself, an illegal act and, therefore, a challenge to authority. Latin American governments have responded in different ways, some taking a generally sympathetic approach through assisting self-help schemes, as in the Peruvian case, but even these may resort to repression. The Peruvian military reacted with force during the Pamplona invasion in May 1971, when they tried to evict the tens of thousands who had participated in this huge squatter invasion in Lima, with the result that there were several injuries and one death (Collier 1975).

Other governments have viewed the spontaneous housing settlements as wretched areas, which not only house society's drop-outs, but are also breeding grounds for crime and radical political activity. The Brazilian government has tried to eradicate the squatter settlements for these reasons, which is especially the case in Rio de Janeiro, because of the added factor that it is an international tourist centre and the *favelas* are so visible on the steep hillsides behind the luxury hotels and beaches. Some of the *favelas* have been knocked down, but there still remains the problem of shelter for their inhabitants. As a result, when shacks disappear, others appear in other parts of the city. The government has attempted some *favela* removal programs, but these have not been very successful, mainly because the new housing schemes are too expensive. The great advantage of spontaneous housing is its cheapness and, until governments can provide adequate housing with the same attraction, they are not likely to be successful. For the government-sponsored Cidade Alta housing project in Rio de Janeiro, only families earning at least three minimum salaries were acceptable, which eliminated about 40–69 per cent of the clientele. In some cases where *favelados* have moved to new housing schemes, they have been unable to meet the payments, which are periodically increased because of inflation and, therefore, had to return to the *favelas*.

Self-help schemes provide Latin American governments with a cheap solution for housing the poor, but the contribution they make to the wider socio-economic structure is more far-reaching. As Gilbert has suggested, 'Self-help keeps the Third World economy functioning' (Gilbert and Gugler 1982: 113). For a start, it allows the poor into the housing market by keeping costs low and not threatening higher-income groups. Where there is consolidation, this offers up opportunities for commercial and industrial companies, for example, where materials such as glass, bricks, cement, tiles and pipes are supplied in large quantities for construction. Marxist arguments support this view, pointing out that cheap housing reduces the pressure on wages, allowing the labour force to reproduce itself despite low wages and in this way contributing to capital accumulation in the capitalist sector. On a political level, these schemes help to maintain the status quo, because they satisfy some of the minimum housing needs of the poor and so reduce pressure for radical reforms. As the satisfaction is just sufficient to prevent people resorting to large-scale political opposition, governments are not pressured into more forceful measures, such as urban reform or progressive taxation.

INFORMAL SECTOR

In the 1970s, partly due to growing criticisms of marginality, which were linked to the increased strength of dependency theories, attention switched away from housing to focus on problems of employment and the economic structure. It became clear that most investment and credits in the urban sector had been used to finance further mechanisation and capitalisation, creating limits to labour absorption of industrial sectors. Since job opportunities in industry have been limited in this way, how do the millions who are coming to the city earn a living?

Although a small number do find work in factories as semi-skilled or unskilled labourers, a significant aspect of the Latin American economy is the large size of the service sector. Table 6.3 shows how

Table 6.3 Latin America: employment characteristics, 1960–79

| | Proportion of population of working age (15–64) | | Proportion of labour force[1] in: | | | | | |
| | | | Agriculture | | Industry | | Services | |
	1960 %	1979 %	1960 %	1979 %	1960 %	1979 %	1960 %	1979 %
Argentina	64	63	20	13	36	28	44	59
Bolivia	55	53	61	50	18	24	21	26
Brazil	54	55	52	40	15	22	33	38
Chile	57	62	30	20	20	20	50	60
Colombia	50	59	51	27	19	21	30	52
Dominican Republic	49	52	67	50	12	18	21	32
Ecuador	52	52	57	52	19	18	24	30
Guatemala	51	53	67	56	14	21	19	23
Honduras	52	50	70	63	11	14	19	23
Mexico	51	51	55	37	20	26	25	37
Nicaragua	50	50	62	40	16	14	22	46
Peru	52	54	53	38	19	20	28	42
Uruguay	64	63	21	11	29	32	50	57
Venezuela	51	55	35	19	22	27	43	54

Source: Armstrong, W., McGee, T, (1985) *Theatres of Accumulation* p. 74
[1] Includes economically active population (plus armed forces and unemployed); excludes housewives, students and economically inactive groups

this sector grew during the 1960s and 1970s. As a result the productive sector is employing a relatively small number of the labour force, while the sector that serves the region absorbs greater numbers. Despite the lack of opportunity in regular wage-earning work, official unemployment figures are not very high (see Table 6.4).

Table 6.4 Urban unemployment

Country	(Average annual rates)					
	1970	1975	1980	1981	1982	1983
Argentina	4.9	2.6	2.3	4.5	4.8	4.1
Bolivia	—	—	7.5	9.7	9.4	12.1
Brazil	6.5	—	7.2	7.9	6.3	6.7
Colombia	10.6	11.0	9.7	8.2	9.3	11.8
Costa Rica	3.5	—	6.0	9.1	9.9	8.5
Chile	4.1	15.0	11.7	9.0	20.0	19.0
Mexico	7.0	7.2	4.5	4.2	4.1	6.9
Panama	10.3	8.6	9.8	11.8	10.3	11.2
Paraguay	—	—	4.1	2.2	5.6	8.4
Peru	6.9	7.5	7.1	6.8	7.0	9.2
Uruguay	7.5	—	7.4	6.7	11.9	15.5
Venezuela	7.8	8.3	6.6	6.8	7.8	10.5

Source: Adapted from ECLA (1985) *Statistical Yearbook for Latin America* 1984 edition

This is largely explained by the statistics for 'disguised' unemployment or underemployment, which often reach striking levels (see Table 6.5).
Since Latin American governments offer no real assistance to the unemployed, many of the poor are compelled to earn a living through irregular and haphazard means. The category of underemployment refers to an area of work that includes street selling, shoe-shining, refuse collecting for sale, prostitution and many other activities which offer no security and bring in very meagre earnings. Table 6.5 reveals a slight contraction in this sector during the 1970s, but nevertheless in 1980 it still represented over a third of the economically active population for the region as a whole. The economic crises of the 1980s have contributed to its expansion in this decade.

Some social scientists have conceptualised these workers in terms of a reserve army of labour. In this case, they would constitute a pool of labour which can be utilised in boom periods and disregarded in recessions. This view sees the experience of the Third World as being little different from that of the industrialised countries. The

Table 6.5 Latin America: segmentation of the economically active population and underemployment coverage: 1950 and 1980 (Percentages)

| | | Share in the total EAP | | | | | | Underemployment coverage |
| | | Non-agricultural | | | Agricultural | | | Mining | |
		Formal (1)	Informal (2)	Total (3)	Modern (4)	Traditional (5)	Total (6)	(7)	(8) = (2) + (5)
Latin America	1950	30.6	13.5	44.1	22.1	32.6	54.7	1.2	46.1
	1980	47.7	19.4	67.1	13.2	18.9	32.1	0.8	38.3
Group A	1950	26.4	12.2	38.6	22.4	38.0	60.4	1.0	50.2
	1980	48.2	18.6	66.8	14.1	18.4	32.5	0.7	37.0
Mexico	1950	21.6	12.9	34.5	20.4	44.0	64.4	1.1	56.9
	1980	39.5	22.0	61.5	19.2	18.4	37.6	0.9	40.4
Panama	1950	34.9	11.8	46.7	6.2	47.0	53.2	0.1	58.8
	1980	51.6	14.8	66.4	11.4	22.0	33.4	0.2	36.8
Costa Rica	1950	29.7	12.3	42.0	37.3	20.4	57.7	0.3	32.7
	1980	54.2	15.3	69.5	20.5	9.8	30.3	0.2	25.1
Venezuela	1950	34.7	16.4	51.1	23.3	22.5	45.8	3.1	38.9
	1980	60.9	18.5	79.4	6.5	12.6	19.1	1.5	31.1
Brazil	1950	28.5	10.7	39.2	22.5	37.6	60.1	0.7	48.3
	1980	51.6	16.5	68.1	12.4	18.9	31.3	0.6	35.4
Colombia	1950	23.9	15.3	39.2	26.2	33.0	59.2	1.6	48.3
	1980	42.6	22.3	64.9	15.8	18.7	34.5	0.6	41.0

Group B	1950	17.1	14.9	32.0	23.2	43.0	66.2	1.8	57.9
	1980	29.1	21.8	50.9	12.0	35.9	47.9	1.2	57.7
Guatemala	1950	16.6	14.0	30.6	20.6	48.7	69.3	0.1	62.7
	1980	23.8	18.9	42.7	19.4	37.8	57.2	0.1	56.7
Ecuador	1950	21.5	11.7	33.2	27.4	39.0	66.4	0.4	50.7
	1980	25.6	28.6	54.2	12.1	33.4	45.5	0.3	62.0
Peru	1950	19.1	16.9	36.0	21.9	39.4	61.3	2.7	56.3
	1980	37.7	19.8	57.5	8.9	31.8	40.7	1.8	51.6
Bolivia	1950	9.1	15.0	24.1	19.0	53.7	72.7	3.2	68.7
	1980	17.9	23.2	41.1	5.2	50.9	56.1	2.8	74.1
El Salvador	1950	18.5	13.7	32.2	32.5	35.0	67.5	0.3	48.7
	1980	28.6	18.9	47.5	22.3	30.1	52.4	0.1	49.0
Group C	1950	54.0	16.6	70.6	20.4	7.6	28.0	1.4	24.2
	1980	61.5	21.4	82.9	9.2	7.0	16.2	0.9	29.4
Argentina	1950	56.8	15.2	72.0	19.9	7.6	27.5	0.5	22.8
	1980	63.5	21.4	84.9	7.8	6.8	14.6	0.5	28.2
Chile	1950	40.8	22.1	62.9	23.1	8.9	32.0	5.1	31.0
	1980	55.5	21.7	77.2	13.2	7.4	20.6	2.2	29.1
Uruguay	1950	63.3	14.5	77.8	17.3	4.7	22.0	0.2	19.2
	1980	63.3	19.0	82.3	9.5	8.0	17.5	0.2	27.0

Source: Data prepared by PREALC. *CEPAL Review* 24 p. 105

large numbers who are unable to find regular work are not seen as a phenomenon characteristic of underdevelopment, but part of the capitalist division of labour and, therefore, a similar feature to the industrialisation process of European countries, differing in terms of quantity rather than quality. For Marx, however, the function of the reserve army of labour was keeping wages low and, to this end, the absolute size of the reserve army need not be very great. The high numbers and continuing growth of this sector in Latin America would suggest that concepts of European analysis are not sufficient.

This sector has also been referred to by some as a lumpenproletariat. The implication here is that these workers have rejected the dominant values of society and are made up of criminals, prostitutes, drug-addicts and other drop-outs (Lloyd 1982). This image clearly does not correspond with the material presented so far in this chapter.

Others use the term sub or proto-proletariat to mean that these members of the urban poor are in the process of becoming a working class, though they have not yet achieved this status. It implies a commitment to the urban way of life and urban employment, and the final development of this sector, at some time in the future, into a proletariat proper (Lloyd 1982). The expansion of the sector in the 1980s presents a genuine difficulty with this concept.

The terms underemployment and 'disguised' unemployment have a negative ring about them and do little to help our understanding of this type of work. In order to shift the emphasis towards a more positive interpretation, Keith Hart in 1973 introduced the concept of the informal sector (Hart 1973). The division between formal and informal is based on the distinction between wage-earning and self-employment, with the key variable being the rationalisation of work, in other words whether or not labour is recruited on a permanent or regular basis for fixed reward. The emphasis on self-employment means that new income-generating activities can be identified. The term informal sector has become widely used.

What are the characteristics of the informal sector? For a start, there is considerable freedom of entry for all involved, unlike the formal sector where barriers exist in the form of qualifications, contracts and other institutional restrictions. Secondly, this sector is highly competitive, there is a complete absence of the monopolies which predominate in the formal sector. Linked to this, is the absence of foreign ownership within the informal sector, the entrepreneurs and pedlars are local people. Finally, pricing mechanisms operate in a different way from the formal sector, where they are fixed. They fluctuate according to the personal factors of those involved in the transaction (Davies 1979).

This sector supplies both the poor and the rich and produces both goods and services. Although all the activities lack security, they vary in the extent of their irregularity and in the nature of the work involved. Street sellers of different kinds are an important group, whether they be street pedlars who manage to buy chewing gum, newspapers, sweets, balloons, ornaments, fruit and any number of miscellaneous items wholesale, or the women who make snacks for sale in the streets. A good illustration of the latter can be found in Domitila Barrios de Chungara's account of the daily lives of a Bolivian miner and his family. She relates how she, like many other miners' wives, sells foodstuffs in the street in order to make up for what her husband's wage does not cover in necessities. Domitila makes and sells pies and because this requires all the tasks of preparing the vegetables, buying the meat, cooking the pies, and then selling them, the children help her. Shopping at the company store often means a long wait in the queue, so the children line up for the groceries, while Domitila sells her pies (Barrios de Chungara and Viezzar 1978).

This sector also includes outworkers for manufacturing and repair operations, who sub-contract work to do in their own homes or small workshops such as shoe manufacturers (Peattie 1982); beggars who are often more organised than they appear (Ruiz-Perez 1979); prostitutes; garbage pickers who can sell various types of waste paper, refuse and bottles; the living-in domestic servants paid low wages and provided with board and lodging who, according to Lloyd, constitute a category which is included within the informal sector by default (Lloyd 1982), and others who work on some sort of irregular basis.

Because of the varied nature of this sector and because of criticism of the term informal sector, itself, other attempts to clarify and analyse this area have been made. Informal sector implies a dualist interpretation of the urban economy, since it proposes a dichotomy between a formal modern capitalist sector in which big businesses and multinationals flourish, and the mass of the poor who are unable to benefit from participation in this sector. The implication is that poverty is due to lack of involvement with successful capitalist enterprise and, though a minority of the poor do become successful entrepreneurs by building up small businesses from street selling, the vast majority are poor because they are excluded from the modern economy.

There is also a problem in delineating this sector since self-employment is considered such a crucial factor. Occupational statistics that deal with categories of employment make no distinctions within the self-employed group. As a result, chewing gum sellers and the successful carpenter who has his own furniture business, fall within the same category.

The important point to focus on is the relationship between the modern economic sector and the informal sector which is clearly not as negative as the formal/informal dichotomy would imply. Many social scientists see a direct link between these sectors similar to that between urban and rural society and between Latin America and the metropolis, that is a relationship of exploitation. It is not because of the poor's isolation from the modern sector that they remain poor, but because they provide a cheap human resource for that sector.

Moser points out that the majority of small-scale enterprises, of the type described in the informal sector, fit into the character of petty commodity production (Moser 1978). This allows us to refer to Marx's analysis of this phenomenon. He argues that petty commodity production exists as a subordinate form in all modes of production, but thrives particularly in the transition from feudalism to capitalism. It contributes to the development of capitalism in two ways. Firstly, it has its roots in commodity production and private ownership of property and, as such, forms the basis for the gradual development of capitalism, through increases in the scale of production. Secondly, it acts as a source of capital and labour which can be indirectly utilised by other forms of capital that may be operating in different spheres of the economy. It is this second point which is especially relevant in the case of Latin America. The Marxist view is that petty commodity production indirectly contributes to the surplus in the modern economy, which is so necessary for capital accumulation (these points are well developed by McEwen Scott 1979). The argument is, then, that a greater surplus can be extracted from this sector by not employing its members on a regular wage-earning basis. This is a similar argument to the Burgess critique of Turner, emphasising the way that self-help shelter houses the poor cheaply, thus making low wages and the resulting capital accumulation more feasible.

Quijano, amongst others, takes this argument a stage further by utilising a modes of production approach. He contests that petty commodity production is a separate mode of production from the capitalist one, but that it articulates with it to facilitate the expanded reproduction of the capitalist mode (Quijano 1974). The relationship between capitalist and non-capitalist modes is one of exploitation, in which the former creams off the surplus from the latter. In this way, it benefits capitalism to maintain non-capitalist modes of production, rather than engulfing them within the rubric of the capitalist mode. In order to fully comprehend the nature of the relationship between these sectors of the economy, it is necessary to look at the empirical material.

THE GARBAGE PICKERS OF CALI

A significant indicator of poverty in any society is the number of people who can be seen poking in rubbish bins looking for something that is still usable, since surviving off society's rubbish epitomises ultimate poverty. Birkbeck's study of garbage pickers in Cali, Colombia, suggests that they should not be viewed as vagrants left behind by economic development but as workers who are part of the industrial system (Birkbeck 1979). He argues that this activity should be seen, not just as an expression of poverty, but as a cause of it. The garbage picker may be excluded from real opportunities within the urban economy, but, nevertheless, his work is closely integrated into the modern economy.

The paper industry in Cali has two sources of raw materials: long-fibred softwood pulp is imported from Canada, Scandinavia and Chile to make the best quality paper, while waste paper is recycled for poorer quality products. In Cali, about 25,000 tons of waste paper are collected each year, of which the garbage pickers contribute some 15,000 tons. Characteristic of LDCs, the paper industry has experienced foreign penetration and is dominated by one giant company. Cartón de Colombia was founded in 1944, largely on the basis of North American capital, that is now in the hands of the Mobil Oil Company. Although laws were passed in the 1960s, reducing the share of United States' capital in the firm, it still remains the major shareholder. The waste paper necessary for the industry is bought from warehouses which are not part of the Cartón de Colombia company. There is a contractual relationship between firm and warehouse, saying that all the waste paper, with a few exceptions, will be sold to the factory at a fixed price. The warehouses are organised in a hierarchical manner with a central one buying from satellite warehouses, which are situated in the poorer residential areas of Cali, so that they are near the homes of the garbage pickers.

The garbage pickers are not employed by Cartón de Colombia or the warehouses, nor do they have any sort of contract with them. The price of goods varies for the same item, in fact Birkbeck noted as many as ten different prices for the same type of waste paper. The price is more likely to relate to the individual picker and the regularity with which he sells to the warehouse. Buyer and seller strike a bargain with each individual purchase. It is difficult to assess the number of garbage pickers, because this fluctuates seasonally and because they are not really enumerated in official statistics, but Birkbeck estimates that at the time of the study, there were between 1,200 and 1,700 garbage pickers in Cali. This is not a startlingly high number but, bearing in mind that each probably supports a family, some 5,000 to 10,000 may well depend on the income from garbage picking. The pickers operate in different ways. The largest group work at the municipal garbage dump near the banks of the river Cauca. They collect here each day when the municipal truck appears and go through the refuse looking for resellable objects, which are put in a sack to be sorted out later. Others intercede at an earlier stage, working along the routes that the municipal trucks take. In between the time the dustbins are put out and the truck arrives, the pickers have been through the contents of the bins. Others go round residential neighbourhoods with their carts collecting different kinds of scrap from shops and houses.

Due to the irregular method of payment, the amount of income is low and variable. Most pickers earn the equivalent to the government minimum daily wage in a day's work, but they do not get any of the benefits of social security payments, minimal though they are, that employed workers receive nor the security of a regular wage.

As most of the domestic waste for recycling is collected by garbage pickers, why do Cartón de Colombia not directly employ the garbage pickers? Clearly, it is cheaper for them to operate like this because they do not have regular wage bills to pay. The income the garbage pickers receive for each item is extremely low and reduced even further by the competition between them, which is encouraged by the system that is very much a buyer's market. The small regular labour force that is employed by the company is relatively well paid, receiving three times the minimum wage. To take the garbage pickers on at this rate would increase their costs and would bring about the additional cost of security benefits. This also gets round problems of fluctuation, when business is slow, they do not have to maintain a regular workforce.

There is another relevant factor. In this way, labour is kept fractionalised. The small but relatively well paid labour force is kept separate from the garbage pickers who are further divided between themselves by intense competition. The labour force realises its relatively privileged position and, therefore, does not embark on serious attempts at collective bargaining. It is significant that the union which represents the employed workers of Cartón has never been on strike.

A final factor contributes to the low income of garbage pickers and this relates to their involvement in the international economy. Of the two materials that are used in the paper industry, pulp is always preferable to waste paper and in Cali, pulp can easily be imported. For waste to be a competitive commodity, it must be distinctly cheaper than the pulp. If garbage pickers were to become regular employees, the price of waste paper would rise by at least three times and it would not be worthwhile the company buying it.

The garbage picker appears to work for himself but is in fact part of an industrial organisation. The nature of his relationship to big industry is to reduce costs through piecework and division of the labour force.

ARTICULATION BETWEEN SECTORS

A related difficulty with the concept of informal sector arises from the range of activities it covers. Bromley points out that there is a great difference between the truly independent street seller and seasonal workers, who work for a regular wage though not on a permanent basis and who would be included in the informal sector category (Bromley 1979). He prefers to use the term casual work to cover this broad area, and defines it as 'any way of making a living which lacks a moderate degree of security in income and employment' (Bromley 1979: 6). Since the similarities between informal sector seasonal workers and formal sector factory workers are greater than between some groups within the informal sector, such as street sellers and seasonal workers, Bromley suggests a continuum of categories as a more useful form of analysis. The continuum stretches from stable wage work to true self-employment. It can be divided into four broad and occasionally overlapping ideal-type categories which, in order of decreasing similarity from stable wage work, are short-term wage work, disguised wage work, dependent work, and true self-employment at the polar extreme of the continuum.

Short-term wage work is work that is paid for and contracted for a specific period of time, whether that be a day or a season. This would include workers employed in tourism for a holiday period, shop assistants who are employed for a Christmas or summer season and construction workers who are employed on a contractual basis.

Disguised wage work refers to work where one or more enterprises appropriate part of the product of a person's work without the person officially being an employee of the firm. Many firms in manufacturing and repair operations use outworkers who perform the work in their own homes, being paid for each completed piece. Small clothing shops in Lima frequently operate in this way. Merchants purchase the materials and prepare the parts ready to be put together as garments, which are either collected by, or delivered to, the outworkers, who sew the pieces together. The garment has to be completed within a certain time, then the outworker is paid the requisite sum. In this case, the firms relinquish responsibility for the instruments of production, which are provided by the workers themselves (McEwan Scott 1979).

With dependent work, the worker appears to work on his own but, in reality, he is dependent on a firm or group of firms for some vital part of his work, such as premises, equipment, supplies, or outlet. In this case, a proportion of the product of the worker's labour is appropriated through the payment of rent, repayment of credit or purchases of supplies at prices disadvantageous to him. Many taxi drivers in Latin America, unable to afford their own vehicle, have to rent one, thus only being able to earn what is left over after deducting fixed rental and running costs. In a similar position would be a street trader, who regularly deals with a certain wholesaler and who could only gain credit from him by guaranteeing to purchase his goods. In this way, he becomes dependent on the wholesaler.

The truly self-employed works quite independently, without involving himself/herself in any form of wage work. This category has the least security, but the greatest freedom of manoeuvre. Street pedlars, who buy from wholesalers according to availability and cost, and those who make up or cook foodstuffs for sale, would fit into this group.

One importance of the continuum is that it is a more precise form of categorisation than the simple dichotomy. But what is more important is that it outlines the links between casual work and the formal economy, setting these out in terms of declining significance. In each case, the links are exploitative. The seasonal workers and outworkers do not receive the security or the minimal benefits that are available to regular workers. The firm saves on this and, at times, provision of facilities or equipment, thus, making it a profitable exercise for the managers. The taxi driver and the street trader, once tied to debts or rental, cannot accumulate sufficient to provide their own capital and can be further exploited. Even the truly independent are dependent on social and economic conditions, which are unfavourable to them. They are operating at the bottom end of the market with no capital and no security.

Poverty is compounded by inflation which has reached extreme levels in the region, as demonstrated by consumer price indices. Between the initiation of the Chilean price index in December 1978 and April 1983, the index registered a 157.5 per cent increase for low-income families and a 142.7 per cent increase for higher income groups. In the twelve-month period from February 1982 to February 1983 alone, consumer prices rose 42.9 per cent (LAWR 1983).

In LDCs in general, the poor are disadvantaged because they have low levels of education and training and therefore have few skills or qualifications to help them. Because of their positon in the class-structure they do not have access to useful connections which, as we have seen, are so valuable in Latin America. Caught in the poverty trap, they are unable to make the savings necessary for business ventures. Their plight is reinforced by their close proximity to wealth.

As capitalism deepens, modifications take place in the informal sector, which in general take the form of an increased articulation between the formal and informal sectors. Safa contrasts the stronger links that exist between the two sectors in Colombia as compared with those between the two sectors in the less-developed economy of an area like northern Nigeria (Safa 1982). Increased articulation will have two principal results.

Firstly, the pattern of poverty already outlined will be the case for the majority. Informal sector activities such as subcontracting will limit the numbers employed in the formal sector, thus curbing permanent, regular employment.

Secondly, for a few, increased articulation will provide entrepreneurial openings. Gwynne suggests that this aspect has been neglected by researchers, who have concentrated on street pedlars and garbage pickers rather than the small-scale manufacturing sector, which does have the potential for growth (Gwynne 1985). He cites the entrepreneurial success of modular furniture makers in Caracas. Because high-rise flats became so popular in the city in the 1970s, the demand for modular furniture appropriate for small residences rose. This was answered in part by a number of small-scale entrepreneurs operating in the shanty towns. Although based in the informal sector, they used some modern sector facilities such as newspapers to advertise their work and because of lower costs were able to compete successfully with large furniture manufacturers. The entrepreneurs in this case were able to take advantage of the low costs of the informal sector, but also use the modern facilities of the formal. This close interlinking of the sectors benefited the entrepreneurs.

The rapid expansion of the informal sector is a feature that Latin America shares with other Third World areas. Calcutta's industrial development in the 1950s occurred without a corresponding expansion in regular employment. Research revealed that, as a result of this, the biggest single occupational groups were petty traders and domestic servants, while only 2.8 per cent of all earners were factory workers (Goldthorpe 1975). Much of the debate that has been discussed, arose from East Africa. The earliest studies were carried out in Kenya, which led policy-makers to suggest self-employment as the answer to lack of formal sector employment (King 1979). Gerry's study in Dakar, Senegal, reveals similar links between apparently independent petty producers and large enterprises, as exist between the garbage pickers and the paper industry (Gerry 1979).

CONCLUSION

Motivated by a desire for a better life, rural populations have migrated to urban areas and the resulting expansion of cities has meant problems of shelter and employment. For many, the movement is one of horizontal mobility rather than vertical. Some of the discussion of the informal sector and the Turner thesis suggest that, for a minority, there may be small improvements in housing or occupation, but the majority remain part of the mass of the urban poor.

Poverty arises because of the lack of remunerative and secure forms of employment. As the large informal sector becomes more entrenched in Third World economies, the articulation between sectors becomes stronger, with resulting poverty for many, but opportunities for a few.

What also emerges from these pages is that the poor are not necessarily apathetic about their situation, nor are they bound by a culture of poverty, but are quite capable of positive action to attempt to solve their problems. The construction of spontaneous housing settlements and the way this has induced several governments to support self-help schemes demonstrates the way squatters have taken the situation into their own hands and provided themselves with some sort of shelter. The inhabitants of the shanty towns have frequently achieved stability and social organisation through the establishment of personal networks and voluntary associations. The informal sector has on occasion generated small businesses and creative enterprises.

In some countries, action has been taken further in the form of political protest movements. This has been especially evident in Peru and Chile, where goals have been fought for and won in this way. Although Gilbert and Ward found little sign of political protest in the areas of Colombia, Venezuela and Mexico where their research was carried out (Gilbert and Ward 1985), Castells documents protest movements in Mexico City (Castells 1982). Social movements, which represent a new and increasing response of urban populations to problems, are analysed in the next chapter.

FURTHER READING

Bromley, R., Gerry, C. (eds) (1979) *Casual work and poverty in Third World cities.* John Wiley, Chichester

Gilbert, A., Gugler, J. (1982) *Cities: poverty and development. Urbanization in the Third World.* Oxford University Press, Oxford

Gilbert, A., Ward, P. (1985) *Housing, the state and the poor.* Cambridge University Press, Cambridge

Gwynne, R. (1985) *Industrialization and urbanization in Latin America.* Croom Helm, London

Moser, C. (1978) Informal sector or petty commodity production: dualism or dependence in urban development? *World Development* 6

Roberts, B. (1978) *Cities of peasants.* Edward Arnold, London

Safa, H. (1982) *Towards a political economy of urbanization in Third World countries.* Oxford University Press, Delhi

Social classes as agents of change

Chapters 5 and 6 have discussed the changes that have been taking place in rural and urban areas and the effects these have had on social structure, poverty and inequality. It is now necessary to situate these in the wider context of the social formation and in particular class structure. The mapping out of social classes is valuable initially in providing a broad picture of society, but more importantly because it helps to explain the dynamics of social change. Change is invariably the result of class struggle and conflict, so that any understanding of social change requires a knowledge of how social classes act. In the analysis of change, the various theorists have focused on different agents of change, which are often social classes. Given the great variation that exists in wealth, social organisation and culture in Latin America, it is not easy to find a simple, but also heuristic schema for class analysis, and perhaps for that reason the exercise has not been attempted very often.

One of the most useful class outlines to appear is that developed by Portes and is used here as a guide to the ramifications of class (Portes 1985). He takes as his criteria for class membership: firstly, the position of individuals in the process of production and their mode of sharing in the distribution of the product; secondly, control over the labour power of others and thirdly, mode of remuneration. These criteria make the concept flexible and appropriate for the study of LDCs, as well as being operational. In this way, Portes distinguishes five social classes. The dominant class, having control over both the means of production and over labour power, derives its remuneration from profits and salaries and bonuses linked to profits. This is the class that enjoys both power and wealth derived from capitalist investment. The bureaucratic-technical class does not have control over the means of production, but does have control over labour power and, unlike the dominant class, finds its remuneration not in profits but in salaries and fees. This refers to the professionals and white-collar workers whose earnings are linked to their skills and qualifications rather than capitalist ventures. The formal proletariat has control over neither the means of production nor labour power, but its members earn regular wages which give them a security that the mass of the poor lack. The informal petty bourgeoisie, like the dominant class, has control over means of production and labour power, since its members own their own small enterprises. Their level of operation, however, is quite different as their irregular profits serve to keep them only slightly above subsistence level. The informal proletariat does not have the independence that control over means of production and labour power implies and must survive at subsistence level on casual wages.

How do the various classes fare in terms of participation in national wealth? This can be assessed by linking class structure to income distribution figures. Portes suggests a correlation between the dominant and bureaucratic-technical classes and the top decile in the income distribution table and also between the informal proletariat and the poorest 60 per cent of the population (Table 7.1).

Table 7.1 Income distribution in Latin America, 1960–75

Income strata	Share of total income (%)	
	1960	1975
Latin America		
Richest 10 per cent	46.6	47.3
20 per cent below richest 10 per cent	26.1	26.9
30 per cent below richest 10 per cent	35.4	36.0
Poorest 60 per cent	18.0	16.7
Poorest 40 per cent	8.7	7.7

Source: Adapted from Portes, A. (1985) Latin American class structures *LARR* 20(3) p. 25

In this case, between 1960 and 1975, the dominant and bureaucratic-technical classes increased their share of national income by about 1 per cent, at the expense of the informal sector, which experienced a decrease of 1.3 per cent. Portes suggests that UN agencies, using a more restricted definition of informal proletariat, would equate it with the poorest 40 per cent. This group has also lost out, its share being reduced from 8.7 per cent to 7.7 per cent.

It should be pointed out that despite increasing income concentration, there has been a general improvement in the quality of life. A Physical Quality of Life Index, which refers to indices of infant mortality, life expectancy at age one, and adult literacy shows an improvement for all the seventeen Latin American countries to which the index was applied in the period from 1950 to the mid-1970s. In 1950, the index ranged from 36 for Guatemala to 77 for Argentina, but by the mid 1970s, it had risen to a range of 43 for Bolivia and 90 for Puerto Rico (Felix 1983).

Portes also suggests figures to show the percentage of the population of each class in each country in 1970 and 1980. This demonstrates class differences between the different areas (Table 7.2). These show that the dominant and bureaucratic-technical classes together do not exceed 15 per cent of the Economically Active Population in any Latin American country and in most their proportion is much lower. The dominant class alone comprises no more than 4 per cent of the EAP in any country and no more than 2 per cent for the whole of Latin America. Despite similarities in size across the continent in these two classes, there is greater variation in the proportion of the population in the formal proletariat, but they relate to levels in economic development. In the southern cone countries of Argentina, Chile and Uruguay, which are highly urbanised and have advanced industrial complexes, the formal proletariat makes up more than half the EAP. In Costa Rica, Panama and Peru, where economic development has taken a distinct path unlike the rest of the continent, the formal proletariat represents a quarter of the EAP. It is worth noting, however, that Brazil is not far off the quarter-mark with 20.5 per cent. Another conclusion that can be drawn from this table is that, apart from the southern cone countries, those who work in the modern sector of the economy comprise a minority of the population. A closer look at class composition and role will put flesh on the bones of distribution statistics and also explain the extent to which the various classes have acted as agents of change.

BENEFICIARIES OF THE SOCIAL ORDER

Traditionally the dominant class had its basis in landownership, but over the years these elites have often shifted their capital to the urban sector because of the possibility of better returns on it, and, on occasion, because of agrarian reform. Today the number of companies

Table 7.2 The Latin American class structure[1]

Country	Dominant		Bureaucratic-technical		Combined dominant and bureaucratic-technical	Formal proletariat	Informal petty bourgeoisie	Informal proletariat	
	1970 (%)	1980 (%)	1970 (%)	1980 (%)	1970 (%)	1972 (%)	1970 (%)	1970 (%)	1980[2] (%)
Argentina	1.5		7.5		9.5	59.0	9.7	22.3	23.0
Bolivia	1.3	0.6		5.7	5.7	3.3	4.8	86.2	56.4
Brazil	1.7	1.2	4.8	6.4	10.2	20.5	7.2	65.8	27.2
Chile	1.9	2.4	7.1	6.6	7.7	60.5	4.5	26.0	27.1
Colombia	0.7	0.7	4.5	4.3	6.6	12.9	15.7	66.2	34.3
Costa Rica	1.7		8.0		9.0	28.5	13.5	48.3	19.0
Dominican Republic	0.3	0.4	2.7	3.1	3.7	6.4	17.3	73.3	
Ecuador	0.8	1.0	5.0	5.1	4.7	10.0	4.1	80.1	52.7
El Salvador	0.2	0.5	3.0	4.2	3.8	5.2	23.1	68.5	39.8
Guatemala	1.6	1.1	3.1	3.7	4.5	22.3	3.3	69.7	40.0
Haiti	0.5		0.5			0.0	[3]	[3]	
Honduras	0.6		2.5		4.5	1.1	13.4	82.4	
Mexico	2.6		6.2		7.7	15.9	11.3	64.0	35.7
Nicaragua	0.9		5.2		5.3	8.7	15.8	69.4	
Panama	2.1	4.4	6.8	10.0	8.7	25.4	5.2	60.5	31.6
Paraguay	0.6		4.2			5.9	[4]	[4]	

Peru	0.4	7.6	1.3	7.3	7.0	27.6		69.5	40.4
Uruguay	1.1	5.6			8.4	88.5	1.0	3.8	
Venezuela	3.6	8.6	3.9	9.5	10.0	12.2	14.0	61.6	20.8
Latin America[6] (N = 93 850 000)	1.7	5.4	1.6	6.0	8.4	22.4	10.2	60.3	30.2

Source: Adapted from Portes, A. (1985) Latin American class structures. *LARR* 20(3) pp. 22–23.

[1] All figures are percentages of the domestic EAP. Figures are for 1970 unless otherwise indicated.

[2] Percentage of the nonagricultural EAP represented by unremunerated family workers and the self-employed.

[3] Insufficient data to differentiate between the informal petty bourgeoisie and the informal proletariat. The total figure for the two classes is 99.0.

[4] Insufficient data to differentiate between the informal petty bourgeoisie and the informal proletariat. The total figure for the two classes is 95.2.

[5] The estimation procedure yields a negative figure in this case.

[6] Averages weighted by the proportion of the regional EAP in each country.

that are privately-owned by Latin Americans is small, because important sectors of industry, agriculture, mining and commerce are controlled by foreign-owned or state enterprises. Top earners in Latin America may be owners or managers, they may work in foreign or local firms and they may work in state or private enterprises. The group that Portes subsumes under the heading of a dominant class are internally divided, but have enough in common for Portes to call them a class.

Potential divisions within the class are numerous. The dependency theorists logically identified the main distinction as being between the national bourgeoisie, whose enterprises were based on local capital and the comprador bourgeoisie, whose interests were tied to foreign capital. They initially thought that competition from powerful foreign interests would encourage the national bourgeoisie to take an anti-imperialist stand. It was soon realised, however, that the national bourgeoisie was too weak to pursue an independent line and being themselves involved in the complexities of dependent development, their orientations remained the same as the rest of the dominant class. In Argentina, for instance, the national bourgeoisie has various indirect links with foreign capital. Many local industrialists rely on credit from international loan agencies, others import essential supplies and the majority import essential equipment. Petras and Cook found that only 4.9 per cent of their sample of the top national bourgeoisie were not dependent on technology that originated from abroad. These industrialists welcomed foreign capital, because they felt that it stimulated economic activity in general, from which they could all benefit (Petras and Cook 1973). In Peru, up-and-coming executives use a period of employment with a multinational as a form of training in the methods and values of big business and then may shift to employment with state or private Peruvian firms or go into business on their own (Becker 1983).

Other commentators have drawn attention to the basic distinction between owners and managers, which is important for a strict Marxist analysis. This distinction, however, carries less weight, where managers of multinationals have control over much greater economic resources and far more people's livelihoods than the owners of small local firms.

One would also expect a difference in attitudes between general managers of state corporations and those of transnationals. The expansion of the state in the economy has led to an increase in the number of state employees, some of whom direct vast industrial complexes. The top personnel in these enterprises have been referred to as a state bourgeoisie. We can, therefore, identify three fractions: domestic capitalists; managers of multinationals and top administrators of public enterprises.

What the different groups all have in common is their control over production processes in the economy and over the labour of a number of subordinates. Their remuneration comes from this position and takes the form of profits or high salaries and bonuses tied to profitability, so that their financial reward is linked very closely to the success of the firm. Since all the members of this class wish to preserve the status quo, they unite politically to support conservative regimes and oppose radical forces that propose significant social changes.

Evans argues that the three fractions have a common interest in capital accumulation and in the subordination of the mass population and therefore cooperate in what he calls a 'triple alliance' between elite local capital, international capital, and state capital. Local capital is not assumed subordinate because the local bourgeoisie has certain economic and political advantages, which can be used when dealing with multinationals. There is some competitiveness within the alliance, but this is reduced by bargaining and a working cooperation is maintained (Evans 1979).

The main feature of the bureaucratic-technical class is that although it lacks effective control over the means of production its members do have control over the labour of others in their subordinate position in bureaucratic structures. Unlike the dominant class, remuneration is tied to specific salaries and fees rather than the profitability of a firm. In Latin America, this class is composed mainly of middle-level management and technical personnel in domestic, state and foreign enterprises, and functionaries of the state bureaucracies, including the armed forces and independent professionals. This class maintains the smooth running of the social order and economic system, but differs from the dominant bourgeois class in that its wealth is not derived from capital. With the dominant class, it shares in the control of the existing social order and benefits from that order (Portes 1985).

The dominant and bureaucratic-technical classes benefit from the system, but how do they act in this privileged position? Do they initiate change and if so, what kind of change? Although the terminology and implications differ, both traditional Marxists and non-Marxists have attached a progressive role to the new entrepreneurial classes that emerge with industrialisation. Marx saw them as promoting the bourgeois state, which was an advance on feudalism and which, in turn, would give rise to the proletarian state. Modernisation theorists, leaning heavily on the experience of Western Europe argued that the middle class erodes the traditional order and promotes economic, political and social progress. In the Latin American context, Johnson took the lead in proposing the middle class as the spearhead of change, by detailing the areas in which he considered they had influenced government in a progressive way in five major republics (Johnson 1958). Empirical research in the 1960s demonstrated that even in the cases where the middle class had been initially progressive, success had given them a conservative outlook and led them to join forces with the traditional elite rather than with the working class (Ratinoff 1967, Sunkel 1965).

A closer look at the bourgeoisie, in terms of their social background, relationships with other classes and political opinions, lends support to the argument that, in practice, they are not the class that is going to bring about radical change. Entrepreneurship has not been a significant mechanism for social mobility in Latin America. Several studies have shown that successful Chilean industrialists since the 1930s, before which immigrants dominated the industrial scene, have come from land-owning or well-to-do families (Johnson 1972, Cubitt 1972). Research on Colombian entrepreneurs reveals a similar pattern, with only 9.5 per cent coming from working-class backgrounds. What is particularly interesting about the latter findings is that four-fifths of the socially mobile were born outside Colombia. Lipman points out that it is easier to gain the necessary qualifications and training for success in Europe. This would suggest that social mobility within Colombian society is more limited than the figures imply (Lipman 1969). The country that has demonstrated the greatest upward mobility through entrepreneurial channels is Argentina, which was one of the first to industrialise and has had probably the greatest influx of immigrants. Imaz found that about a quarter of the Argentine industrial elite, at a time when industrialisation was getting well under way, were self-made men from neither middle- nor upper-class backgrounds (Imaz 1964).

Explanations for this lack of mobility lie in the international context. Initially, the immigrants provided too much competition for the aspiring local working class, as, coming from countries where the process of industrialisation was under way, they were able to use their knowledge and experience to seize the initiative in entrepreneurial activity.

More recently, multinationals and foreign capital, with all their implications, have made vertical upward mobility difficult. The promising entrepreneur finds it very hard to compete with multinationals, which can always outproduce him and undercut his prices because of the very scale of their operations and capital. To compete successfully with multinationals, the entrepreneur must acquire knowledge, qualifications and specialised training similar to the managers and technical staff that the foreign company can afford to employ. Higher education is expensive in Latin America, and especially so the education, such as business qualifications from the United States, that is desired for running large firms. Only the offspring of the wealthy can afford to benefit. These factors again demonstrate why the wealth produced by productivity, on the basis of foreign capital and in a situation of unequal opportunity of access to qualifications, does not produce the desired trickle-down effect.

Given their social background, it is not surprising that the bourgeoisie, in most Latin American countries, has close links with landowners. Research in both Argentina and Chile has revealed the close links between industrialists and agrarian interests (Chilcote and Edelstein 1974, Petras 1969).

In the case of Chile, it is argued that the successful new urban groups have been coopted by the land-owning oligarchy. According to Sunkel, the major changes have been industrialisation, urbanisation and an expansion of the economic and social activities of government which have, together, brought an improvement in the standard of living of urban middle-sector groups. Chilean social structure has always had a small elite, with a great concentration of power and, instead of presenting a challenge to them, the successful industrial and commercial groups have become incorporated into their ranks. This social fusion has taken place through intermarriage and access to the social circles and institutions which denote prestige in society, such as organisations, clubs and landed estates (Sunkel 1965).

This point is supported by Johnson, who goes on to demonstrate that, as a result, Chilean industrialists have not developed their own independent ideology and value system. Questions about their politics elicited answers which were, generally, conservative and not in favour of progressive ideas. Johnson found little support among them for the reformist policies of the government of the day. Less than a quarter were in favour of the government having the power to expropriate land, which offers little support to the opposition to the landed elite thesis (Johnson 1972).

Considerable evidence shows that, to date, those who have been successful through industrialisation and urbanisation have not been an independent, dynamic and progressive force in Latin America, but why? Chilcote and Edelstein argue that it is because of the type of industrialisation that has taken place. Industrialisation was prompted by the failures of Europe and the United States during the Great Depression and the Second World War, leading to import substitution, rather than a conscious development policy. The implication is that industrialisation was not the planned result of a dynamic, forward-thinking group but a reaction to a crisis (Chilcote and Edelstein 1974). The point is that so much economic growth in Latin America, from the enclave economy to contemporary multinationals, has been brought about by foreign concerns, which has denied the local entrepreneurial groups their historic role in leading, organising and financing this process. The only time they had the opportunity was, almost by default, during import substitution, but Latin Americans were soon overshadowed by the transnationals. Since so much capital has external sources, the bourgeoisie have not come through the same phase of saving and investment, as did their European counterparts, but have moved straight to a consumption stage. One argument states that the Latin American bourgeoisie has never had sufficient capital to promote the economic development it wanted and has, therefore, had to import capital. The counter-argument is that it is precisely the importation of capital that has prevented the local bourgeoisie accumulating its own on a grand scale.

As a possible agent of change, the bourgeoisie was discarded by dependency theorists, but in the wave of post-dependency criticism, there have been attempts to resuscitate this role for them. Becker says that it is expecting too much of Third World bourgeoisies to think they can bring about societal transformations on a grand scale or act in the 'heroic' way of entrepreneurs a century ago (Becker 1983). He characterises the mining bourgeoisie in Peru as a corporate national bourgeoisie, which he considers to be progressive as it is nationalist and developmentalist. This new bourgeoisie is innovative technologically; internationalist, since its members partake of universalistic norms of technocracy and the managerial ideology; and it promotes development, through a desire to compete with transnational companies. The group is strong because it has access to power through its institutional involvement with the state, which is why Becker calls it a corporate bourgeoisie. Becker asserts that greater social mobility is possible in a society where the new corporate bourgeoisie is the dominant class than where family firms predominate in the economic sector. The conservative aspect of the new bourgeoisie is that it establishes a more durable form of capitalism, but as Becker does not see socialism as the only way of ushering in progress, this does not present a problem for him in his depiction of the new corporate bourgeoisie as promoters of development.

THE WORKING CLASS

The formal proletariat is defined by its lack of control over both the means of production and the labour of others (Portes 1985). Its remuneration in the form of wages may not be very high, but does offer a measure of security, in that wages are contractually established and regulated under existing labour laws, which means that in theory they can not be arbitrarily withdrawn or altered. The formal proletariat is basically urban in composition and along with the dominant class and the bureaucratic-technical class, makes up (what is referred to as) the modern sector of Latin American economies. The Latin American working class has its similarities to and differences from the working class in other Third World areas. Where the nature of development has been capital intensive in LDCs, the proletariat will be small. The previous chapter showed how so much of the rural-urban influx has been absorbed by the informal sector, rather than regular working-class employment. Even if development is not capital intensive, but relies on labour power, what is emerging in Latin America is a pattern of part-time employment, whether it be seasonal work in rural areas or informal-sector activities in urban. To survive in this situation, it is necessary to have more than one economic activity. Though small, the working class in Latin America, because of higher levels of urbanisation and industrialisation, is relatively larger and better established than in most other Third World regions. The pattern of increasing underemployment, both rural and urban, may be one that will be followed by the other LDCs.

Figures for the proportion of the total population in the labour force are quite revealing. In the mid 1970s, while almost half the population of the United Kingdom and the United States, 47 per cent and 45 per cent respectively, were in the labour force, in Mexico, with its very young population, only 28 per cent were. Chile had a similar 28 per cent and Peru 29 per cent, while Venezuela and Brazil fared a little better with 31 per cent and 32 per cent of the total population in the labour force (*World in Figures* 1978). What this means is that only a relatively small proportion of the population is earning and has the burden of supporting a large number of old and young. Portes using statistics for 1972, has assessed the proportion of the Latin American economically active population that constitute the formal proletariat as being 22.4 per cent (see Table 7.2).

Although the working class is of recent formation, it operates in a variety of different working situations. The Latin American economy is characterised by a large number of very small firms and yet some workers are employed by large transnationals using the most modern technology and employing thousands of workers. Where mineral-extracting enclaves still exist, the workforce lives in its own community, a long way from major urban centres. The various levels of technology employed also mean that workers have very different skills and qualifications.

It has been argued that these divisions within the working class are unreconcilable and prevent it acting as a strong, united, radical force. The proposition put forward by this view is that technology shapes the problems, demands and forms of organisation of workers and it is precisely the levels of technology that vary so much between the modern, dynamic, industrial sector and traditional areas. The better off within the working class have often been referred to as a labour aristocracy, though the term has been used differently by various social scientists. Some use it generally to refer to those workers whose income is higher than most others. Arrighi and Saul more specifically consider the labour aristocracy to comprise the skilled technicians in large factories and sub-elite of clerks and teachers (Lloyd 1982). Others identify the labour aristocracy as workers who have high earnings because they are employed by multinationals or foreign firms which, as Roxborough points out, is closest to Lenin's original meaning (Roxborough 1979). The implication of the term is not only that it is a privileged group but that, as a result, its members will not desire change and so be a conservative force in society. The two issues at stake with the labour aristocracy thesis are: can this relatively privileged sector of society be a militant force for change or will it want to maintain the status quo? Can this group remain within a united working class or will it pursue selfish interests, separating itself further from the remainder of the working class?

Humphrey's research on workers in the Brazilian motor industry in the 1970s shows that, in this particular case, a group of relatively highly paid workers in a modern sector of the economy did not behave as a labour aristocracy, but took on a vanguard role in providing political leadership for the working class as a whole (Humphrey 1982). He also points out similar situations in Argentina in the 1960s, when car workers were involved in revolutionary unionism and urban insurrection, and in Mexico, where they have fostered some of the stronger, independent unions.

In the Brazilian situation, it was the auto workers who took the leading role in the industrial disputes of the 1970s and early 1980s. They took full advantage of the general liberalisation, that was the government's policy at the time, to fight against the constraints imposed by the labour system. Despite their relatively high wages, these constraints had imposed burdens on working conditions. Through their militancy, they won union autonomy and union reform. Humphrey says 'in the seventies, at least, factors which distinguished auto workers from other sections of the working class enabled them to adopt a vanguard role' (Humphrey 1982: 231). Because they worked for large, modern firms, the state was closely involved with their employers, which meant their industrial grievances led them into conflict with the state. To challenge their employers, they had to challenge the labour system itself. Their activities were supported by, and benefited, the rest of the working class. Support can be seen in the upsurge of working-class activity that accompanied the strikes of 1978 and 1979 and the way that the union's leader, Lula, became such a popular figure. The union reform that was won by these workers benefited the working class in general.

Humphrey calls the differentiation of the working class thesis technologically determinist because he says it attaches too much importance to technology. The development of industry is part of a process of the accumulation of capital that involves not only technological changes, but also other factors. The working class are affected by the changing relationship between labour and capital, the changing role of the state and new forms of labour legislation. The aim of management is to make profits and, therefore, its strategy with the labour force is directed to this end, not dominated by technology. The factory, too, is not solely a technical institution, it is a social organisation, influenced by political, social and economic aspects of society at large.

Although Humphrey emphasises that one can not rule out the possibility of auto workers being a conservative force in the future, he does demonstrate that, at this particular historical-political conjuncture, their militant action provided a catalyst for change for the working class. The political stance of the working class will rely heavily on the nature, size and development of the labour movement. It is the union movement which has, in the industrialised countries, been the basis of action. A look at the development of the labour movement in Latin America will lead us into the debate over the radical/conservative nature of the working class.

Spalding has divided the period of growth of the labour movement into different stages (Spalding 1977). The formative period from 1850 to 1914 witnessed the birth of a clearly identifiable movement, with labour organising for the first time on a massive scale. Prior to that, guilds had been the only groupings of workers. In Argentina, the formative period began with the formation of mutual aid associations for shoemakers and printers and ended with the foundation of the General Workers' Union and three general strikes. The period from 1914 to 1933 Spalding identifies as the expansive and explosive period. This was a time of peak union activity for many countries, for both qualitative and quantitative advances were made. New ideologies from Europe provided workers with different organisational concepts. In the southern cone countries, the union movement, having spread to white-collar workers and peasants, erupted in large-scale worker protest.

All this union activity did not occur without any reaction from the elite. For them, the expansion of the labour movement was perceived as a threat of communism, so various measures were resorted to in order to control labour, ranging from crude repression to legal limitations on union activity. At the same time, many governments offered social reforms to ease the plight of workers and give them fewer grounds for opposition. This labour legislation included laws governing female and child labour, improvements in working conditions and social security provisions. But, even where there were legal improvements, enforcement was often limited and, given the nature of the labour market in Latin America, many workers remained outside the legal framework, which applied only to industrial workers.

Spalding calls the period from 1930 to the present day the cooptive period because of the attempts made by the elite to integrate labour into the established political and social framework. By this time, politicians had realised that organised labour represented a bloc of votes, which could be very valuable to candidates. Control from above was won by the use of various mechanisms. Ideologies, such as nationalism and developmentalism, were used to counter the influence of communism. Nationalism encouraged workers to identify with their nation rather than their class, while developmentalism asked the worker to sacrifice short-term gains, such as better working conditions and remuneration, for long-term interests, on the basis that industrialisation benefits all in the long run. Labour codes as a mechanism of control were introduced in most countries. These included: the power to intervene in labour federations and unions; control over candidates in union elections; provisions governing the legality of strikes and unions; legal distinctions between white- and blue-collar workers which have the effect of dividing workers; and the prohibition of certain groups (often government employees) to form unions. Spalding also suggests that the introduction of highly technologised industry, leading to high levels of unemployment, has weakened the labour movement and made political alliances necessary.

Spalding concludes that, with few exceptions, such as the tin miners in Bolivia, labour has been coopted by these mechanisms and not proved itself to be a revolutionary force. It is true that the very process of mobilising labour by elites for their own support has brought workers together for political action and this could form the basis for the development of an independent labour movement, but this has, so far, been prevented by the mechanisms of control (Spalding 1977). Spalding's stages could be criticised for being somewhat vacuous. The term formative is fairly obvious for the beginning of a development process so, also, the term expansion for the next stage. Nor do the stages neatly fit all Latin American countries. Nevertheless they do provide a rough scheme for organising the multitude of empirical facts concerning the growth of unions. What is more polemical, is the conclusion that the labour movement, despite periods of radicalism and fervent political activity, has become a conservative force in Latin America.

THE ROLE OF THE PROLETARIAT DEBATE

For Marx, class consciousness, which develops with the increasing struggles that the workers have with management, is a key factor contributing to the revolutionary role of the proletariat. In Latin America, the supporters of Spalding's view would argue that the working class has not developed into a fully fledged class for itself. Much of this can be explained by the cooptation which has taken place through the mechanism of clientelism. As with the peasantry, strong ties of loyalty and obligation tend to prevent the development of permanent horizontal links. These may shape the activities of unions, so that their political manoeuvring is based on clientelist relationships, rather than class relationships. Payne argues that in Peru, this method has been very successful, for by using it, the organised workers realised a greater improvement in wages than the unorganised white-collar workers, and achieved a rise in their real income, even in the face of inflation (Payne 1965). These tactics have been used by unions in Mexico, where cooptation through the state bureaucracy has taken place as the labour movement is integrated into the organisation of the governing party. Mexico's electoral system has given power continuously to the party that emerged triumphant from the revolution, the Revolutionary Party or PRI. One of the three major sectors of PRI represents labour and within this, the CTM, the main confederation uniting Mexican unions, predominates. The CTM has a complex organisation of state-wide, regional and local federations, based on geographical cohesion and industry-wide unions on a national and regional level. In any industrial plant, there is a local union headed by a general delegate. The close integration of labour with the ruling party means that labour has no independent base. It assumes that the interests of workers are national, rather than class interests, which may not always be best for the workers, as a class. Mexico is often depicted as being characterised by '*charrismo*', the phenomenon of trade unions being controlled by the state, in order to keep wages down in the service of capital accumulation and accelerated economic growth. It is frequently argued that the political stability and rates of economic growth of the post-war period rest on the control of subordinate classes by the Mexican state.

Since the union organisations are part of PRI, they have a dual function: firstly, as a pressure group lobbying for a greater share of social benefits for labour; secondly, as an apparatus of political control of the working class. These functions are coordinated through clientelism, which exists between local leaders and their fellow members, and also between local leaders and national and regional leaders, with the local leaders this time being the clients. In San Cosme, as elsewhere in Mexico, union leaders have an important say in job placements in factories and can exert influence on behalf of their members at regional and national levels. Control of jobs and access to political leaders can be used to win political support for themselves. In the role of clients, these local leaders bring in their own supporters behind their patron, in return receiving political advancement for themselves and small benefits for the union (Rothstein 1979). Lomnitz argues that this situation is exacerbated and class identity weakened by the lack of informal ties and solidarity between workers. She says that as Mexican workers socialise mostly with the extended family, there is little personal contact with co-workers (Lomnitz 1982).

The linking of the national President of Mexico with the workers through clientelist relationships can be seen in the pattern of strikes over the years. Gonzalez-Casanova, using statistics for numbers of strikes per year, suggests that these follow the presidential-type policy of the government of the day. He found that the greatest number of large-scale strikes broke out when the presidents were known for their populist and pro-worker policies. This implies that workers and union leaders felt themselves protected and even encouraged by the presidential power. Presidents who followed less radical policies or more open alliances with the property-owning national and foreign sectors, they felt to be less sympathetic to their cause and, therefore, less likely to respond to their wishes. It was clearly patronage that they were seeking, rather than a confrontation with another class. The unions had sought and relied on government policy, rather than developing mass working-class organisations characterised by class consciousness (Gonzalez-Casanova 1968).

Roxborough criticises the standard account of the Mexican labour movement, for its one-sided emphasis on the aspect of control over the rank and file (Roxborough 1984). He argues that the extent of this control has been exaggerated, and as evidence documents a number of cases of successful, although sometimes shortlived, insurgent labour movements that have taken place. He found in his research on Mexican unions that there was no direct link between union affiliation and militancy, in other words the unions that were controlled from above were not less likely to be militant. This is not to say that the Mexican unions are likely to become revolutionary tools to be used against a capitalist state, but nor are they conservative in supporting the status quo. Roxborough believes it unrealistic to expect unions to play such a revolutionary role in Latin America today and predicts that with the growing economic crisis in Mexico, the unions will become more militant (Roxborough 1984).

From the point of view of Spalding and Gonzalez-Casanova, the working class is seen to have been coopted by the political elite, offering them political support in the form of votes of union members and receiving, in return, favours such as improved wages or working conditions. This strategy is not necessarily unsuccessful and, indeed, in Peru (Payne 1965) and Mexico, workers have received some definite material rewards through this procedure. There is no doubt, too, that the time during which the working class did best in Argentina was the Peronist period, when clientelism linked the labour force with the powerful. In 1954, the last full year of the Peronist era, the wage-earners' share of the national income was 30.6 per cent, an all-time high (LAWR 1983). Peron was a political patron at the highest level, who offered his workers definite improvements in return for their support on which he depended.

Although these mechanisms may provide short-term micro-level benefits, they do not encourage the development of an independent organisation with its own ideology, which would then be in a position to spearhead change to bring about real and long-lasting improvements. Favours are won through reciprocity, not through militant industrial action.

Contrasting views, based on different areas, portray the working class as having greater potential for radical action. Lloyd points out that it is often those who are called a labour aristocracy, who are the most militant. 'It is they who are most exploited and they are conscious of this. Bargaining, however, tends to be confined within the company. Selfishness is also seen in their apparent lack of concern for the poor but what, in effect, could they do?' (Lloyd 1982: 119.) Among the African poor, this militancy is often seen as leadership, rather than being viewed antagonistically.

Argentine unions, which were shaped from above, are some of the strongest in Latin America. Peron needed the union movement for support and, indeed, it was the labour movement who brought him back from exile and won him the presidency. Workers' organisations were then created and expanded, with the assistance of patronage, but in order to defend workers' interests. When Peron was overthrown, these organisations were strong enough to resist opposition. To this day, despite periods of extreme repression, they have survived, often having to spend long periods underground.

The Bolivian tin miners and the Chilean unions have demonstrated that it is possible for the labour movement to develop a revolutionary role in Latin America. The Bolivian miners performed the classic vanguard role when they participated in the Bolivian revolution and became a significant partner in the revolutionary party that took control. Today, however, the power of one of the most militant movements in the region is threatened by the decline of the tin market (Martin 1986).

Along with Argentina, Chile was one of the first countries in Latin America to experience union organisation and by 1970, the labour movement had emerged as a strong and ideologically independent organisation. The new left-wing government, under the leadership of Allende, restructured the economy into three sectors: the social-property sector, made up of state enterprises and those to be expropriated; the private-property sector; and the mixed-property sector, made up of enterprises where the capital was owned jointly by the state and private individuals. The workers, wanting participation in management, exerted pressure on the union leadership and the government, who came to an agreement in December 1970, that ensured the participation of workers in the running of enterprises in the social and mixed sectors of the economy. Concrete modes of putting this into operation were discussed by a commission and put into effect by June 1971. The expropriated firms were run by an administrative council, made up of eleven members, five elected by the workers, five appointed by government, and a director appointed by the President. Of the workers' representatives, three were elected from the shop floor, one from the administrative workers and one from the technicians, engineers and graduate staff.

Worker participation was a notable achievement, but the Chilean proletariat went further in their radical actions, by setting up the *cordones*. These were the result of spontaneous revolutionary activity from the base, which even embarrassed the union leadership, and demonstrate a high level of class consciousness among the mass of workers. The *cordones* were units of industrial organisation made up of workers from various enterprises, which were brought into being by the Bosses' strike in October 1972. A left-wing party outside government had, for some time, been calling for the workers to seize factories and, when they found themselves shut out by the closing of firms by management in the Bosses' strike, the workers were prompted to action. They seized firms and, having taken them over, set up a *cordón* in the area. They made an inventory of the industries in the zone and then made contact with union members in them. It was, frequently, these groups that were responsible for worker take-overs for, if any of the firms in the area were still in the private sector, the local *cordón* would encourage the workers to take control. One such *cordón* was the Cordón O'Higgins which in 1973, grouped fifteen enterprises and, with a base of 11,000 workers, mobilised 5,000 of them.

This activity worried the union leadership and the government because, although they were committed to a strong social-property sector, the government was adamant that this should be achieved by legal and orderly means. The government was, also, committed to a private sector as, in its manifesto, it had pledged support for the small businessman, of whom there were many in Chile. Legality was important to the President because, although he had won the presidential election, he did not have a majority in Congress. He, therefore, could not afford to support illegal methods, which would give the opposition in parliament and the middle class, in general, genuine grounds for opposing him.

The Chilean case shows that the working class were prepared to take the situation into their own hands and adopt radical action over the heads of their own leaders. They were highly organised and ideologised and, prompted by a sympathetic political situation and finally by the political actions of management, they became a powerful militant force. Chile's previous period of democracy and the way that the labour movement had developed its independent, political base and strong organisational structure during that time, made possible the development of militant collective action on the part of the proletariat.

'The political stance adopted by a class at any given time will be in part a function of the structure of the political system as a whole and the concrete possibilities which exist in a specific situation for the application of various kinds of class alliances' (Roxborough 1979: 82). This is true of the working class in Latin America, whose political stance has varied across the region. Most of the evidence from Mexico lends support to the Spalding view, while the data on the Allende period in Chile show very distinct revolutionary potential. Humphrey stresses that his conclusions relate only to the Brazilian auto workers under study at that particular time. The next chapter looks at the way in which the working class has been involved in class alliances in order to capture the state and exert influence that way.

POPULAR SOCIAL MOVEMENTS

Portes' last two class categories both belong in the informal sector. The informal petty bougeoisie is a term that is rarely found in attempts to outline class structure in Latin America, but Portes' usage refers to small-scale entrepreneurs, who have similar characteristics in the class analysis to the dominant class, but who operate at a very different level and have a somewhat precarious existence. Since petty entrepreneurs make use of casual labour, often in the form of unremunerated family workers, they can be classified as informal unlike the dominant class, who hire workers through contractual mechanisms. There is a distinct rural segment of this class which is made up of small commercial farmers, who depend on a casual labour supply.

The development of the urban informal proletariat has been discussed fully in the previous chapter, its rural counterpart being the agricultural semi-proletariat. There is some disagreement about the size of the informal proletariat, which is not surprising given that its informal nature does not lend itself to the gathering of statistics, but most commentators see it representing about 40–60 per cent of the economically active population. Since the 1950s, its composition has altered, in that there has been a shift from the rural informal proletariat to the urban. Whatever disagreement there may be about size, there can be no doubt that this sector will not disappear easily and there is every evidence to show that with the economic crises of the 1980s, it has been increasing.

In the early days of shanty-town development, there were suggestions that the squatters would become a strong political force with the potential for threatening the status quo. Land invasions are a highly militant form of action, which require courage on the part of those involved. But in most cases, the land invasion represented the peak of political activity. In general, further energies went into consolidation, as the struggle for day-to-day survival offered little time or opportunity for political mobilisation. Exceptions to this were the case of the Chilean urban poor before and during the Allende period and Peruvian collective action during the 1960s and 1970s. Although this sector has rarely produced a highly organised and successful political movement, it is becoming more of a source of protest, that is gaining significance in contemporary Latin America. Popular protest movements are becoming more common and although they are usually multi-class in membership, they often originate in poor urban neighbourhoods.

These social movements express new forms of social struggle, which have arisen out of the relative failure of other sectors of society to make significant changes and out of changing socio-economic conditions. They are not confined to Latin America, nor even to the LDCs, as they represent a common response to some of the problems of contemporary capitalism. Three major processes are identified as being responsible for new forms of subordination that inspire resistance in the form of new movements: firstly, a commodification of society as individuals are increasingly brought into a market system; secondly, bureaucratisation resulting from increasing state intervention into daily life and finally cultural massification as the influence of mass media becomes more pervasive (Slater 1985).

The term social movement refers to a wide range of groups with certain characteristics in common. Firstly, they are multi-class, which does not mean that class struggles do not exist. These are new antagonisms which emerge as social conflict is diffused to more social relations. Secondly, instead of being located in a work situation, these groups are usually based in a community, often a neighbourhood or some form of local grouping. They bring together people with a shared experience of suffering the same problems. Thirdly, social movements are organised around specific demands such as the need to defend the legality of land-holdings; the desire to get access to water and electricity; or the need to protect human rights. Fourthly, the movements are based on a principle of democracy, so that they have very little in the way of hierarchy or authoritative positions. Finally, Portes suggests that in the struggle, the groups rarely come into direct confrontation with the dominant class, but usually with members of the bureaucratic-technical class who staff the agencies of the state (Portes 1985).

There are a number of different groupings, which may be included under the rubric of social movement: neighbourhood councils, which include the gamut of barrio and community organisations aimed at solving problems of urban facilities and also those that are concerned with living standards, particularly in the form of rising prices of food, transport and other necessities; women's movements, which have become particularly prominant in Grenada and Nicaragua, but which also exist in more localised forms in other countries; human rights groups, which have become so well-known on a national scale in Argentina, but are also active at neighbourhood level as for example in São Paulo, where one was formed in 1978 in the barrio of São Miguel after one of the inhabitants was victimised by police brutality (Singer 1982); CEBs, as described in Chapter 4, are spreading now throughout the continent; regional movements have emerged in countries where the interests of one region have been subordinated to those of other areas as in Peru; and political protest groups, which in the extreme become guerrilla groups, such as Sendero Luminoso in Peru.

In general these movements have operated only at grass-roots level, but in some areas they have been joining up to form networks of organisations of the urban poor. In Mexico in the early 1980s these networks had joined to form the National Council of Popular Urban Movements, with their main demand being that every poor family had a right to a piece of land for a dwelling (Cockroft 1983).

One grass-roots group of this kind, which has been relatively successful is the Cost of Living Movement (MCV) in São Paulo (Singer 1982). It originated in the Mothers' Clubs in a parish in the southern part of the city. The members wrote a letter to the authorities protesting at the increases in the cost of living, which had exacerbated problems of nutrition, health and transport. After the letter was published in the press during some local elections, the inhabitants decided to continue with the campaign by carrying out research on the effects of these rises on lifestyles. Seventy Mothers' Clubs distributed 2,000 questionnaires, which showed that the average worker in that part of São Paulo earned one and a half minimum salaries, which was not sufficient to cover costs of food, rent, mortgage of land payments, clothing, transport, medicine, school equipment, electricity and water for their families. This was followed by a demonstration, to which the Governor of the state was invited, but he did not attend. Various suggestions were made, but little was done, leading to disillusionment, which almost ended the movement. The following year, however, it was revived with the aim of extending it to other neighbourhoods of the city. Gradually the movement spread until by 1978, it was able to assemble 5,000 people with a petition for which almost 1,300,000 signatures had been collected, but the petition received little attention from the authorities. Although the petitioners realised that it was government policies which were responsible for the impoverishment of the masses, the movement did not oppose government, it appealed to it for improvements. Although the MCV failed in its immediate objectives, it can claim some achievements. It had managed to reach the mass of people and make them aware of possible means of tackling their problems. Consciousness-raising of this type has spread, as the MCV has emerged in other cities and in other states.

The new social movements represent a very positive force, they unite people in different occupations to confront a problem and in so doing, they raise consciousness. Because they operate at grass-roots level, they involve people in the issues that really matter to them, which may be the reason why they have often been so dynamic. The problem is that the factors which contribute to their dynamism are also disadvantages. Because they focus on local-level, small-scale issues, their achievements must by definition be limited to that level, and success, that is the accomplishment of the task, may even mean the disbandment of the movement. Also the lack of organisation, although contributing to the involvement of members, makes it difficult to expand and develop these movements to any sort of state or national level. How much notice the authorities will take of them remains to be seen.

CONCLUSION

The changes that have been taking place in Latin America and the economic growth that the region has experienced have not brought about any redistribution of income in favour of the low-income groups, the trend has been if anything slightly towards a greater polarisation of wealth. The dominant and bureaucratic-technical classes, through lack of motivation and the organised working class, due to its size and nature, resulting from peripheral capitalist development, have not been revolutionary forces in the region. Perhaps as Becker has suggested for the bourgeoisie (Becker 1983) and Roxborough for the proletariat (Roxborough 1984), it is expecting too much to place the burden of revolution on the shoulders of any one class. The two major revolutions of modern times in the region,

Cuba (1959) and Nicaragua (1979), were both brought about by multi-class coalitions. It is more realistic to look for advances which are significant for those concerned. The new social movements represent a multi-class force for change, but so far, have in general been limited in their achievements.

FURTHER READING

Becker, D. (1983) *The new bourgeoisie and the limits of dependency: mining, class and power in 'revolutionary' Peru*. Princeton University Press, Princeton

Evans, P. (1979) *Dependent development: the alliance of multinational, state and local capital in Brazil*. Princeton University Press, Princeton

Felix, D. (1983) Income distribution and the quality of life in Latin America: patterns, trends and policy implications. *Latin American Research Review*, Vol. 18 No. 2

Humphrey, J. (1982) *Capitalist control and workers' struggle in the Brazilian auto industry*. Princeton University Press, Princeton

Lloyd, P. (1982) *A Third World proletariat?* Allen and Unwin, London

Portes, A. (1985) Latin American class structures: their composition and change during the last decades. *Latin American Research Review*, Vol. 20 No. 3

Slater, D. (1985) *New social movements and the state in Latin America*. Latin American Studies 29. CEDLA, Amsterdam

Chapter

8

The state

There are various reasons for the importance of the state in contemporary Latin America. Since industrialisation and economic growth have so often been perceived as the motor forces of development, one of the major concerns of development theory has been the source of capital necessary for these processes.

It is not just the bourgeoisie and multinationals who provide the investment for capital accumulation but also, in many countries, the state. This triple alliance of capital has become very important for economic growth in the more industrialised of the Latin American countries, with the state in some cases playing the dominant part. The state is able to manipulate such a role, for not only can it direct its own capital into the economic sectors where growth is required, but it can also influence its powerful partner, foreign capital, into the desired areas of the economy.

The state has emerged as such an important institution, not only because of its role in capital investment, but also as an employer. The expansion of state education and health facilities, as well as its economic activities and general growth of bureaucracy, mean that far more Latin Americans now work for the state. Their salaries, conditions of service and prospects for the future depend on the continuing prosperity of the state. The state bourgeoisie has expanded in numbers and increased its influence. Such was the expansion of the government sector in Ecuador, following the state's appropriation of oil revenues, that by 1982, employees of the state made up 22.9 per cent of the EAP (ISS-PREALC 1983).

It has been shown that one of the fundamental problems facing the poor is lack of access to secure well-paid work. As job opportunities are shaped by government policies, as well as educational opportunities, these are other areas in which the state has the power to make important contributions to development.

Is the state, then, becoming the new promoter of development? This chapter examines the explanations that have been put forward for the growth of the strong state and then looks at the role of the state towards development. It has been stressed that the 1960s and 1970s were periods of economic growth for Latin America, during which levels of growth at times surpassed those of the developed nations. In many Latin American countries, this growth has been characterised by state-sponsored industrialisation. The stronger the state the more able it is to influence the economy and so the development of the authoritarian state has facilitated state sponsorship. In most cases, it is military governments that have been responsible for the authoritarian nature of the state, but not all.

Mexico has frequently been considered authoritarian, despite the existence of an election process to provide the ruling party and the government of the day. The apparently elected ruling party has been the same one for about fifty years and has gained and maintained considerable control over the state apparatus in that time. Control is exercised through the integration of potential sources of opposition into the state apparatus, where they can be managed from above. The reciprocity which keeps this system going has already been described in the case of the labour movement. If for any reason these mechanisms fail to curb an insurrection, the army can be called upon, as the events of 1968 showed. In that year, hundreds were killed by the army, after a massive student demonstration.

The argument of this chapter is that the policies of the authoritarian state have encouraged economic growth but at the same time exacerbated the accompanying social costs, a pattern of development which is characteristic of the region as a whole, but which is exaggerated by those republics with authoritarian states. This is partly due to monetarist policies, which authoritarian regimes are able to implement so fully because they can use force to put into practice the less palatable aspects. For society, these policies have meant increased production and wealth and the development of a substantial, wealthy and European-style middle class, but they have also contributed to poverty, unemployment and underemployment and increasing inequality. Many of the military regimes have now given way to democracies, but the legacy of the military has made development programs difficult for the new governments. After looking at the evidence for the social costs of this type of development and the potential in the new democracies for resolving them, two case studies, which represent two very different situations, are examined.

Peru is the exception to the argument, providing us with a very unusual example of military policies. Brazil epitomises the growth of the strong state and economic modernisation with its associated problems. This example demonstrates the mechanisms by which the state is able to promote high levels of growth, but at the same time how these same mechanisms have encouraged problems of underdevelopment. As Brazil is often seen as a leader in development in the Third World, it is appropriate to end with this case-study as an indicator of a development path which other LDCs may be following.

THE AUTHORITARIAN STATE

Explanations for the growth of authoritarianism first focused on the military. In 1964, the military seized power in the largest country in Latin America, Brazil, a scenario which was soon repeated in perhaps the most advanced (in terms of economic development and indices of modernisation) Latin American country at the time, Argentina, and in one which had enjoyed an unprecedented period of constitutional governments, Bolivia. In 1968, Peru, too, experienced a military coup and in 1973, the two countries in which democratic institutions were widely regarded as being securely planted, Chile and Uruguay, succumbed to the military. By that year, ten Latin American countries were governed by the armed forces. At first it was thought that the officers in power would adopt a 'caretaker' role, maintaining law and order for a short spell until the country was ready again for democratic rule but, contrary to these views, the military stayed in power.

The first comprehensive theories of the military emphasised their increasing professionalisation and argued that military governments would become more infrequent with the expansion of the middle class (Lieuwen 1961, Johnson 1964). Johnson believed that military influence on politics could be beneficial to society because they were able to mobilise modernisation programs, such as the colonisation of virgin territories and the building of roads. Jose Nun, however, having witnessed the military coups of the middle of the decade, saw the officers' regime as a more permanent feature of Latin American societies (Nun 1967). He distinguished between military intervention in the more backward and the more advanced republics, suggesting that in the latter it takes the form of a middle-class military coup. He argued that the army officers who came to power were allied to, and controlled by, the middle class. The latter were not strong enough on their own to fill the power vacuum left by the declining oligarchy but, through the armed forces, they could implement their policies.

Unlike Johnson, Nun considered the middle class to be conservative and so he characterised the military as being unfavourable to progress and social reforms.

The permanence of the armed forces in power required a rethinking of the role of the state. The move from democracy to authoritarianism did not fit the stages of modernisation theory, for it represented a move backwards to a more traditional order. On the other hand, some sociologists pointed out that these governments were embarking on modernising programmes. The Brazilians were in the process of developing Amazonia, by clearing the jungle and building settlements there, as well as encouraging highly technological and sophisticated industrial development. This led to the view that authoritarian regimes are not necessarily part of a traditional order, but have a part to play in the development of the LDCs (Malloy 1977).

O'Donnell was concerned to show that these regimes were the outcome of precisely those processes, such as the expansion of market relations, industrialisation and increasing political participation, that modernisation theorists had identified as leading to democracy (O'Donnell 1973). But O'Donnell emphasised that these processes resulted in government policies which were not democratic, redistributive or humanitarian, thus adding more evidence to disprove the modernists. O'Donnell's term 'bureaucratic-authoritarianism' was first used by him to refer to the state in Argentina and Brazil after the mid-1960s, but has later been used by other social scientists to refer to various military states.

The applications of authoritarianism to Latin America have been based on the original model developed by Linz to explain Franco's Spain (1970). His definition is 'Authoritarian regimes are political systems with limited, not responsible, political pluralism: without elaborate and guiding ideology (but with distinctive mentalities); without intensive nor extensive political mobilization (except some points of their development); and in which a leader (or occasionally a small group) exercises power within formally ill-defined limits but actually quite predictable ones'. (Linz 1970: 255)

The main features of the 'bureaucratic-authoritarian' state are, firstly, a form of government which ensures the domination of society through a class structure, by a bourgeoisie that is externally oriented. Institutionally, it is made up of a coalition of coercive and technocratic agencies and is technically rational. It involves a system of political exclusion which denies the mass of people the rights of citizenship. Moreover, this system encourages foreign capital and promotes high levels of social inequality (Philip 1985). The links with foreign capital, encouraged by the 'bureaucratic-authoritarian' state, gave O'Donnell some affinity with dependency theorists, though most of

his other ideas have developed independent of a dependency framework.

O'Donnell's very influential ideas have aroused some criticisms.
Munck argues that these states, and in particular Argentina, are not
so much bureaucratic in a Weberian sense, as technocratic. He adds
that authoritarianism is too vague a word, especially as it really acts
as a euphemism for repression (Munck 1985a).

Others, theorising about the state, have developed the theme of
authoritarianism, emphasising in particular the structures of corporatism that are so often an aspect of authoritarian regimes. This mode
of organising state and society has been aptly described by Malloy
in the following way:

> ... that each of these regimes is characterised by strong and relatively
> autonomous governmental structures that seek to impose on the society
> a system of interest representation based on enforced limited pluralism.
> These regimes try to eliminate spontaneous interest articulation and
> establish a limited number of authoritatively recognised groups that
> interact with the governmental apparatus in defined and regularised
> ways. Moreover, the recognised groups in this type of regime are
> organised in vertical functional categories rather than horizontal class
> categories and are obliged to interact with the state through the
> designated leaders of authoritatively sanctioned interest associations.
> (Malloy 1977: 4)

Malloy suggests that corporatism has become a dominant feature
of the contemporary Latin American state, especially in the more
industrially advanced countries and that modernising authoritarian
regimes with corporatist structures are likely to remain part of political
life.

Since the corporatism of Latin America is distinct from the forms
of the state featured in the capitalist and socialist paths of development, it needs some explanation. It has been argued that this mode
reflects a Hispanic-Catholic tradition which has always existed
beneath the surface, while it has been fashionable for other constitutional forms to come and go. But this reasoning does not explain
why corporatism should have come to the fore at this particular
point in time, nor does it account for its orientation towards
modernisation.

Malloy argues that two other processes have been crucial in the
growth of corporatism, delayed dependent development and populism
(Malloy 1977). His explanation for the growth of corporatism is very
similar to O'Donnell's account of the factors underlying the development of the 'bureaucratic-authoritarian' state. According to Malloy,
delayed dependent development brought about a general crisis of
public authority, which democratic regimes have been unable to
resolve. The crisis arose because modernisation was brought to Latin

America from abroad and imposed on traditional structures of patronage and particularism. This created a multiplicity of societal interests which could not easily be integrated into one political structure with a guarantee of stability. The big difference between Malloy and O'Donnell is that while the former emphasises modernisation, O'Donnell stresses the social costs of modernisation.

Malloy's main argument, however, is that populism was the response to the first crisis of delayed dependent development and that this, in turn, laid the foundations for corporatism. Since populism has been a prominent feature of Latin American political systems in certain historical periods, it is worth turning attention, briefly, to this political form.

Populism is a movement that is organised on the basis of community rather than class, with a charismatic figure as a leader. But, because a movement claims to be classless, this is not necessarily so and, indeed, in Latin America, populism has usually taken the form of class alliances. Initially a response to the collapse of the export-oriented economy, populism briefly united the middle and working classes in order to fill the power vacuum that had developed.

The disruption of export-based economies, brought on by the depression of the 1930s and 1940s, led to a desire for autonomous national development and the implementation of import substitution. The economic crisis engendered the collapse of hegemonic control of the oligarchy, who lost the support of the middle class, some of whom were losing their jobs. Although sometimes internally divided, as in Argentina between the export bourgeoisie and the small industrialists, the bourgeoisie pushed to the front of the political struggle. In order to strengthen their weak position, they sought allies elsewhere, the obvious choice being the working class. Populism, by using ideology that offered rewards to the workers, was the way in which the bourgeoisie attempted to construct a coalition and win support of the working class. The aim was to create coalitions powerful enough to control the state and then, having gained power, the bourgeoisie could assert itself and the subordinate position of the working class.

The populists saw the problems of Latin America stemming from dualism, oligarchic control, dependence and a weak state. Thus, they wanted economic independence, an end to the semi-feudal structures of the countryside and social justice for all sectors, and the agency which was to try and achieve this was the state. Populism was, therefore, 'statist' but the state was to be controlled by a multi-class alliance. Although populism advocated a pluralist coalition to achieve reform, the bourgeoisie were to be the paternalistic leaders in this, offering education and improvements to their followings, in return for their support. This uneven exchange was, clearly, clientelist rather than one reflecting an equal relationship between classes. The strong ties in populism were, therefore, vertical between patron and clients, rather than horizontal and, because of the emphasis on the state, populism was based on an implicit corporatist image of socio-political organisation. With populism, the state actively brought the masses into politics, giving a minority certain benefits, as is characteristic of clientelism.

Populism had its achievements, the Peronist period in Argentina brought about very definite improvements for the working class, Brazilian workers gained better working conditions from Vargas, and APRA has remained a strong political party for a long time in Peru. In general, populism had, by the 1950s, weakened the power of the traditional elites; promoted import substitution, which increased the significance of the industrialists and organised labour; and stimulated a general increase in political mobilisation.

But, despite the expansion of the state apparatus by the populists, the state itself did not increase its power or efficiency, mainly because of the continuation of dependency. The economic crises of the 1960s showed that the problems had not been solved and dependency still continued, though now often in the form of multinationals. The bourgeoisie had not proved strong enough in filling the power vacuum left by the declining oligarchy. Radicalised by the Cuban revolution, some Latin American groups were using political protest to push for reform in society. Under the guise of nationalism and security, the military stepped into the gap, seizing control of the extensive state apparatus that the populists had previously set up.

The military's seizure of power represented a move from the potentially democratic corporatism of the populists to the authoritarian corporatism of the soldiers and technocrats (Malloy 1977). Populism had paved the way by setting up vertical corporatist structures, but the armed forces have adapted these to more authoritarian ends. The military have wanted to achieve state-sponsored industrial growth and, in order to attain this, they have had to increase the power and autonomy of the state and to consciously favour the groups they feel most likely to be successful at the expense of others, which has meant the need for authoritarianism and repression. Unlike the populist period, the state in the 1960s became powerless to prevent benefits being drained off by multinationals. In order to gain a measure of control over both transnationals and society, the bourgeoisie have favoured policies that are incompatible with liberal democracy.

The corporatist nature of the Mexican state can be seen in the way that groups are linked to the governing party. Enforced limited pluralism exists in the form of the various influential groups, such as business associations, unions and peasant organisations, having vertical ties with the ruling party. The resulting network that links the president of Mexico with peasants and factory workers acts more as a form of control, than a means of interest representation.

The idea that the state has increased its power and autonomy challenges the crude interpretation of Marx that the state is the tool of the ruling class. Poulantzas, taking a more rigorous Marxist stand, argues that relative autonomy of the state can strengthen capitalism and therefore is not necessarily bad news for the dominant class (Poulantzas 1975). He points out that the function of the state in a determinate social formation and the interests of the dominant class in this formation coincide because of the system itself. The direct participation of members of the ruling class in the state apparatus is not the cause but the effect. Thus, for Poulantzas, the social background of the ruling class is not really relevant because, whatever their background, members of the ruling class want to preserve the society in which they are successful. Capitalist society requires a bourgeoisie and a proletariat to function and, since the ruling class wishes to preserve and prosper capitalism, it must protect the class relations of capitalism and must, therefore, ensure the continued supremacy of the bourgeois ruling group. Since the role of the state is to preserve the class system of capitalist society, the interests of the state and the ruling class are entwined and ensure the continuing power of the ruling class.

This argument leads Poulantzas to his concept of the relative autonomy of the state. He suggests that capitalist society might benefit from a state bureaucracy, whose members are not drawn from the same dominant social class. Poulantzas argues that a ruling group might suffer divisions according to the different interests of the factions within it. If the members of the state apparatus are not drawn from the dominant social class, they will not identify with one particular faction nor try to promote its interests in opposition to another faction. Instead, standing outside these differences, they will be able to see what actions would best serve the development of capitalist society and, since they share interests with the state, act accordingly. In this way, they can organise the hegemony of the whole class more successfully.

THE SOCIAL COSTS OF AUTHORITARIANISM

The policies of authoritarian regimes have only served to intensify the existing concentration of income in the region. The growing polarisation of wealth has been vigorous in Brazil and Mexico. In Argentina, it was slight until the 1970s when it was exacerbated by the decline in real wages. The decline of real wages has had the same effect in Chile and Uruguay in the 1970s (Felix 1983). In the 1960s,

Uruguay was one Latin American country which did not display extremes of income concentration, but by the late 1970s this situation had changed. In 1968, the wealthiest 5 per cent of households accounted for 17 per cent of income, but by 1979 their share had almost doubled, expanding to 31 per cent (Gillespie 1985). In Guatemala, which has experienced a succession of military dictators since 1954, income concentration is extreme. In 1980, 5 per cent of the population received 59 per cent of the national income, while the poorest 50 per cent received 7 per cent (Howes 1986). In Chile, the poorest 40 per cent of the population now receive about half as much of total income as they did before the militarisation of politics. In 1968, their share of national income was 13.4 per cent, but by 1983 it had dropped to 6.4 per cent while, in that year, the wealthiest 10 per cent received over 50 per cent of national income. This was partly due to falling real wages, which dropped by 15 per cent in 1981 and by another 16 per cent in 1982, and unemployment (LAWR 5 Aug. 1983).

Eckstein points out that despite Mexico's revolution, her income distribution is no more egalitarian than other Latin American countries, since about 80 per cent of the population receive little more than 40 per cent of the national income. More significantly, their share of national income has not increased with the expansion of domestic production (Eckstein 1977).

One of the characteristics of monetarist policies, as practised by the Latin American authoritarian regimes, has been to raise levels of unemployment. In Chile, unemployment rose from 4.6 per cent in the early 1970s, before militarisation, to 24 per cent in 1983 (LAWR 5 Aug. 1983). In Santiago, it is now estimated at more than 25 per cent (Grugel 1986).

One of the major problems to emerge in the 1980s has been the debt crisis. Many factors have helped to bring this about: the oil shocks of 1974 and 1978; the consequent increase in commercial bank lending; the further economic crisis of the 1980s; rising population; the pressure on governments to provide work; and the policies of the authoritarian states. These policies have been to encourage industrial growth on the basis of foreign capital and loans, as this was considered the best way to find the necesssary capital. Between 1974 and 1978, for example, the GDP of seven of the most industrially advanced countries (Argentina, Mexico, Brazil, Chile, Colombia, Peru and Venezuela), increased by the enormous amount of 74 per cent. But at the same time annual net external borrowing doubled and in the next three years, when annual GDP increased 37 per cent, net external borrowing doubled again (IADB 1985). The authoritarian regimes were able, through their control of the state apparatus, to ensure cheap labour and substantial profits to attract investment, multinationals and foreign loans. Many Latin American governments supposed that the resulting economic growth would be quite sufficient to cover the debts incurred from borrowing. International trends, amongst other things, have thwarted these expectations. Interest rates have risen, due to the monetarist policies of the industrialised countries and the growing US budget deficit, which has meant that not only is it more difficult for the LDCs to meet their debt service requirements, but that new lending, which would have helped them to do this, has been reduced. Moreover, the world recession has led to a fall in commodity prices affecting the LDCs' exports and protectionist policies on the part of the industrialised world, who fear competition from low-priced Third World goods. It has now become very difficult for many of the debtor countries to continue servicing their debts. Interest payments leapt from 17 per cent of export earnings in 1978 to 42 per cent in 1982, the year when the full effect of the external debt crisis was felt (IADB 1985). These have reached such a level that during the period 1982 to 1984, Latin American countries made a net transfer of US $80 billion to industrialised countries. This is equivalent to 8 per cent of the region's total output of goods and services, 50 per cent of the amount devoted to investment and 25 per cent of its export income (IBT 1985).

Although many LDCs have incurred problems of indebtedness, it is in Latin America that these have reached such extreme levels. Of the world's ten largest debtors, seven are Latin American: Brazil, Mexico, Argentina, Venezuela, Chile, Peru, and Colombia. By 1983, Latin America's total external debt was US $256,669 million (IADB 1985).

To try and tackle the issue, the Latin American debtors put forward proposals which included the separation of old from new debt, the restoration of US interest rates to historic levels, flexible negotiations and recognition of the need for development. The USA, prompted by fears of political destabilisation, responded with the Baker plan which, although it promised new loans in 1986–88 by multilateral financial institutions and commercial banks in return for some economic 'liberalization', was clearly inadequate.

The real burden of the debt crisis falls on the mass of the poor. They are the people who ultimately suffer from the resulting increased unemployment, falling output, inflation and balance of payment crises. The solution is often seen in terms of approaching the IMF, whose prescriptions usually include stringent measures, such as setting higher prices for basic goods and services, controlling wages, cuts in government expenditure on public services, 'privatisation' of public sector activities and encouragement for exports. These sorts of measures are frequently unacceptable to the LDCs, with the result that economic recession gets worse and the plight of the poor, who number over 40 million in a country like Brazil, is exacerbated.

The immense repayments that took place between 1981 and 1984 were obtained at the cost of great sacrifices in living standards for the workforce of most countries. According to the Inter-American Development Bank, the main burden during this period fell on wage-earners because of the increase in inflation and real depreciation of currencies. The largest cumulative declines in real wages occurred in Brazil and Mexico, which have the largest debts, the declines in Chile, Peru, and Venezuela being somewhat smaller (IADB 1985). The resulting drop in economic activity during this period had repercussions throughout society, in particular unemployment rose and the informal sector expanded. Standards of living were further eroded by programs of fiscal austerity, which reduced expenditure on public services. The comment of the Inter-American Development Bank on this situation is worth noting:

> In view of the substantial losses in real income suffered by the region in recent years, and the evidence that a disproportionate part of these losses have been concentrated in the lower income strata, to the extent that real wage containment remains a necessary element of the adjustment process, mechanisms will have to be found to shift some of the burden to the higher income groups in the interests of social justice and domestic peace. (IADB 1985: 12–13)

The discontent aroused by the debt and general economic malaise has seriously shaken governments. In Chile, the financial collapse in 1983 compelled the military junta to start renegotiating the foreign debt with the banks and the IMF, and opened the door to opposition from sectors as varied as elements of the business community and the trade union movement. A number of protest movements arose culminating in the first day of National Protest, in May 1983, which marked a real challenge to the regime. The military have remained in power, though over a deeply-divided nation. The early 1980s in Brazil were marked by unprecedented food riots, especially in the poorest parts of the country, where supermarkets and stores were ransacked by uncontrollable mobs.

DEMOCRATISATION

After a lengthy period of military rule, twenty years in the case of Brazil, most South American countries have now returned to civilian regimes. Ecuador was the first (1979), followed by Peru (1980), Bolivia (1982), Argentina (1983), Uruguay (1985), and Brazil (1985). This leaves Chile and Paraguay with generals at their head. Venezuela and Colombia have experienced continuous civilian rule since 1958. Paul Cammack optimistically sees this as marking the end of a fifty-year cycle of political instability and the beginning of a long-term period of democracy for South America (Cammack 1985). He does, however, point out that the type of democracy on offer is elitist and limited in its aims. He suggests that the power vacuum which has existed in the class structure since the 1930s has been filled and that Latin America now has a civilian elite 'which is capable of ruling on behalf of the dominant classes with the consent of the majority, and of perpetuating its rule through the mechanism of competitive party politics'. (Cammack 1985: 39). Cammack implies that the failure of the armed forces is the last of the unsuccessful attempts at development since the export crisis of the 1930s and that it has ushered in a period of bourgeois hegemony. This hegemony is bolstered by the ability of the new elite to present left-wing moves for change as threats to law and order and, therefore, to thwart them

Cammack is optimistic about the continuation of democracy, but these newly-elected leaders have some very pressing problems to solve. Apart from the immense financial task of paying the debt and interest on it, the burden that it imposes undermines any real attempts at development for the mass of society. It is very difficult to fulfil election promises when resources which could be harnessed for economic growth are flowing abroad to service debt payments. Moreover, democracies are of different kinds and may be authoritarian, as has been suggested in the case of Mexico. The two major issues that arise have to do with, firstly, the viability of the new regimes (is there a likelihood of further military coups?) and, secondly, the extent of genuine democracy (are authoritarian states masquerading as democracies?).

In Argentina, quite strenuous attempts have been made to demilitarise society and confine the armed forces to the barracks. Discredited by their failures in the running of the economy, their abuses of human rights, corruption and above all by the defeat in the Falklands/Malvinas war, the military lost the support of the general public. In 1982–83, demilitarisation was kept at the forefront of the electoral campaign for the first time since the 1930s (Makin 1984). Unlike other retiring military governments in the region, the Argentine officers were unable to secure an amnesty law for themselves before the elections. The fact that leading generals were put on trial demonstrated not only the government's very genuine commitment to human rights, but also the weakness of the military. Although Alfonsin's government has been concerned to demilitarise politics and reduce the influence of the officers in social and economic affairs, it has not attacked the armed services as an institution. The military have been excluded from politics but not undermined in their own sphere (Little

1986). The threat of a coup by the demoralised remaining officers seems unlikely. As to the content of Argentina's new democracy, there has been a shift away from corporatism towards an emphasis on political parties and parliament as the main protagonists in the political arena, with the demise of the political role of the army. Certainly there is a mandate from the people for a reduction in authoritarianism, as 52 per cent of the electorate voted for the candidate who most obviously expressed a desire for democratisation (Munck 1985b).

Peru's return to democracy has been coloured by a faltering economy. Overwhelmed by its foreign debt, in 1983 the country suffered what has been referred to as 'the worst economic crisis of the century'. (LAB 1985: 88). The strikes and demonstrations brought about by the following recession made the government turn to repressive measures. Complaints about worsening social and economic conditions were met by the riot police, revealing the fragility of Peru's democracy. The major challenge to the government comes from the radical guerrilla group, Sendero Luminoso which, despite five years of repression, is gaining strength. Its supporters are now to be found not only in its rural stronghold around Ayacucho, but also in many urban areas. Increasing support for the left might provoke the generals to step in again. Aware of the presence of the military in the wings, it is unlikely that any Peruvian head of state will do much to upset the armed forces.

In Ecuador, the period of military rule was shorter than elsewhere, but it coincided with the oil boom and resulting economic changes. The newly-elected government could not, therefore, simply return to the pre-1972 situation, but had to create the structures and institutions that would legitimise the political system. Attempts at political modernisation have been only partially successful and the maturation of Ecuadorian democracy may have been slowed down with the election to power of the conservative Leon Febres in 1984 (Corkill 1985). The new democracies are fragile, but it is to be hoped that the strength of the desire for democracy, which has brought them back, will keep them in power and that they will not feel a need to use authoritarian measures to try and solve their many social and economic problems.

PERU 1968–80, A REVOLUTIONARY MILITARY?

In 1968, a military coup brought a group of officers with professed radical aims, and led by General Juan Velasco Alvarado, to power in Peru. They embarked on a path of development which they declared to be neither capitalist nor socialist. This 'revolution from above' was marked by two distinct phases: firstly, 1968–75, the period of major reforms and, secondly, 1975–80, the period of consolidation until power was handed over to an elected government. The changes initiated by the military have stimulated considerable debate about the extent of change involved, but there is no doubt that some major reforms were carried out under the auspices of authoritarian rulers. Some commentators, writing in the early days of military rule, classified it as a bourgeois revolution, arguing that the policies being implemented were anti-oligarchic, but benefited Peruvian managers, professionals and white-collar workers (Quijano 1971, Petras and Rimensnyder 1970). Looking at the period as a whole, it is usually interpreted as a bourgeois revolution which became state capitalism.

One of the factors underlying the rise to power of the officers was a crisis of hegemony, and the early policies of the Velasco regime implied that they intended the bourgeoisie to fill the power vacuum. Petras and Rimensnyder have pointed out that as the army officers who formed the initial government were not from elite backgrounds or those families associated with industrial wealth, they could afford to be anti-oligarchic (Petras and Rimensnyder 1970). Early measures had the effect of shifting Peru away from semi-feudal structures and towards a more capitalist-dominated society.

Agrarian reform was a very full and complex programme but only the aspects relevant to the argument will be discussed here. Expropriation of agricultural properties began with the large estates but, prompted by the strikes and rural agitation of 1970 and 1971, the programme became more radical and expropriations easier. What is particularly interesting about this reform is the compensation that was given. The expropriated landlords were entitled to bonds which could be exchanged for shares of stock in industrial enterprises belonging to the state and/or investment in new industrial plant. The object of this was to transfer private capital from agriculture, often seen as a backward sector of the economy, to the sectors of industry which the government wished to encourage, that is, the state sector and modern, dynamic enterprises. At the same time, the traditional landed elite were, at a stroke, converted into industrial capitalists. This meant that their financial interests were now in industry rather than agriculture. Those who took shares of stock in state enterprises maintained their income, but lost the power that derives from control over land (Quijano 1971).

The middle-sized rural estates were not expropriated, thus leaving the rural bourgeoisie intact. The expropriated lands were turned into cooperatives of different types, but all of which were linked to government bureaucracy and so involved an expansion of administrative middle-class occupations. The peasantry who were brought into cooperatives did, in general, benefit. Those who remained outside the cooperative system, however, estimated at about four-fifths of the Peruvian peasantry, received virtually no attention from government and were therefore excluded from the benefits of agrarian reform. The net result was to expand and aid the middle levels of rural society, at the expense of the elite, and offering little assistance to the really poor.

Policies towards the industrial sector had similar results for urban society. Here, the government embarked on a program of state control of basic industries and economic infrastructure, leaving the modern, dynamic sector of the economy to private enterprise. This involved a process of expropriation which undermined foreign capital in areas where it was dominant. One of the most notable examples was the International Petroleum Company for, when this giant corporation was expropriated, considerable American wrath was aroused. Domestic capital was affected in other areas. Expansion of the role of the state, therefore, took place at the expense of both foreign and local capitalists but the national bourgeoisie was encouraged to participate with the state in areas of economic activity previously monopolised by foreign capital and in the dynamic manufacturing sector.

There is considerable discussion over why the shift to state capitalism occurred. Economists such as Fitzgerald, Thorp and Bertram have argued that the military were compelled to make moves in this direction because of the failure of the bourgeoisie to respond positively to their policies and become a new dynamic social and economic force (Fitzgerald 1976, Thorp, Bertram 1978). Others argue that the reforms themselves unleashed processes of class struggle and political mobilisation which, in turn, radicalised the reforms beyond the initial intentions of the generals (Havens, Lastarria-Cornhiel, Otero 1983). For example, in the countryside, rural strikes and agitation encouraged more radical agrarian reform. Booth and Sorj imply that the officers' policies were governed by a more genuine commitment to agrarian reform than they are often credited with, pointing out that many of their actions provoked the hostility of the bourgeoisie (Booth, Sorj 1983).

The nationalisation of firms proceeded apace in the first half of the 1970s and it was this state control of so many enterprises that gave Peru its state capitalist nature. By 1975, state firms were responsible for two-thirds of the banking system, half of the total productive investment, a fifth of industrial production and more than 50 per cent of mining output. As well as this, under Velasco, the state's share of production doubled to reach 21 per cent in 1975 (LAB 1985).

Private enterprises which were left untouched by the nationalisation programme, had to modify their labour relations. Laws were passed to compel all firms with more than five employees to set up an industrial community comprising all those who worked for the enterprise. Members of the industrial community were to participate in the distribution of profits and be represented on the board of directors. These laws clearly offered advantages to the working class who were in regular employment but, like the rural sector, the beneficiaries were very much a minority. By 1974, nearly all of the 3,700 eligible firms had set up an industrial community, but this only covered 38 per cent of the industrial labour force (Fitzgerald 1976). The great majority of the urban poor try to make a living in the informal sector, which was not affected by these innovations. It should, however, be remembered that the military did much to improve material conditions in the shanty towns, by extending urban facilities to these areas and encouraging self-help schemes there.

The social property programme, which represented the culmination of the government's proposals, was to extend to all the main areas of economic activity. These state-sponsored workers' cooperatives were run on the basis of self-management and the 'subordination of capital to labour'. They were essentially based on a combination of the characteristics of participation and solidarity (Palacios 1983). The sector, however, was never properly financed and promoted, with the result that no more than fifty cooperatives were set up (LAB 1985). When Bermudez replaced Velasco in 1975, ambitious plans concerning the social property sector were put aside and a period of reappraisal followed.

The interests of the officers did not coincide with any one class. They probably did not intend the advance of the popular classes, but their reforms raised expectations and, because these changes weakened the controls formerly used by the dominant class, the masses gained opportunities to mobilise and act. The reforms of the period were numerous, varied and in some cases very radical, though not all of them left the drawing-board. There is no doubt that major adjustments were made in Peruvian society, but the mass of poor in both town and country were excluded from the benefits.

BRAZIL

Brazil, since the 1960s, represents the 'modernising authoritarian' state *par excellence*. As it is the largest country in Latin America and has developed some of the most highly industrialised areas of the continent, it is often taken as the country that is leading the way for the rest of Latin America's development. Many of the characteristics of modern Brazil, such as the polarisation of society that has accompanied economic growth and the emergence of the strong state, do epitomise a type of development that is taking place in Latin

America. For these reasons, it is worth taking a closer look at Brazil, state and society.

The authoritarian aspect of the state has flourished under the military. The social changes that were taking place in the early 1960s disturbed the bourgeoisie, who viewed them as expressions of confusion and disorder. The military took the opportunity to seize power, adopting the image of a salvationist mission to restore law and order. When change is perceived as chaotic, the military has an appeal for the privileged groups, because the armed services, above all, have the power to maintain internal peace and can offer national security. The Brazilian coup was brought about by two major groups, the hard liners and the moderates, led by General Castello Branco. Although Branco became president, it was the more authoritarian element who gradually came to dominate and they compelled Branco to adopt more hard-line policies.

It took ten years for the nature of the regime to become clearly established but, by then, its corporatist characteristics had become clear. The Latin American Bureau's characterisation of the main features depict many corporatist factors:

- a highly centralised federal government controlled by the military, dominating weak state governments with little or no military participation;
- the widespread appointment of retired military officers to influential and often leading roles in the state machinery and state companies;
- rotation of the presidency every five years, a process usually preceded by a crisis of succession as different groups within the armed forces struggle for power. In this 'dictatorship without a dictator', only four-star army generals are eligible to become president;
- a large and lavishly paid civilian technocracy, the 'expert' section of the bureaucracy, particularly well entrenched in economic policy-making, an area in which the military have virtually no say;
- the dominance of business interests over most other interests.
- the maintenance of some of the usual political institutions, in particular a functioning congress and regular elections, to provide the regime with some basis for legitimacy;
- frequent changes in the rules of the political game, and periodic purging of potential leaders thrown up by popular movements or the popular vote, so as to maintain control of the political process. (LAB 1982: 38–9)

The system is dominated from above, allowing for no genuine representation from grass-roots level, by relying on certain interest groups such as the business community, which has strong vertical links with government.

Authoritarian measures began soon after the coup, with the labour movement being one of the first areas of attack. There were massive purges of the urban labour unions, leaders were arrested, records were confiscated and the rural syndicates and peasant leagues closed down. The political and judicial arenas also suffered. In 1969, Congress was closed, which allowed the president almost unlimited powers, in the name of protecting national security but this, in fact, inaugurated a wave of repressive acts. Political rights were suspended for a large number of people, forcing political dissidents and intellectuals into exile. Eventually the supreme court itself was purged, with the result that all opposition to the government went underground, setting in motion a period of terrorist activity and brutal repression of anyone suspected of opposition. The military and police were now able to impose controls.

Once the labour movement had been purged, the government were able to control it by enforcing the existing labour code, which had been initiated by Vargas during an earlier populist period and institutionalised in 1943 and which embodied a corporatist system of labour relations. The code compelled workers in certain industries to pay union dues, which were deducted from workers' pay cheques, but the dues then went to the ministry of labour, who retained control of them, by only releasing them to unions whose budgets the ministry approved. Only one syndicate could be recognised in each industry and the minister of labour had the legal authority to validate the elections of syndicate officials. The right to strike, which had been forbidden in the 1943 code, was either excluded for some groups or made subject to revocation by the labour courts for others. The code clearly gave control of the labour movement to the government, emphasising the vertical links between union members, their leaders and the military.

The officers in power believed that authoritarianism was necessary in order to carry out their economic policies, which they realised would be very unpopular, but which they considered necessary for economic growth. The military were supported by a bureaucracy, composed of technocrats, who wished to introduce advanced technology and modern methods to the running of their society. They accepted the authoritarian aspects of a military regime because it made it possible for them to implement their ideas. The alliance between them succeeded because the military needed the technocrats to make the economy work and the latter needed the former to have the power to carry out their policies.

The so-called modernising policies of the Brazilian generals produced levels of economic growth, which became world famous as the 'Brazilian miracle'. There is no doubt that the rate of economic growth achieved between the mid-1960s and the 1970s was extremely impressive, gross domestic product rose from US $52 billion in 1963 to US $134 billion in 1978 and, from 1968 to 1974, gross domestic product grew by an average yearly rate of 10 per cent, more than double the rate of growth of advanced countries. (LAB 1982). During the 1970s Brazil became the tenth largest economy in the world, with the thirteenth largest industrial sector. Such was the country's economic development that, by the mid-1970s, the notion that Brazil might reach major-power status, became acceptable. By the late 1970s it was being suggested that Brazil might be integrated into the Organisation of Economic Cooperation and Development, which would have been a sign of developed-nation status (Selcher 1981). There can be no doubt that this demonstrates very real and profound economic growth.

The social costs of this economic growth, however, were immense, the new wealth was concentrated in the hands of a few, thus increasing inequalities in society.

> The proportion of total income going to the poorest 5 per cent of the economically active population fell from 1.51 per cent in 1960, to 0.54 per cent in 1972. The share of total income of the poorer half of the population fell from 15.87 per cent in 1960 to 10.49 per cent in 1970, then recovered somewhat to 12.94 per cent in 1976. The increased share of the richer half was taken almost entirely by the richest 10 per cent, whose slice of the cake grew from 41.28 per cent to 51.15 per cent. (LAB 1982: 49–50)

The economic boom was brought about by the government's monetary and fiscal policies. The period of 1964–67 was seen as one of stabilisation, in which the government was successful in gaining control of wages, especially among the lower paid. The resulting fall in the real value of the minimum wage between 1963 and 1973, estimated at about 25 per cent in São Paulo and Rio de Janeiro (LAB 1982: 47), ensured that a mass of cheap labour was available for the multinationals and large Brazilian firms. Moreover, in the countryside, many landowners, rather than pay their labourers the minimum wage, laid off their workers on a massive scale, thus driving great numbers of unskilled labourers to the city in search of work. Despite the clamp down on wages, prices of goods such as food, fuel, public transport and housing, rose, with the redistributive consequences of a transfer of wealth from the working class to the middle class. Capital was transferred to those who might invest in industry, cheap labour was available and the country was ready for the boom which began in 1968. But the extreme polarisation that had occurred in the middle of the decade was never reduced by the increasing prosperity.

When the boom came and economic growth was high, more people were able to join the labour force in unskilled and semi-skilled jobs.

This encouraged internal migration so that, at the height of the 'miracle', as many as 500,000 people a year moved from rural areas to São Paulo. However, because of inflation and the decline in the minimum wage, even those in paid work were barely able to support themselves and their families. For those who lived in extreme poverty in the depressed North East, the 'miracle' had little relevance.

As the small and inefficient Brazilian firms had been put out of business by government policies, it was the multinationals in the motor industry, electronic household goods, plastics, pharmaceutical and tyre and rubber industries that dominated the dynamic sector and featured most prominently in the 'miracle'. The prosperous middle class provided a market for these goods and the personnel to manage the new factories. The increasing demand for professionals and businessmen to run the rapidly expanding economy was not met by the state, but by private capital which financed the setting up of schools, colleges and universities on a massive scale. Exports also prospered during the boom years, though coffee lost its dominating role, giving way to soya, which took the lead, and exports of manufactured goods (shoes and machinery), processed goods (cocoa products) and minerals.

The military, who had needed to use authoritarian measures to make their unpalatable policies of wage squeezes and worker lay-offs possible, were led during the years of the 'miracle' and the worst repression by General Garrastazú, who took power in 1969. The resulting wealth that was generated never produced a 'trickle-down effect', but only served to reinforce the position of the wealthy.

The economic growth that took place was prompted by state intervention in the economy and the penetration of foreign capital. Despite the declaration of support for the private sector, the public sector grew, 200 new state firms being created between 1966 and 1975 and many of them among the largest in Brazil. As is clear from the 'miracle', however, private enterprise clearly benefited. What happened was that all three sectors of capital – private, state and multinational – experienced growth. By the end of the 1970s the state was becoming the dominant one in this triple alliance because it could act as a regulator. In this way, the state was able to participate with multinationals in profitable projects and get a measure of influence. It could, also, ensure the survival of local national firms by aiding them with capital or getting cooperation with the multinationals. The government, therefore, made the state sector more effective while, at the same time, creating conditions in which private business could prosper. As a regulator, however, the state was able to choose which private firms and which sectors of the economy to support, a feature which alienated the unfavoured sectors of the bourgeoisie.

The authoritarian state had achieved a degree of relative autonomy.

It had emerged controlled by military men and bureaucrats, who were not clearly identifiable with the dominant socio-economic class, the bourgeoisie and, therefore, their personal interests were not closely tied to any one sector of the bourgeoisie. They were, however, very determined to promote capitalism and, therefore, preserve the class relations of capitalist society.

Since capital investment enabled them to manipulate power in the economic sector, they used this to strengthen the sectors of the economy which they considered advantageous for the advancement of capitalism in Brazil. Unhindered by any personal loyalties or interests, the state could use its position as regulator to direct economic growth.

Brazil's economic 'miracle' came to an end with the tripling of oil prices in the mid-1970s, for this was one natural resource which Brazil, despite its size, could not produce. A massive vote for opposition candidates was witnessed in 1974. The Catholic Church had, for many years, been the major institution to oppose the excesses of the military, but now other forms of opposition began to appear. By the end of the 1970s, student demonstrations, which had long been absent from the streets, were visible, strikes among the better-paid workers in the dynamic motor industries took place and social movements were developing in urban areas. By 1983, hunger had reached such proportions that food riots, involving thousands of people, were taking place in different parts of the country. Several food warehouses, stores and supermarkets, especially in the drought-ridden North-East, were ransacked (LAWR 26 Aug. 1983). But, perhaps, the major crisis for Brazil at the end of the generals' rule was the enormous debt, which had been run up as a result of foreign borrowing to finance economic growth. The debt, which reached over US $100,000 million by the end of the military regime, was the largest in the world (IADB 1985). The long-awaited event of redemocratisation and the apparent end to modernising authoritarianism, occurred in 1985.

Brazil had achieved its modernisation programme by keeping wages low and yet spending the minimum on state provision of health and education facilities and, at the same time, allowing the wealthy to benefit from high profits and salaries and low taxes, not to mention the availability of sophisticated consumer goods. As a result, the poorest half of the population, who received 4 per cent of national income in 1968, had had this reduced to 3 per cent by 1984, while the richest 10 per cent increased their share from 39 per cent to 51 per cent during that period (IBT 1985).

It could be argued that Brazil has achieved a First World economy and a Third World society. Before the debt crisis, Brazil's economy had reached such a level, that it had seriously been considered for

First World membership. It is true that the enormous debt is a characteristic of LDCs, but it has now reached such a proportion in some
Latin American countries, that First World banks are seriously
worried. The size of the debt is forcing the industrialised countries
to take steps; the international capitalist economy is vulnerable as well
as the Latin American countries. At the same time, while about one-
quarter of the population correspond to a First World society, the
majority of the population does not, in terms of standard of living.
This is not a dual society, because no clear demarcation can be made
separating two societies. Peripheral groups are being brought into
society, but that society has a disparate number of interlinked social
situations, a few of which benefit from the fruits of economic growth,
but the majority do not.

CONCLUSION

The strong state has been shown to be a characteristic of the more
industrially-advanced Latin American countries. Many of the military
governments which were associated with this development have withdrawn from the political stage, leaving a legacy of economic malaise.
The state has been modernising in the sense of promoting economic
growth, but the social costs of this policy have been great. Increasing
concentration of income, rising unemployment, an expanding informal
sector and falling real wages have been compounded by the debt
crisis. The policy of extensive borrowing to finance the economic
growth has brought about an intolerable burden of repayments and
debt servicing. Democratisation has been welcomed with considerable
optimism in some quarters, but the tasks which the new democracies
face are formidable and even the most hopeful of views suggests that
governments will continue to be elitist.

The growth of the strong state has meant policies from above. The
hallmark of the military was that they could impose their development
plans, without any fears of democratic mechanisms preventing them
being put into practice. This enabled them to implement the most
stringent aspects of monetarist policy. The corporatist aspects of the
state undermined the power of institutions, such as trade unions, to
provide any meaningful opposition. Since governments gained control
of organised groups, protest has occurred in the form of social movements. The incapacity of the state to provide adequate services, their
economic failings and continual abuse of power, have all contributed
to the growth of these movements.

As has already been pointed out, these movements have, so far,
been limited in their achievements, but they must have contributed
to the growing pressure to demilitarise society. In one area at least,

human rights, a movement has challenged the state, and with some success. In Argentina, a group of mothers of the 'disappeared' (men and women who had been secretly killed or abducted by the armed forces) began to parade every week outside the government palace, protesting at injustices and asking for information about their missing sons and daughters. Their numbers grew and soon they were advertising to the world the repressions of the officers. The human-rights movements that developed helped to fuel the general feeling of revulsion at the excesses of the generals. It is worth noting that, the candidate who won the elections was the one who took the strongest line on the human rights issue and, for the first time in Latin America, generals have been tried for their misdeeds when in power. All this suggests that a formidable and influential human-rights movement has been at work.

FURTHER READING

Booth, D., Sorj, B. (1983) *Military reformism and social classes. The Peruvian experience 1968–80.* Macmillan, London
Bulletin of Latin American Research 1985 vol. 4 no. 2
Latin America Bureau 1982 *Brazil state and struggle.* Latin American Bureau, London
Malloy, J. (ed) (1977) *Authoritarianism and corporatism in Latin America.* University of Pittsburgh Press, London
Ó'Maoláin, C. (1985) *Latin American political movements.* Longman, Harlow
Philip, G. (1985) *The military in South American politics.* Croom Helm, Beckenham, Kent

Chapter
9

Conclusion

Contrary to much popular imagery, Latin America is a dynamic continent, where considerable social and economic change is taking place. This book has examined how far these changes represent development for Latin American society. The emphasis has been on social aspects, rather than economic indicators, in an attempt to examine what benefits the people of Latin America have gained from recent changes.

BROAD TRENDS

Although Latin America has been experiencing a variety of changes across the region, certain broad themes emerge from these processes. On the one hand, there is an increasing integration of society, as groups, such as Indian communities, which were peripherally located, become more involved with the market economy and the spread of mass media incorporates a wider range of people into a universal value-system. On the other hand, processes of change have brought about greater differentiation and produced a more complex social structure than existed prior to this century. This differentiation can be seen at all levels and in various distinct areas. It is a significant indicator that development theory now offers no orthodox global theory which can be widely applied. Instead, theory has become related to specific issues.

Differentiation has been documented in this book in a number of ways. In economic terms there is a widening gap between the newly industrialising countries and the poorer republics of the region. In the countryside, the traditional forms of labour have given way to increasing discrepancies in the size of smallholdings, a variety of forms of semi-proletarianisation and permanent agricultural labour, ranging from work for agribusiness to employment with well-to-do peasantry. Ethnic groups have become internally differentiated by growing class affiliation. In the urban environment, the expansion of the informal sector has meant a rise in the forms of livelihood which involve varying degrees of irregularity and different types of links with the modern economy. In class terms, this has meant a more complex class structure, with the growth of the informal proletariat and informal petty bourgeoisie, but it has also brought about increasing income concentration.

Economic growth has taken place in the region, sometimes at very rapid rates. Statistics reveal distinct levels of economic growth for the 1960s and 1970s although, due to the economic crises linked to the debt problem, figures for the early 1980s are negative for many countries in the region, but recovering by 1984 (see Appendix). The very impressive rates of growth, in some countries in particular, reveal in some areas levels of economic development which are similar to those of the industrialised world.

This has resulted in increased wealth for a minority of the population and an expanded middle class, with greater purchasing power, whose aspirations and role models are based on the middle class of the industrialised countries. There have also been improvements in some areas, such as nutritional levels (Chapter 5) and the quality of life as expressed by physical indices (Chapter 7) which affect a majority of the population.

There has clearly been a shift from feudal to capitalist institutions, which can most clearly be seen in the agrarian structure, with the reduction of the number of *haciendas*. Agrarian reform has provided a more equitable distribution of land-holding in some areas.

But the deepening of capitalism has also brought about the trend of social and economic differentiation. In many of the situations described in this book, a small minority have benefited, while the majority have suffered, thus increasing the difference in the levels of participation and widening even further the gap between the very rich and the very poor. Inequality, demonstrated by income distribution figures and class structure in Chapter 7, is softened, but also supported by the system of personalistic social relations described in Chapter 4. The rural and urban poverty that this inequality implies can be seen in Chapters 5 and 6.

Linked to this is the trend towards more informal and, therefore, less secure forms of employment. In the countryside, semi-proletarianisation is on the increase and indeed a greater number of different types of semi-proletarianisation are appearing. In the Latin American towns, the informal sector has expanded in all countries. This means a flexible supply of labour for managers, but greater insecurity and low wages for workers. The insecurity lies in the lack of regular guaranteed work, the absence of benefits in the case of sickness and the mobility that may be necessary to move from job to job, which entails the disruption of supportive networks for the whole family.

The problems of underdevelopment have not been passively accepted by Latin American populations, but have frequently been met by a positive response from very different sectors of society, in the form of social movements. These movements, with their strengths in democracy and involvement of members, have some potential for change, although so far they have been limited in their achievements. Social movements give people a mechanism for protest and a means through which they can organise themselves when faced with a crisis.

It is notable that the Mexican earthquake of 1985 brought forth a very positive popular response, despite the vacillations of government which led to criticisms of inadequacy at the top. It was the popular organisation in four different sectors of Mexico City that made possible the creation of rescue teams, the speedy organisation of temporary shelters for the homeless and the development of programs of mutual assistance between and within the different areas. The scale and seriousness of these groups impressed international bodies to such an extent that UNICEF channelled its campaign of preventative vaccination through a neighbourhood association.

Protest has even been expressed as part of what must symbolise the ultimate in leisure activity, Brazilian carnival. In 1983, one samba school presented a Brazilian-style menu for each region to protest at the lack of foodstuffs and the high price of beans. The following year, several groups put the country's troubles to music, producing floats with the themes of hunger, poverty, inflation, economic and social problems and the scarcity of money (LARR 1984).

PROBLEMS OF UNDERDEVELOPMENT

Chapter 1 posed the questions, what kind of economic development is necessary to enable welfare goals to be achieved and can industrial growth be achieved without inequality? In order to attempt answers, the development process needs to be examined to see why and how problems have arisen.

One of the major sources of difficulty is that industrial growth has taken place on the basis of foreign capital. The great value of dependency theory lies in the way in which it pointed a finger at foreign capital and exposed the way that the centre had developed at the expense of the periphery. Others have argued, however, that industrialisation is necessary for development, capital is necessary for industrialisation and, therefore, foreign or multinational capital is the motor force of development. The linking of investment from outside Latin America with economic growth and the lack of welfare achievements, can be seen in different areas.

One answer for why economic growth has not reduced inequalities is because of the ways that foreign capital, whether in the form of multinationals or loans, has contributed to polarisation. Firstly, while this has produced wealth, it has also brought about concentration (of wealth; income; productive forces; the benefits of development such as education, health facilities, etc.). The levels of capital accumulation and advanced technology that foreign capital makes possible act as a magnet for further investment and for people, at the same time producing the benefits in society. Secondly, much of the profit has gone abroad and now there is the situation of large sums leaving the region to pay debts. Because of these two factors, the beneficiaries of development are few in number. Wealth has not trickled down to the mass of people because the types of employment available are structured towards the maximisation of profit and, therefore, where labour is plentiful, they represent cheap forms of labour, which offer little remuneration. Chapters 5 and 6 showed the ways in which the mass of people in rural and urban areas are limited in their opportunities. The growth of the strong state has only encouraged these processes, as governments have produced policies of development, financed by foreign capital and loans, which promote economic growth with social costs.

Inequalities have not been reduced, also because economic growth has not produced sustainable development. If the level of economic development reached at peak periods could be maintained, those who benefited would be able to consolidate their improvements and turn them into long-lasting achievements, which could be passed on to later generations as an acceptable level of prosperity. Sustainable development also means the growth of a class with sufficient savings and confidence in the economy to provide the local capital that is needed. The lack of sustainable development can frequently be traced to the international context. Examples in this book have demonstrated bursts of real economic development, which could not be sustained, at both micro and macro levels.

At the former level, sectors of the peasantry have at times been able to take advantage of market opportunities in international boom years and lost out in the downward fluctuations of the market. It was the global swings of the coffee market that meant a period of prosperity, only to be followed by poverty, the forced sale of land and migration for the Oaxacan peasantry. The Ecuadorian peasants benefited from the oil boom, in that the demand for food which this generated gave a boost to their production. But the ensuing economic crisis eroded their gains, demonstrating the flimsiness of development based on externally-generated growth. The oil boom and decline in general in Latin America has had a considerable affect on employment. In the Mexican state of Tabasco, employment opportunities expanded from 1978–81 but, with the subsequent prices promoted by falling oil prices, many lost their jobs and had to migrate or return to subsistence agriculture to survive.

At national level, the Brazilian miracle, financed by multinational and foreign investment, produced very impressive growth rates in the late 1960s and early 1970s. The miracle came to an end because of rising oil prices and Brazil's inability to produce a cheap source of energy and because the repressive structure on which growth was built, was vulnerable to any economic weaknesses. The motor force of change, foreign capital, generated its own problems in the form of massive debts.

This brings us on to another problem in financing development with borrowed capital – debt. The borrowing which countries such as Brazil, Mexico and Argentina relied on to finance the development process, has brought almost as many problems as it sought to dispel. In Mexico, they say 'the devil gave us oil' to depict how the once-thought-of panacea has brought a multiplicity of problems. The changing world economy and increased interest rates have together made the large debts of the Latin American countries virtually unbearable. Latin American countries are managing to pay off some of the debts in stages, but the real burden of this is falling on those who are least able to shoulder it.

PATHS OF DEVELOPMENT

The countries which have produced the highest rates of economic growth, but which have also experienced extremes in terms of social costs, are those characterised by growth from above. They have been governed by authoritarian regimes which have been in a position to impose their model of development. They are also areas where social movements, which epitomise change from below, as they represent attempts to bring about improvements at grass-roots level, have become active, which might suggest a growing impatience with the growth-from-above model. Growth from above has characterised socialist as well as capitalist societies, for Cuba, too, has a strong state and development follows a central plan. Does this mean that the focus of development for those involved should shift to the local level?

Perhaps development policies should be oriented more towards a basic-needs approach and look towards social movements for the identification of these needs, as indeed has already happened in Brazil, as quoted in the São Paulo Cost-of-Living-Movement example. Detailed research into basic needs has been carried out in Ecuador (ISS-PREALC 1983). This has provided a quantity of information about income levels, purchasing power, housing facilities, consumption patterns and other aspects of everyday requirements. More research of this kind is needed in Latin America, where there is still a surprising lack of empirical data on aspects of living standards and nutritional levels, although these are so fundamental to any understanding of development. It has been argued that, in Asia and Africa, development should be focused on the rural areas rather than encouraging industrialisation and urbanisation, and the emphasis placed on local communities as the unit of development. For much of Latin America it would not be feasible to try such an approach and reverse the urbanisation process. But it might be possible to link the growth-from-below approach to social movements, whether in urban or rural areas.

Alternatively, since industrialisation financed by foreign capital has not only created problems of underdevelopment, but also contributed to economic growth, the wealth produced by that growth could be used to greater mass advantage by radical, thorough and wide-ranging policies of redistribution. Gwynne has argued that the way forward for Latin America is further industrialisation, one of his points being that it is the most industrialised republics of the region that have best been able to confront the debt crisis (Gwynne 1985). It is precisely these countries, however, Mexico and Brazil where, as pointed out earlier, the poor have made the greatest sacrifices in order that repayments can be made. It is clear that not only have the poor not benefited from industrialisation, they are the ones paying the highest price to right the national level-problems that have arisen. If wealth does not automatically filter through to the rest of society, fundamental governmental redistribution programs need to be implemented.

The radical and innovative redistribution programmes which have been tried, such as the Allende reforms in Chile and, at a different level, Mexico's attempt to utilise oil revenues through SAM, have often appeared attractive in theory, but failed for a number of reasons. Redistribution programs of this kind could be supported and aided by government policies of encouraging, through financial incentives, the growth of local-level, labour-intensive industries based on indigenous capital. If this were initiated on a small scale, sufficient investment might be found. The emphasis on labour-intensive activities would make a contribution towards easing the proliferation of irregular forms of labour.

Whatever paths of development Latin American countries follow, will depend on the political colour of their governments, international forces and the particular configuration of local, social and economic characteristics. One thing that is certain is that more research is wanted in the form of local-level studies of the day-to-day requirements of the needy.

Appendix

COUNTRY PROFILES

Argentina

Area (km^2)		2 776 656
Population: Total 1984 (83.3 per cent urban)		30 097 000
Annual growth rate 1970–84		1.7
Birth rate (1984)		24.6
General mortality (1984)		8.7
Infant mortality (1984)		36.0
Life expectancy (1984)		69.7
Literacy (1982)		94.2

Percentage of households in   8.0
conditions of poverty (1970)

Labour force (1980)   (Percentages)
Labour force in Agriculture   15.2

Women in total labour force   25.6

	1982	1983	1984
Real production		(Growth rates)	
Total GDP (market prices)	−5.1	2.9	2.0

	1981	1982	1983
External public debt outstanding, including the undisbursed portion (millions of dollars)	14,427	18,303	26,449

Bolivia			

Area (km^2)			1 098 581
Total population 1984 (thousands of inhabitants)			6 253
(Percentage of urban population 47.1; rural 52.9)			
Annual rate of growth of total population			2.7
Average 1970–84 (percentage)			
Birth rate per 1,000 inhabitants (1984)			43.2
Mortality per 1,000 inhabitants (1984)			15.4
Infant mortality per 1,000 live births (1982)			124.4
Years of life expectancy at birth (1984)			54.0
Percentage of literacy (1980)			67.7
Labour force (1980)			(Percentages)
Labour force in Agriculture			56.1
Women in total labour force			20.4
	1982	1983	1984
Real production		(Growth rates)	
Total GDP (market prices)	−8.7	−7.6	−3.0
	1981	1982	1983
External public debt outstanding, including the undisbursed portion (millions of dollars)	3,139	3,158	3,849

Brazil

Area (km^2)		8 511 965	
Population: Total 1984 (73.1 per cent urban)		131 185 000	
Annual growth rate 1970–84		2.5	
Birth rate (1980)		23.3	
General mortality (1980)		6.8	
Infant mortality (1980)		68.1	
Life expectancy (1976)		60.5	
Literacy (1980)		68.7	
Percentage of households in conditions of poverty (1972)		49.0	

Labour force (1980)	(Percentages)		
Labour force in Agriculture	29.9		
Women in total labour force	21.6		

	1982	1983	1984
Real production	(Growth rates)		
Total GDP (market prices)	0.9	−3.2	4.5

	1981	1982	1983
External public debt outstanding, including the undisbursed portion (millions of dollars)	57,476	64,233	71,985

Chile

Area (km^2)		756 629		
Population: Total 1984 (83.1 per cent urban)		11 878 000		
Annual growth rate 1970–84		1.7		
Birth rate (1983)		22.3		
General mortalit (1983)		6.4		
Infant mortality (1983)		21.9		
Life expectancy (1980–85)		67.0		
Literacy (1983)		95.6		

Percentage of households in conditions of poverty (1968)   17.0

Labour force	(Percentages)
Labour force in Agriculture (1983)	14.3
Women in total labour force (1980)	23.4

	1982	1983	1984
Real production		(Growth rates)	
Total GDP (market prices)	−14.3	−0.6	5.9

	1981	1982	1983
External public debt outstanding, including the undisbursed portion (millions of dollars)	5,017	5,957	7,862

Latin American Society

Colombia

Area (km^2)		1 138 338	

Population:	Total 1984 (74.7 per cent urban)		28 473 000
	Annual growth rate 1970–84		2.1
	Birth rate (1981)		30.0
	General mortality (1981)		5.9
	Infant mortality (1981)		45.7
	Life expectancy (1981)		62.5
	Literacy (1981)		81.0

Percentage of households in conditions of poverty (1972)	45.0

Labour force (1980)	(Percentages)
Labour force in Agriculture	34.5
Women in total labour force	24.6

	1982	1983	1984
Real production		(Growth rates)	
Total GDP (market prices)	0.9	1.0	3.0

	1981	1982	1983
External public debt outstanding, including the undisbursed portion (millions of dollars)	8,018	9,962	10,799

Costa Rica

Area (km^2)	50 000
Total population 1984 (thousands of inhabitants)	2 460
(Percentage of urban population 48.7; rural 51.3)	
Annual rate of growth of total population	2.6
Average 1970–84 (percentage)	
Birth rate per 1,000 inhabitants (1984)	30.8
Mortality per 1,000 inhabitants (1984)	3.9
Infant mortality per 1,000 live births (1984)	18.8
Years of life expectancy at birth (1980–85)	73.1
Percentage of literacy (1981)	89.8
Percentage of households in conditions of poverty (1971)	24.0
Labour force (1983)	(Percentages)
Labour force in Agriculture	27.7
Women in total labour force	25.1

	1982	1983	1984
Real production		(Growth rates)	
Total GDP (market prices)	−7.3	2.3	6.6

	1981	1982	1983
External public debt outstanding, including the undisbursed portion (millions of dollars)	3,104	3,372	4,153

Dominican Republic

Area (km^2)	48 442
Total population 1984 (thousands of inhabitants)	6 102
(Percentage of urban population 52.0; rural 48.0)	
Annual rate of growth of total population	2.5
Average 1970–84 (percentage)	
Birth rate per 1,000 inhabitants (1984)	34.7
Mortality per 1,000 inhabitants (1984)	4.6
Infant mortality per 1,000 live births (1984)	31.0
Years of life expectancy at birth (1980–85)	62.6
Percentage of literacy (1981)	69.4

Labour force (1980)	(Percentages)
Labour force in Agriculture	41.3
Women in total labour force	11.9

	1982	1983	1984
Real production		(Growth rates)	
Total GDP (market prices)	1.7	4.0	0.6

	1981	1982	1983
External public debt outstanding, including the undisbursed portion (millions of dollars)	2,067	2,400	2,983

Ecuador

Area (km²)	270 670
Total population 1984 (thousands of inhabitants)	9 115
(Percentage of urban population 50.7; rural 49.3)	
Annual rate of growth of total population Average 1970–84 (percentage)	3.1
Birth rate per 1,000 inhabitants (1984)	36.7
Mortality per 1,000 inhabitants (1984)	8.0
Infant mortality per 1,000 live births (1984)	68.4
Years of life expectancy at birth (1982)	64.3
Percentage of literacy (1982)	85.6

	(Percentages)
Labour force (1980)	
Labour force in Agriculture	51.6
Women in total labour force	20.1

	1982	1983	1984
		(Growth rate)	
Real Production			
Total GDP (market prices)	1.8	−3.3	3.0

	1981	1982	1983
External public debt outstanding, including the undisbursed portion (millions of dollars)	5,100	4,932	7,347

El Salvador

Area (km^2)	20 935
Total population 1984 (thousands of inhabitants) (Percentage of urban population 40.8; rural 59.2)	4 756
Annual rate of growth of total population Average 1970–84 (percentage)	2.2
Birth rate per 1,000 inhabitants (1983)	30.5
Mortality per 1,000 inhabitants (1983)	6.9
Infant mortality per 1,000 live births (1983)	43.8
Years of life expectancy at birth (1983)	64.8
Percentage of literacy (1983)	57.1
Labour force (1980)	(Percentages)
Labour force in Agriculture	47.2
Women in total labour force	28.8

	1982	1983	1984
Real production		(Growth rates)	
Total GDP (market prices)	−5.6	−0.7	1.5

	1981	1982	1983
External public debt outstanding, including the undisbursed portion (millions of dollars)	1,050	1,357	1,414

Guatemala

Area (km^2)	108 889
Total population 1984 (thousands of inhabitants)	7 740
(Percentage of urban population 32.7; rural 67.8)	
Annual rate of growth of total population	2.9
Average 1970–84 (percentage)	
Birth rate per 1,000 inhabitants (1984)	42.0
Mortality per 1,000 inhabitants (1984)	10.3
Infant mortality per 1,000 live births (1984)	64.4
Years of life expectancy at birth (1984)	59.0
Percentage of literacy (1984)	56.4

	(Percentages)
Labour force (1980)	
Labour force in Agriculture	55.4
Women in total labour force	13.5

	1982	1983	1984
Real production		(Growth rates)	
Total GDP (market prices)	−3.6	−2.7	0.1

	1981	1982	1983
External public debt outstanding, including the undisbursed portion (millions of dollars)	1,380	1,548	1,834

Haiti	
Area (km^2)	27 750
Total population 1984 (thousands of inhabitants)	5 358
(Percentage of urban population 27.6; rural 72.4)	
Annual rate of growth of total population	1.7
Average 1970–84 (percentage)	
Birth rate per 1,000 inhabitants (1980–85)	35.6
Mortality per 1,000 inhabitants (1980–85)	13.0
Infant mortality per 1,000 live births (1980–85)	117.7
Years of life expectancy at birth (1980–85)	54.5
Percentage of literacy (1982)	36.9

Labour force	(Percentages)		
Labour force in Agriculture (1982)	65.4		
Women in total labour force (1980)	47.2		

	1982	1983	1984
Real production	(Growth rates)		
Total GDP (market prices)	−3.9	0.9	1.8

	1981	1982	1983
External public debt outstanding, including the undisbursed portion (millions of dollars)	499	531	612

Honduras

Area (km^2)	112 088
Total population 1984 (thousands of inhabitants) (Percentage of urban population 39.0; rural 61.0)	4 232
Annual rate of growth of total population Average 1970–84 (percentage)	3.2
Birth rate per 1,000 inhabitants (1983)	36.7
Mortality per 1,000 inhabitants (1983)	4.7
Infant mortality per 1,000 live births (1983)	17.5
Years of life expectancy at birth (1980–85)	59.9
Percentage of literacy (1982)	59.5
Percentage of households in conditions of poverty (1967)	65.0

Labour force (1982)	(Percentages)
Labour force in Agriculture	54.1
Women in total labour force	13.3

	1982	1983	1984
Real production	(Growth rates)		
Total GDP (market prices)	−1.8	−0.5	2.8

	1981	1982	1983
External public debt outstanding, including the undisbursed portion (millions of dollars)	1,969	2,032	2,314

Mexico

Area (km^2)		1 967 183		

Population:	Total 1984 (61.1 per cent urban)	77 043 000		
	Annual growth rate 1970–84	3.0		
	Birth rate (1980–85)	33.9		
	General mortality (1980–85)	7.1		
	Infant mortality (1980–85)	53.0		
	Life expectancy (1980–85)	65.7		
	Literacy (1983)	87.9		

Percentage of households in conditions of poverty (1967)		34.0		

Labour force (1980)		(Percentages)		
Labour force in Agriculture		37.6		

Women in total labour force		18.5		

	1982	1983	1984	
Real production		(Growth rates)		
Total GDP (market prices)	−0.5	−5.3	3.5	

	1981	1982	1983
External public debt outstanding, including the undisbursed portion (millions of dollars)	46,812	55,552	72,465

Nicaragua

Area (km^2)	139 000
Total population 1984 (thousands of inhabitants)	3 163
(Percentage of urban population 56.6; rural 43.4)	
Annual rate of growth of total population	3.6
Average 1970–84 (percentage)	
Birth rate per 1,000 inhabitants (1984)	44.2
Mortality per 1,000 inhabitants (1984)	9.7
Infant mortality per 1,000 live births (1984)	76.4
Years of life expectancy at birth (1980–85)	59.8
Percentage of literacy (1981)	87.9
Labour force (1980)	(Percentages)
Labour force in Agriculture	41.8
Women in total labour force	21.3

	1982	1983	1984
Real production		(Growth rates)	
Total GDP (market prices)	−1.2	4.7	−1.4

	1981	1982	1983
External public debt outstanding, including the undisbursed portion (millions of dollars)	2,615	3,164	4,105

Panama

Area (km^2)			77 082
Total population 1984 (thousands of inhabitants)			2 134
(Percentage of urban population 56.0; rural 44.0)			
Annual rate of growth of total population			2.5
Average 1970–84 (percentage)			
Birth rate per 1,000 inhabitants (1983)			26.4
Mortality per 1,000 inhabitants (1983)			4.1
Infant mortality per 1,000 live births (1983)			20.4
Years of life expectancy at birth (1980–85)			71.0
Percentage of literacy (1981)			88.1
Percentage of households in conditions of poverty (1970)			39.0

Labour force (1980)			(Percentages)
Labour force in Agriculture			33.7
Women in total labour force			25.9

	1982	1983	1984
Real production		(Growth rates)	
Total GDP (market prices)	5.5	0.4	−1.2

	1981	1982	1983
External public debt outstanding, including the undisbursed portion (millions of dollars)	3,144	3,403	3,853

Paraguay

Area (km^2)	406 752
Total population 1984 (thousands of inhabitants)	3 576
(Percentage of urban population 43.9; rural 56.1)	
Annual rate of growth of total population	2.6
Average 1970–84 (percentages)	
Birth rate per 1,000 inhabitants (1984)	38.9
Mortality per 1,000 inhabitants (1984)	7.2
Infant mortality per 1,000 live births (1984)	52.9
Years of life expectancy at birth (1984)	68.0
Percentage of literacy (1984)	92.0
Labour force	(Percentages)
Labour force in Agriculture (1982)	43.3
Women in total labour force	22.5

	1982	1983	1984
Real production		(Growth rates)	
Total GDP (market prices)	−1.0	−3.0	2.9

	1981	1982	1983
External public debt outstanding, including the undisbursed portion (millions of dollars)	1,527	1,904	1,988

Peru				
Area (km^2)		1 280 219		
Population:	Total 1984 (66.6 per cent urban)	19 198 000		
	Annual growth rate 1970–84	2.6		
	Birth rate (1984)	36.4		
	General mortality (1984)	10.3		
	Infant mortality (1984)	94.9		
	Life expectancy (1984)	59.6		
	Literacy (1984)	84.5		

Percentage of households in conditions of poverty (1972) 50.0

Labour force (1980) (Percentages)
Labour force in Agriculture 40.0

Women in total labour force 21.9

	1982	1983	1984
Real production		(Growth rates)	
Total GDP (market prices)	0.9	−11.8	3.5

	1981	1982	1983
External public debt outstanding, including the undisbursed portion (millions of dollars)	8,480	9,960	11,022

Uruguay	
Area (km^2)	176 215
Total population 1984 (thousands of inhabitants) (Percentage of urban population 85.2; rural 14.8)	2 990
Annual rate of growth of total population Average 1970–84 (percentage)	0.6
Birth rate per 1,000 inhabitants (1983)	19.0
Mortality per 1,000 inhabitants (1983)	8.7
Infant mortality per 1,000 live births (1983)	32.0
Years of life expectancy at birth (1983)	70.3
Percentage of literacy (1983)	96.3
Labour force	(Percentages)
Labour force in Agriculture (1982)	17.0
Women in total labour force (1980)	28.5

	1982	1983	1984
Real production		(Growth rates)	
Total GDP (market prices)	0.7	−4.8	−1.7

	1981	1982	1983
External public debt outstanding, including the undisbursed portion (millions of dollars)	1,932	2,256	3,077

Venezuela

Area (km^2)	898 805

Population:	Total 1984 (85.2 per cent urban)	16 857 000
	Annual growth rate 1970–84	3.0
	Birth rate (1980)	35.4
	General mortality (1981)	5.6
	Infant mortality (1981)	35.2
	Life expectancy (1980)	68.6
	Literacy (1982)	89.0

Percentage of households in conditions of poverty (1971)	25.0

Labour force	(Percentages)
Labour force in Agriculture (1983)	15.1
Women in total labour force (1980)	22.6

	1982	1983	1984
Real production	(Growth rates)		
Total GDP (market prices)	9.7	−4.8	−1.7

	1981	1982	1983
External public debt outstanding, including the undisbursed portion (millions of dollars)	11,535	12,957	13,516

Source: Data are taken from: *Economic and Social Progress in Latin America. External Debt: Crisis and Adjustment* Inter-American Development Bank 1985 Report; *World Tables*: Social Indicators and *Statistical Yearbook for Latin America* 1984 edition, ECLA.

Glossary

Boias-frías	rural workers who live in urban areas and have to take their food with them each day and eat it cold.
Cacique	rural boss.
Callampas	Chilean shanty towns.
Coca	Coca, a plant whose leaves when chewed act as a mild stimulant.
Colono	resident estate worker allotted a piece of land for subsistence farming.
Compadrazgo	ritual sponsorship of children by godparents, instituting a set of permanent, personal ties between parents, children and godparents.
Compadres	parents and godparents, who have a special relationship.
Ejido	unit of agrarian reform in Mexico.
Encomienda	a mechanism introduced by the Spaniards, which flourished in the 16th and 17th centuries, to control and extract tribute and labour services from the indigenous population.
Favela	Brazilian shanty town.
Favelado	inhabitant of the favelas.
Fazenda	hacienda in Brazil.
Hacienda	large estate often producing for export, which represents a social as well as an economic system.

Inquilinos	service tenants in Chile.
Ladino	mestizo in Middle America.
Latifundia	large estate.
Machismo	cult of male dominance, derived from the word macho, meaning male.
Macumba	Brazilian spirit possession cult.
Maquiladoras	American-owned assembly plants in Mexico near the US border.
Marianismo	cult of female subordination in general, but superiority in spiritual matters.
Mestizo	someone of mixed European and Indian stock.
Mulatto	someone of mixed negro and European stock.
Palanca	intermediary, often between patron and client (literally a lever).
Panelinha	informal group made up of people linked by personal ties, but in different occupations.
Tortilla	Mexican maize pancake.
Umbanda	Brazilian spirit possession cult.
Villas miserias	Argentine shanty town.
Voladores	flying men in Mexico, who perform a ritual, whereby tied by a strap to a central pole, they whirl round.

Bibliography

Allardt, E., Rokkan, S. (eds) (1970) *Mass politics: studies in political sociology*. Free Press, New York and London

Archetti, E., Cammack P., Roberts B (1986) *Sociology of 'developing societies': Latin America*. Macmillan, London

Armstrong, W., McGee, T. (1985) *Theatres of accumulation: studies in Asian and Latin American urbanization*. Methuen, London and New York

Bailey, F. (1971) The peasant view of the bad life. In **Shanin, T.** (ed) *Peasants and peasant society*. Penguin, Harmondsworth

Banton, M. (1967) *Race Relations*. Tavistock, London

Baran, P. (1957) *The political economy of growth*. Monthly Review Press, New York

Barke, M., O'Hare, G. (1985) *The Third World: conceptual frameworks in Geography*. Oliver and Boyd, Edinburgh

Barrios de Chungara, D., Viezzar, M. (1978) *Let me speak! Testimony of Domitila, a woman of the Bolivian mines* (translated from Spanish by Ortiz, V.). Monthly Review Press, New York and London

Baster, N. (ed) (1972) *Measuring Development: the role and adequacy of development indicators*. Frank Cass, London

Bauer, P. (1981) *Equality, the Third World and economic delusion*. Weidenfeld and Nicolson, London

Beals, R. (1969) Indian-mestizo-white relations in Spanish

America. In **Tumin, M.** (ed) *Comparative perspectives on race relations.* Little, Brown and Co, Boston

Becker, D. (1983) *The new bourgeoisie and the limits of dependency: mining, class and power in 'revolutionary' Peru.* Princeton University Press, Princeton

Binder, L. (1986) The natural history of development theory, *Comparative Study of Society and History* Vol 28 No 1

Birkbeck, C. (1979) Garbage, industry and the 'vultures' of Cali, Colombia. In **Bromley, R** and **Gerry, C.** (eds) *Casual work and poverty in Third World cities.* John Wiley, Chichester

Bonilla, F. (1970) Rio's favelas: the rural slum within the city. In **Mangin, W.** (ed) *Peasants in cities: readings in the anthropology of urbanization.* Houghton Mifflin Co, Boston

Booth, D. (1976) Cuba, color and the revolution. *Science and Society* Vol XL No 2

Booth, D. (1985) Marxism and development sociology: interpreting the impasse, *World Development* Vol 13 No 7

Booth, D., Sorj, B. (1983) *Military reformism and social classes: the Peruvian experience 1968–80.* Macmillan, London

Booth, C. (1899) *Life and labour of the people in London,* Vol 1. Williams and Norgate, London

Bossen, L. (1984) *The redivision of labor: women and economic choice in four Guatemalan communities.* State University of New York Press, Albany

Bossert, T. (1980) The agrarian reform and peasant political consciousness in Chile, *Latin American Perspectives* Issue 27 vol 7 No 4

Bourricaud, F. (1967) *Power and society in contemporary Peru* (translated from French by Stevenson P). Faber and Faber, London

Brain, R. (1972) *Into the primitive environment: survival on the edge of our civilization.* George Philip and Son, London

Brandt, W. (1980) *North-South: a programme for survival.* Pan Books, London

Bromley, R., Gerry, C., (eds) (1979) *Casual work and poverty in Third World cities.* John Wiley, Chichester

Bronstein, A. (1982) *The triple struggle: Latin American peasant women.* WOW Campaigns Ltd. London

Brookfield, H. (1975) *Interdependent development: perspectives on development.* Methuen, London

Burbach, R., Flynn, P. (1980) *Agribusiness in the Americas.* Monthly Review Press, New York and London

Burgess, R. (1978) Petty commodity housing or dweller control? A critique of John Turner's views on housing policy, *World Development* Vol 6 No 9/10

Cammack, P. (1985) Democratisation: a review of the issues, *Bulletin of Latin American Research* Vol 4 No 2

Cancian, F. (1965) *Economics and prestige in a Maya community: the religious cargo system in Zinacantan.* Stanford University Press, Stanford, California

Cardoso, F. (1972) Dependency and development in Latin America. *New Left Review* 74 July/August

Cardoso, F. (1973) Associated-dependent development: theoretical and practical implications. In **Stepan, A.** (ed) *Authoritarian Brazil: origins, policies and future.* Yale University Press, New Haven

Cardoso, F., Faletto, E. (1979) *Dependency and development in Latin America* (translated from Spanish by Mattingly M). University of California Press, London

Castells, M. (1982) Squatters and politics in Latin America: a comparative analysis of urban social movements in Chile, Peru and Mexico. In **Safa, H.** (ed) *Towards a political economy of urbanization in Third World countries.* Oxford University Press, Delhi

Castillo, L., Lehmann, D. (1982) Chile's three agrarian reforms: the inheritors, *Bulletin of Latin American Research* Vol 1 No 2

CEPAL Review (1984) No 24

Chaney, E. (1979) *Supermadre: women in politics in Latin America.* University of Texas Press for the Institute of Latin American Studies, Austin and London

Chapman, R. (1975) The first ten years. In **Goodsell J** (ed) *Fidel Castro's personal revolution in Cuba: 1959–1973.* Alfred Knopf, New York

Chilcote, R., Edelstein, J. (1974) *Latin America: the struggle with dependency and beyond.* John Wiley, New York

Chinchilla, N. (1977) Industrialization, monopoly capitalism and women's work in Guatemala. In **The Wellesley Editorial Committee** (ed) *Women and national development: the complexities of change.* The University of Chicago Press, Chicago and London

Clayton, E. (1983) *Agriculture, poverty and freedom in developing countries.* Macmillan, London and Basingstoke

Cockroft, J. (1983) *Mexico: class formation, capital accumulation and the state.* Monthly Review Press, New York

Collier, D. (1975) Squatter settlements and policy innovation in Peru. In **Lowenthal, A.** (ed) *The Peruvian experiment: community and change under military rule.* Princeton University Press, Princeton and London

Colman, D., Nixon, F. (1978) *Economics of change in less developed countries.* Allan Publishers, Oxford

Commander, S., Peek, P. (1986) Oil exports, agrarian change and the rural labor process: the Ecuadorian Sierra in the 1970s, *World Development* Vol 14 No 1

Coraggio, J. (1985) Social movements and revolution: the case of Nicaragua. In **Slater, D.** (ed) *New social movements and the state in Latin America*. Latin American Studies 29, CEDLA, Amsterdam

Corkill, D. (1985) Democratic politics in Ecuador, 1979–1984, *Bulletin of Latin American Research* Vol 4 No 2

Crabtree, J. (1985) Peru: from Belaunde to Alan Garcia, *Bulletin of Latin American Research* Vol 4 No 2

Cubitt, D., Cubitt, T. (1980) National minorities, cultural identity and class differentiation in Latin America: some methodological notes, *Journal of Area Studies* No 1 Spring

Cubitt, T. (1972) *The role of kinship and friendship links among Chilean industrialists*. Paper presented to the kinship and social networks seminar at the Institute of Latin American Studies, June.

Cubitt, T. (1983) Women in the Latin American labour force, *Journal of Area Studies* 7

Cubitt, V. (1979) *Supplement to the urban poverty datum line in Rhodesia: a study of the minimum consumption needs of families*. Faculty of Social Studies, University of Rhodesia, Salisbury

Cubitt, V., Riddell, R. (1974) *The Urban poverty datum line in Rhodesia: a study of the minimum consumption needs of families*. Faculty of Social Studies, University of Rhodesia, Salisbury

Curtis, R. (1983) *Two agrarian reforms: a case study of Nicaragua*. Dissertation submitted for the BA Honours degree in Latin American Studies, Portsmouth Polytechnic

Davies, R. (1979) Informal sector or subordinate mode of production? A model. In **Bromley, R., Gerry, C.** (eds) *Casual work and poverty in Third World cities*. John Wiley, Chichester

de Janvry, A. (1981) *The agrarian question and reformism in Latin America*. The Johns Hopkins University Press, Baltimore, London

de Janvry, A., Ground, L. (1978) Types and consequences of land reform in Latin America, *Latin American Perspectives* Issue 19 Vol 5

Dos Santos, T. (1973) The crisis of development theory and the problem of dependence in Latin America. In **Bernstein, H.** (ed) *Underdevelopment and development*. Penguin, Harmondsworth

Durkheim, E. (1915) *The elementary forms of the religious life* (translated from the French by Swain J). Allen and Unwin, London

Eckstein, S. (1977) *The poverty of revolution: the state and the urban poor in Mexico.* Princeton University Press, Princeton

ECLA (1975) *Participation of women in development in Latin America.* United Nations World Conference of the International Women's Year E Conf. 66/BP/8/Add 1

ECLA (1985) *Statistical Yearbook for 1984.* UN, Santiago de Chile

ECLAC/FAO (1985) The agriculture of Latin America: changes, trends and outlines of strategy. *CEPAL Review* 27

Elkins, S. (1976) *Slavery: a problem in American institutional and intellectual life.* The University of Chicago Press, Chicago, London

Evans, P. (1979) *Dependent development: the alliance of multinational, state and local capital in Brazil.* Princeton University Press, Princeton

Felix, D. (1983) Income distribution and the quality of life in Latin America: Patterns, trends and policy implications, *Latin American Research Review* 18 No 2

Fernandes, F. (1974) A counter-ideology of racial unmasking. In **Heath, D.** (ed) *Contemporary cultures and societies of Latin America* 2nd edn. Random House, New York

Figueroa, M. (1985) Rural development and urban food programming. *CEPAL Review* 25

Filet-Abreu de Souza, J. (1980) Paid domestic service in Brazil. *Latin American Perspectives* 7 No 1

Filgueira, C. (1983) To educate or not to educate: is that the question? *CEPAL Review* 21

FitzGerald, E. (1976) *The state and economic development: Peru since 1968.* Cambridge University Press, Cambridge

Foster, G. (1967) *Tzintzuntzan: Mexican peasants in a changing world.* Little, Brown and Co. Boston

Foster-Carter, A. (1985) *The Sociology of development.* Causeway Press, Ormskirk

Frank, A. (1967) *Capitalism and underdevelopment in Latin America: historical studies of Chile and Brasil.* Monthly Review Press, New York

Frank, A. (1969) Sociology of development and underdevelopment of sociology. In **Frank, A.** *Latin America: underdevelopment or revolution.* Monthly Review Press, New York

Freire, P. (1968) *Educacão e Conscientizacão.* Cuaderno No 25, CIDOC, Cuernavaca, Mexico

Freyre, G. (1946) *The master and the slaves (Casa-Grande and Senzala):a study in the development of Brazilian civilization* (translated from the Portuguese by Putnam S.). Alfred Knopf, New York

Galjart, G. (1964) Class and 'following' in rural Brazil. *America Latina* 7 No 3

Garcia, N. (1982) Growing absorption with persistent underemployment. *CEPAL Review* 18

Geofile 1982 No 1

George, S. (1976) *How the other half dies: the real reasons for world hunger.* Penguin, Harmondsworth

Germani, G. (1972) Stages of modernization in Latin America. In Halper, S., Sterling, J. (eds) *Latin America: the dynamics of social change.* Allison and Busby, London

Gerry, C. (1979) Small-scale manufacturing and repairs in Dakar: a survey of market relations within the urban economy. In Bromley, R., Gerry, C. (eds) *Casual work and poverty in Third World cities.* Wiley, Chichester

Gilbert, A. (1974) *Latin American development: a geographical perspective.* Penguin, Harmondsworth

Gilbert, A., Gugler, J. (1982) *Cities: Poverty and Development. Urbanization in the Third World.* Oxford University Press, Oxford

Gilbert, A., Ward, P (1985) *Housing, the state and the poor.* Cambridge University Press, Cambridge

Gillespie, C. (1985) Uruguay's return to democracy, *Bulletin of Latin American Research* Vol 4 No 2

Goldthorpe, J. (1975) *The sociology of the Third World: disparity and involvement.* Cambridge University Press, Cambridge

Gonzalez-Casanova, P. (1968) Dynamics of the class structure. In Kahl, J. (ed) *Comparative perspectives on stratification, Mexico, Great Britain, Japan.* Little, Brown and Co. Boston

Goodman, D., Redclift, M. (1981) *From peasant to proletarian: capitalist development and agrarian transitions.* Basil Blackwell, Oxford

Griffin, K. (1981) Economic development in a changing world, *World Development* Vol 9 No 3

Gracierena, J., Franco, R. (1978) Social formations and power structures in Latin America, *Current Sociology* Vol 26 No 1

Grugel, J. (1986) *Some reflections on 'successful' authoritarianism: the Chilean phenomena.* Paper presented to the annual conference of the Society for Latin American Studies, Liverpool

Gwynne, R. (1985) *Industrialization and urbanization in Latin America.* Croom Helm, London

Hamilton, N. (1982) *The limits of state autonomy: post-revolutionary Mexico.* Princeton University Press, Princeton

Harris, M. (1971) *Town and country in Brazil.* W Norton and Co. New York

Hart, K. (1973) Informal income opportunites and urban

employment in Ghana. *Journal of Modern African Studies* Vol 11

Havens, A., Lastria-Cornhiel, S., Otero, G. (1983) Class struggle and the agrarian reform process. In **Booth, D., Sorj, B.** (eds) *Military reformism and social classes: the Peruvian experience 1968–80.* Macmillan, London

Hellman, J. (1986) Migration and urbanization. *Latin American Research Review* Vol 21 No 1

Henfrey, C. (1984) Between populism and Leninism – the Grenadian experience, *Latin American Perspectives* Issue 42 Vol II No 3

Hewitt de Alcántara, C. (1984) *Anthropological perspectives on rural Mexico.* Routledge and Kegan Paul, London

Hoetink, H. (1973) *Slavery and race relations in the Americas: an inquiry into their nature and nexus.* Harper and Row, New York, London

Hopkins, T., Wallerstein, I. (eds) 1982 *World systems analysis: theory and methodology.* Sage Publications, Beverly Hills, California

Howes, M-C. (1986) *Guatemala: the rise of the military and the growing response of the Catholic church.* Dissertation submitted for the BA Honours degree in Latin American Studies, Portsmouth Polytechnic

Huberman, L., Sweezy, P. (1969) *Socialism in Cuba.* Monthly Review Press, New York

Huizer, G. (1973) *Peasant Rebellion in Latin America.* Penguin, Harmondsworth

Humphrey, J. (1982) *Capitalist control and workers' struggle in the Brazilian auto industry.* Princeton University Press, Princeton

Hurtado, M. (1986) Teeming cities: the challenge of the urban poor. *Latin America and the Caribbean Review.* World of Information, Saffron Waldon

IADB (1985) *Economic and social progress in Latin America, external debt: crisis and adjustment.* Washington

Ianni, O. (1970) Research on race relations in Brazil. In **Morner, M.** (ed) *Race and class in Latin America.* Columbia University Press, New York, London

IBT (1985) *Brazil, Brazil.* London

ILO (1976) *Employment, growth and basic needs: a one world problem.* Geneva

Imaz, J. (1964) *Los que mandan.* Editorial Universitaria, Buenos Aires *International Labour Review* July–August 1961

ISS-PREALC (1983) *Planning for basic needs in Latin America. Urban poverty, access to basic services and public policies: a case study*

of the marginal suburbs of Guayaquil, Ecuador. Working paper
No 7, Quito

Jiménez, M. (1979) *Caracteristicas de la demanda de mano de obra
femenina en sectores seleccionados de la industria de transformación.*
Instituto Nacional de Estudios del Trabajo, Mexico
Johnson, D. (1972) The national and progressive bourgeoisie in
Chile. In **Cockroft, J., Frank, A., Johnson, D.** (eds) *Dependence
and underdevelopment: Latin America's political economy.* Anchor
books, New York
Johnson, J. (1958) *Political change in Latin America: the emergence of
the middle sectors.* Stanford University Press, Stanford
Johnson, J. (1964) *The military and society in Latin America.*
Stanford University Press, Stanford

Kahl, J. (1970) *The measurement of modernism.* University of Texas
Press, Austin, London
Kay, C. (1978) Agrarian reform and the class struggle in Chile.
Latin American Perspectives Issue 18 Vol 5 No 3
King, K. (1979) Petty production in Nairobi: the social context of
skill acquisition and occupational differentiation. In **Bromley, R.,
Gerry, C.** (eds) *Casual work and poverty in Third World cities.*
John Wiley, Chichester
Kitching, G. (1982) *Development and underdevelopment in historical
perspective.* Methuen, London

Laclau, E. (1971) Feudalism and capitalism in Latin America. *New
Left Review* 67
Lall, S. (1975) Is dependence a useful concept in analysing
underdevelopment? *World Development* Vol 3 No 11
Lambert, J. (1967) *Latin America: social structure and political
institutions* (translated from the French by Katel H). University of
California Press, Cambridge University Press, London
Landsberger, H. (ed) (1969) *Latin American peasant movements.*
Cornell University Press, Ithaca, London
LARR (Latin American Regional Report) Jan 1980
LARR Oct 1983
LAWR (Latin American Weekly Report) Aug. 5 1983
Latin American and Caribbean Women's Collective (1980) *Slaves of
Slaves: the challenge of Latin American women.* Zed Press, London
Latin America Bureau 1982 *Brazil: state and struggle.* LAB, London
Latin America Bureau 1985 *Peru: paths to poverty.* LAB, London
Leeds, A. (1974) Brazilian careers and social structure: a case
history and model. In **Heath, D.** (ed) *Contemporary cultures and
societies of Latin America.* Random House, New York

Lehmann, D. (1982) Agrarian structure, migration and the state in Cuba. In **Peek, P.** and **Standing, G.** (eds) *State policies and migration.* Croom Helm, London

Lenin, V. (1970) Imperialism the highest stage of capitalism. In **Lenin, V.** *Selected works* Vol 1. Progress Publishers, Moscow

Lewis, O. (1966) The culture of poverty, *Scientific American* Vol 215 No 4

Lieuwen, E. (1961) *Arms and politics in Latin America.* Praeger, New York

Linz, J. (1970) An authoritarian regime: Spain. In **Allardt, E.** and **Rokkan, S.** (eds) *Mass politics: studies in political sociology.* Free Press, New York and London

Lipman, A. (1969) *The Colombian entrepreneur in Bogota.* University of Miami Press, Coral Gables, Florida

Lipton, M. (1977) *Why poor people stay poor: a study of urban bias in world development.* Temple Smith, London

Little, W. (1986) Paper presented to the annual conference of the Society for Latin American Studies

Lloyd, P. (1979) *Slums of Hope?* Penguin, Harmondsworth

Lloyd, P. (1982) *A Third World proletariat?* Allen and Unwin, London

Lobo, S. (1982) *A house of my own: social organization in the squatter settlements of Lima, Peru.* University of Arizona Press, Tucson

Lomnitz, L. (1977) *Networks and marginality: life in a Mexican shanty town* (translated from the Spanish by **Lomnitz, C.**). Academic Press, New York, London

Lomnitz, L. (1982) Horizontal and vertical relations and the social structure of urban Mexico, *Latin American Research Review* Vol 17 No 2

Long, N. (1977) *An introduction to the sociology of rural development.* Tavistock, London

López Cordovez (1982) Trends and recent changes in the Latin American food and agriculture situation. *CEPAL Review* 16

MacEwen Scott, A. (1979) Who are the self-employed? In **Bromley, R., Gerry, C.** (eds) *Casual work and poverty in Third World cities.* John Wiley, Chichester

Makin, G. (1984) The Argentine process of demilitarization, *Government and Opposition* Vol 19 No 2

Malloy, J. (ed) (1977) *Authoritarianism and corporatism in Latin America.* University of Pittsburgh Press, London: Feffer and Simmons

Mangin, W. (ed) (1970) *Peasants in cities: readings in the anthropology of urbanization.* Houghton Mifflin Co. Boston

Martin, G. (1986) Carrying the can: Bolivian labour and the international tin crisis, *Journal of Area Studies* No 13

Martinez-Alier, J. (1970) The peasantry and the Cuban revolution from the spring of 1959 to the end of 1960. In **Carr, R.** (ed) *Latin American Affairs* St. Antony's Papers no 22. Oxford University Press, Oxford

Mattelart, A. (1978) The nature of communications practice in a dependent society. *Latin American Perspectives* Issue 16 Vol 5 No 1

Miró, C., Rodriguez, D. (1982) Capitalism and population in Latin American agriculture. Recent trends and problems. *CEPAL Review* 16

Mitchell, S. (ed) (1981) *The logic of poverty: the case of the Brazilian Northeast.* Routledge and Kegan Paul, London

Montgomery, T. (1983) The church in the Salvadoran revolution, *Latin American Perspectives* Issue 36 Vol 10 No 1

Morner, M. (1970) *Race and class in Latin America.* Columbia University Press, New York, London

Morse, R. (1971) Trends and issues in Latin American urban research 1965–70, *Latin American Research Review* Vol 6 No 1

Moser, C. (1978) Informal sector or petty commodity production: dualism or dependence in urban development? *World Development* 6

Munck, R. (1985a) The 'modern' military dictatorship in Latin America. The case of Argentina (1976–1982), *Latin American Perspectives* Issue 47 Vol 12 No 4

Munck, R. (1985b) Democratization and demilitarization in Argentina 1982–1985, *Bulletin of Latin American Research* Vol 4 No 2

Muñoz, H. (1980) *From dependency to development: strategies to overcome underdevelopment and inequality.* Westview Press, Boulder, Colorado

Muñoz, H. (1981) The strategic dependency of the centres and the economic importance of the Latin American periphery, *Latin American Research Review* Vol 16 No 3

Murdoch, W. (1982) *The poverty of nations.* Johns Hopkins University Press, Baltimore, London

Nash, J. (1977) Women in development: dependency and exploitation. *Development and Change* Vol 8

Nelson, M. (1945) The negro in Brazil as seen through the chronicles of travellers 1800–1868, *Journal of Negro History* Vol 30

Nun, J. (1967) The middle-class military coup. In **Veliz, C.** (ed) *The politics of conformity in Latin America.* Stanford University Press, Stanford

O'Brien, P. (1975) A critique of Latin American theories of dependency. In **Oxaal, I., Barnett, T., Booth, D.** (eds) *Beyond the sociology of development.* Routledge and Kegan Paul, London

O'Brien, P., Cammack, P. (eds) (1985) *Generals in retreat; the crisis of military rule in Latin America.* Manchester University Press, Manchester

O'Donnell (1973) *Modernization and bureaucratic-authoritarianism: studies in South American politics.* University of California Press, Berkeley

Ó'Maoláin, C. (1985) *Latin American political movements.* Longman, Harlow

Ortega, E. (1982) Peasant agriculture in Latin America: situations and trends, *CEPAL Review* 16

Oxaal, I., Barnett, T., Booth, D. (1975) *Beyond the sociology of development: economy and society in Latin America and Africa.* Routledge and Kegan Paul, London

Palacios, M. (1983) Social property in the political project of the military regime. In **Booth, D., Sorj, B.** (eds) *Military reformism and social classes: the Peruvian experience 1968–80.* Macmillan, London

Palma, G. (1981) Dependency: a formal theory of underdevelopment or a methodology for the analysis of concrete situations of underdevelopment? In **Streeten, P., Jolly, R.** (eds) *Recent issues in world development: a collection of survey articles.* Pergamon Press, Oxford

Parkinson, F. (1984) Latin America, her newly industrialising countries and the new international economic order, *Journal of Latin American Studies* Vol 16 Part 1

Parsons, T. (1949) *The structure of social action.* Free Press of Glencoe, New York

Parsons, T. (1951) *The social system.* Routledge and Kegan Paul, London

Parsons, T., Shils, E. (eds) (1951) *Toward a general theory of action.* Harvard University Press, Harvard

Payne, J. (1965) *Labor and politics in Peru.* Yale University Press, New Haven, London

Pearce, J. (1986) *Promised land: peasant rebellion in Chalatenango, El Salvador.* LAB, London

Pearse, A. (1975) *The Latin American peasant.* Frank Cass, London

Pearse, A. (1980) *Seeds of plenty, Seeds of Want: social and economic implications of the green revolution.* Oxford University Press, Oxford

Peattie, L. (1982) What is to be done with the 'informal sector'? A case study of shoe manufacturers in Colombia. In **Safa, H.** (ed)

Towards a political economy of urbanization in Third World countries.
Oxford University Press, Delhi

Perlman, J. (1976) *The myth of marginality: urban poverty and politics in Rio de Janeiro.* University of California Press, Berkeley

Petras, J. (1969) *Politics and social forces in Chilean development.* University of California Press, Berkeley, London

Petras, J., Rimensnyder, N. (1970) The military and the modernization of Peru. In **Petras, J.** (ed) *Politics and social structure in Latin America.* Monthly Review Press, New York

Petras. J., La Porte, R. (1971) *Cultivating revolution: the United States and agrarian reform in Latin America.* Vintage Books, New York

Petras, J. (1981) Nicaragua: the transition to a new society. *Latin American Perspectives* Issue 29, Vol 8 No 2

Petras, J., Cook, T. (1973) Dependency and the industrial bourgeoisie: attitudes of Argentine executives toward foreign economic investments and US policy. In **Petras, J.** (ed) *Latin America: from dependence to revolution.* Wiley, Chichester

Philip, G. (1985) *The military in South American politics.* Croom Helm, Beckenham

Pitt-Rivers, J. (1977) *The fate of shechem or the politics of sex: essays in the anthropology of the Mediterranean.* Cambridge University Press, Cambridge

Poblete, R. (1970) The church in Latin America: a historical survey. In **Landsberger, H.** (ed) *The church and social change in Latin America.* University of Notre Dame Press, London

Portes, A. (1970) Los grupos urbanos marginados: nuevo intento de explicación, *Aportes* No 18

Portes, A. (1985) Latin American class structures: their composition and change during the last decades, *Latin American Research Review* Vol 20 No 3

Poulantzas, N. (1975) *Political power and social classes.* New Left Books, London

PREALC, 1981 *Dinámica del subempleo en América Latina.* Estudios e informes de la CEPAL series 10, ECLAC, Santiago

Preston, D. (ed) (1980) *Environment, society and rural change in Latin America: the past, present and future in the countryside.* Wiley, Chichester

Quijano, A. (1971) *Nationalism and capitalism in Peru: a study in neo-imperialism.* Monthly Review Press, New York, London

Quijano, A. (1974) The marginal pole of the economy, and the marginalised labour force. *Economy and Society* Vol 3 No 4

Rama, G. (1983) To educate or not to educate: is that the question? *CEPAL Review* 21

Ratinoff, L. (1967) The new urban groups: the middle classes. In **Lipset, S., Solari, A.** (eds) *Elites in Latin America*. Oxford University Press, London

Redclift, M. (1984a) 'Urban bias' and rural poverty: a Latin American perspective, *Journal of Development Studies* Vol 20 No 3

Redclift, M. (1984b) *Development and the environmental crisis: red or green alternatives?* Methuen, London

Redfield, R. (1941) *The folk culture of Yucatan*. University of Chicago Press, Chicago

Redfield, R. (1947) The folk society, *The American Journal of Sociology* 52

Reyna, J., Weinert, R. (eds) (1977) *Authoritarianism in Mexico*. Institute for the Study of Human Issues, Philadelphia

Roberts, B. (1978) *Cities of peasants: the political economy of urbanization in the Third World*. Edward Arnold, London

Rostow, W. (1960) *The stages of economic growth: a non-communist manifesto*. Cambridge University Press, Cambridge

Rothstein, F. (1979) The class basis of patron-client relations. *Latin American Perspectives* Issue 21 Vol 6 No 2

Roxborough, I. (1979) *Theories of underdevelopment*. Macmillan, London

Roxborough, I. (1984) *Unions and politics in Mexico: the case of the automobile industry*. Cambridge University Press, Cambridge

Rubbo, A. (1975) The spread of capitalism in rural Colombia: effects on poor women. In **Reiter, R.** (ed) *Toward an anthropology of women*. Monthly Review Press, New York, London

Ruiz-Pérez, S. (1979) Begging as an occupation in San Cristobal de las Casas, Mexico. In **Bromley, R., Gerry, C.** (eds) *Casual work and poverty in Third World cities*. Wiley, Chichester

Safa, H. (1977) The changing class composition of the female labor force in Latin America, *Latin American Perspectives* Issue 15 Vol 4 No 4

Safa, H. (1982) *Towards a political economy of urbanization in Third World countries*. Oxford University Press, Delhi

Saffioti, H. (1978) *Women in class society* (translated from the Portuguese by Vale M.). Monthly Review Press, London

Sanders, J., Lynam, J. (1981) New technology and small farmers in Latin America. *Food Policy* Vol 6 No 1

Schmink, M. (1977) Dependent development and the division of labour by sex: Venezuela. *Latin American Perspectives* Issues 12 + 13 Vol 4 Nos 1 + 2

Selcher, W. (1981) Brazil in the world: multipolarity as seen by a peripheral ADC middle power. In **Ferris, E., Lincoln, J.** (eds) *Latin American foreign policies: global and regional dimensions*.

Westview Press, Boulder, Colorado

Shanin, T. (1971) Peasantry as a political factor. In **Shanin, T.** (ed) *Peasants and peasant societies*. Penguin, Harmondsworth

Simmons, A., Diaz-Briquets, S., Laquian, A. (1977) *Social change and internal migration: a review of research findings from Africa, Asia and Latin America*. International Development Centre, Ottawa

Simmons, A., Vlassoff, C. (1982) Industrialisation and urbanisation in Colombia. In **Peek, P., Standing, G.** (eds) *State Policies and migration*. Croom Helm, Beckenham, Kent

Singer, H., Ansari, J. (1982) *Rich and poor countries* (third edition). Allen and Unwin, London

Singer, P. (1982) Neighbourhood movements in São Paulo. In **Safa, H.** (ed) *Towards a political economy of urbanization in Third World countries*. Oxford University Press, Delhi

Slater, D. (ed) (1985) *New social movements and the state in Latin America*, Latin American Studies 29. CEDLA, Amsterdam

Smith, B. (1982) *The church and politics in Chile*. Princeton University Press, Princeton

Spalding, H. (1977) *Organized labor in Latin America: historical case-studies of workers in dependent societies*. Harper Row, New York

Stavenhagen, R. (1970) Classes, colonialism and acculturation. In **Horowitz, I.** (ed) *Masses in Latin America*. Oxford University Press, New York

Stavenhagen, R. (1974) The future of peasants in Mexico. In Institute of Latin American Studies, *The rural society of Latin America today*. Almqvist and Wiksell, Stockholm

Stavenhagen, R. (1978) Capitalism and the peasantry in Mexico. *Latin American Perspectives* Issue 18 Vol 5 No 3

Stein, S. (1957) *Vassouras: a Brazilian coffee county, 1850–1900*. Harvard University Press, Cambridge, Massachusetts

Stein, S., Stein, B. (1970) *The colonial heritage of Latin America: essays on economic dependence in perspective*. Oxford University Press, New York

Stein, W. (1961) *Hualcán: Life in the highlands of Peru*. Cornell University Press, Ithaca, New York

Stepan, A. (1973) *Authoritarian Brazil: origins, policies and future*. Yale University Press, New Haven and London

Streeten, P. (1981) *Development Perspectives*. Macmillan, London

Strickon, A., Greenfield, S. (eds) (1972) *Structure and Process in Latin America: patronage, clientage and power systems*. University of New Mexico Press, Albuquerque

Sunkel, O. (1965) Change and frustration in Chile. In **Veliz, C.** (ed) *Obstacles to change in Latin America*. Oxford University Press, London

Tannenbaum, F. (1946) *Slave and citizen: the negro in the Americas*. Vintage, New York

Thorp, R., Bertram, G. (1978) *Peru, 1890–1977: growth and policy in an open economy*. Macmillan, London

Todaro, M. (1981) *Economic development in the Third World*. Longman, New York

Tokman, V. (1982) Unequal development and the absorption of labour, *CEPAL Review 17*

Tullis, F. (1970) *Lord and peasant in Peru: a paradigm of political and social change*. Harvard University Press, Cambridge, Massachusetts

Tumin, M. (1969) *Comparative Perspectives on race relations*. Little, Brown. Boston

Turner, J. (1965) Lima's barriadas and corralones: suburbs versus slums, *Ekistics* 112

Turner, J. (1970) Barriers and channels for housing development in modernizing countries. In **Mangin, W.** (ed) *Peasants in cities: readings in the anthropology of urbanization*. Houghton Mifflin Co. Boston

UNICEF 1981 *New dimensions, fair conditions*. UN, Geneva

Uno Mas Uno Mexico

Unwin, T. (1982) *Integration, who benefits? The development of post-revolutionary relations between the government and the indigenous groups of Mexico*. Dissertation submitted for the BA Honours degree in Latin American Studies, Portsmouth Polytechnic

Vallier, I. (1967) Religious elites: differentiations and developments in Roman Catholicism. In **Lipset, S., Solari, A.** *Elites in Latin America*. Oxford University Press, London

Vasquez de Miranda, G. (1977) Women's labor force participation in a developing society: the case of Brazil. In **the Wellesley Editorial Committee** (ed) *Women and national development. The complexities of change*. The University of Chicago Press, Chicago, London

Wagley, C. (1953) *Amazon Town*. Macmillan, New York

Wagley, C. (1968) *The Latin American tradition*. Columbia University Press, New York, London

Wagley, C. (1969) From caste to class in North Brazil. In **Tumin, M.** (ed) *Comparative Perspectives on race relations*. Little, Brown, Boston

Wagley, C., Harris, M. (1958) *Minorities in the New World: six case studies*. Columbia University Press, New York, London

Wallerstein, I. (1974) *The modern world system 1: capitalist agriculture and the origins of the European world-economy in the*

sixteenth century. Academic Press, New York, London

Wallerstein, I. (1980) *The modern world system 2: mercantilism and the consolidation of the European world economy, 1600–1750.* Academic Press, New York, London

Warren, B. (1973) Imperialism and capitalist industrialisation, *New Left Review* 81

Weber, M. (1965) *The protestant ethic and the spirit of capitalism.* Allen and Unwin, London

Weber, M. (1947) *The theory of social and economic organization* (edited and with an introduction by **Parsons, T.**). Free Press of Glencoe, London

Weffort, F. (1970) Notas sobre la 'teoría de la dependencia' Teoría de clase o ideología nacional, *Revista Latinoamericana de Ciencia Política* 1/3 Dec

Wolf, E. (1959) *Sons of the shaking earth*. University of Chicago Press, Chicago

Wolf, E. (1969) *Peasant wars of the twentieth century*. Harper and Row, New York

Wolf, E., Hansen, E. (1972) *The human condition in Latin America.* Oxford University Press, New York

World Bank (1982) *World Development Report*

Young, K. (1978) Changing economic roles of women in two rural Mexican communities, *Sociologia Ruralis* Vol 18 2/3

Subject Index

38, 49, 50, 51, 54, 60, 77,
100–1, 121, 125, 131, 139,
140, 169, 175, 182, 184,
185, 186, 193, 195, 199,
201–4, 205, 208, 210–12,
214–32
autonomous, 8, 37, 44, 45,
46–7
economy
enclave, 44, 169, 171
international, 6, 37, 41, 51,
105, 115–16, 156, 205, 211
modern, 153–4, 155, 163, 172,
208
national, 2, 6, 40, 115, 130
plantation, 59, 62, 73–5
subsistence, 6, 67, 114, 116,
117, 121
education, 1, 2, 6, 11, 16–17, 19,
24, 60, 64, 67, 72, 78, 79,
86, 87, 90–4, 95, 97, 98,
104, 107, 108, 109, 110, 111,
114, 115, 129, 135, 139, 141,
144, 158, 168, 184, 185,
189, 204, 210
elite, 13, 35, 43, 78, 86, 90, 92,
95, 96, 101, 108, 110, 111,
112, 121, 134, 163, 167,
168, 169, 173, 174, 176,
186, 190, 195, 197, 198, 205
intellectual, 17
land-owning, 34, 100, 169
entrepreneurship, 13, 34, 45, 69,
77, 115, 119, 152, 153, 159,
167–70, 179
ethnicity, 2, 57–73, 80–3, 135,
208

feudal institution, 36, 38, 39, 74,
121, 208
feudalism, 42, 134, 154, 167

green revolution, 10, 129–30

hacienda, 36, 63–4, 66, 118, 120,
121, 124, 208, 233
health, 10–11, 14, 17, 18, 19, 24,
67, 86, 100, 108, 122, 135,
181, 184, 204, 210
hunger, 4, 9–10, 14, 15, 28, 29,
67, 127, 129, 131, 204, 209

illiteracy, 16–17, 91, 99, 102–3
imperialism, 48, 96, 134
anti-, 166
cultural, 95–7
economic, 40, 41, 43
theories of, 40–1, 48
Inca, 61, 62, 80, 86
income redistribution, 2, 11–13,
19, 20, 38, 54, 93, 124, 182
industrialisation, 3, 13, 16, 19, 21,
22, 27, 29, 30, 32–4, 37–8,
39, 45, 47, 48, 53, 55, 77,
90, 100, 101, 104, 105, 108,
109, 120, 139, 152, 167,
168, 169, 171, 174, 184,
185, 187, 190, 192, 209–10,
212
inequality, 1, 2, 7, 9, 11–13, 15,
16, 19, 27, 28, 29, 30, 46,
54, 72, 91–2, 97, 109, 110,
111, 161, 185, 187, 202,
208–10
informal sector, 2, 73, 147–60,
162–3, 171, 179, 194, 199,
205, 208–9

labour aristrocracy, 171–2, 177
labour movement, 2, 54, 107, 114,
124, 126, 135, 156, 172–9,
185, 190, 194, 201, 205
literacy, 6, 16–17, 21, 22, 72, 88,
91, 93, 96, 141, 163, 214–32

machismo, 103–4, 108, 110, 234
marginality, 65, 105, 107, 143–4,
146, 147
marianismo, 104, 234
Marxism, 88, 89
Marxists, 38, 123, 132–3, 146,
147, 154, 167

Marxist theory, 40, 41, 42, 48, 93, 166, 191
mass media, 2, 94–7, 102, 110, 114, 180, 207
Maya, 61, 69
middle class, 2, 33–5, 37, 45, 49, 54, 79, 83, 92, 108, 109, 114, 167–8, 178, 185, 186–7, 189, 197, 202, 203, 208
migration, 2, 57, 60, 76–7, 116, 120, 168, 210–11
   rural-urban, 2, 45, 60, 73, 101–2, 117, 130, 137–46, 159, 203
   seasonal, 115, 119
   wage, 117
military, 94, 186–7, 190, 196
   regimes, 26, 39, 54, 87, 104, 124, 145, 146, 185–7, 192, 194–206
   theories of the, 186–7
modernisation, 65, 76, 95, 110, 112, 113, 128, 134, 186, 188–9, 196, 199, 201, 204, 205
   theories of, 33–9, 45–6, 55, 94–5, 101, 104, 117, 121, 167, 187
modes of production, 42, 52–3, 66, 76, 79, 117, 121, 134, 135, 146, 154
multinational corporations, 6, 25, 44–5, 47, 48, 50–1, 105, 112, 118, 120, 135, 153, 166–72, 184, 190, 192, 202, 203, 210, 211

national debt, 22, 25, 29, 51, 128, 139, 192–6, 204–5, 208, 210, 211–12, 214–32
newly-industrialising countries, 30, 53, 208

oligarchy, 33, 38, 69, 189, 190, 197
Otavalo, 69

patriarchal family, 74–5, 102, 117
peasantry, 2, 15, 16, 18, 35, 42, 45, 47, 52, 63–6, 68–72, 87, 92, 94, 96, 99–100, 101, 103, 109, 110, 112–35, 137, 141, 142, 173, 175, 190–1, 197, 208, 210–11
   peasantisation, 117–21
   peasant mobilisation, 2, 72, 113, 132–5
Peronism, 177, 190
personalism, 68, 71, 85, 97–101, 110–111, 133, 152, 208, 234
polarisation of society, 7, 29–30, 45, 182, 191–2, 199, 202, 210
population growth, 14–15, 17, 72, 102–3, 113, 120, 137, 192, 214–32
populism, 188–90, 201
proletariat, 2, 33, 38, 47, 108, 134, 152, 162–5, 167–8, 170–9, 182, 189, 190, 191, 199, 202
   informal, 162–5, 179–80, 208
   lumpen, 152
   proletarianisation, 65, 79, 114, 116–21, 125, 134
   proto-, 152
   semi-proletarianisation, 47, 73, 117, 118–21, 208–9
   sub-, 152
poverty, 1, 2, 7, 8–16, 19, 23–4, 29, 46, 54, 56, 66, 72, 88, 93, 94, 96, 103, 118, 121, 122, 125, 127, 130, 134, 135, 139, 142, 144, 146, 153–5, 158–60, 161, 185, 203, 208–10, 214, 216–19, 225–6, 228, 230, 232
   culture of, 143, 160
   Poverty Datum Line, 23–4
   poverty trap, 158

SAM, 131–2, 212
Sandinista, 88, 104, 135
slavery, 42, 58, 59, 62, 74–80, 86
social class, 2, 43, 47, 52–3, 57,

64–5, 83, 92, 108, 116, 133,
161–83, 188, 189–91, 199,
204, 208, 210
bureaucratic-technical, 162–5,
167–70, 181, 182
class consciousness, 100,
133–4, 174, 176, 178
class structure, 2, 46, 65, 73,
144, 158, 161, 162, 164–5,
179, 187, 195, 208
class struggle, 133, 161, 180,
198
colour class, 73, 78–83
dominant, 43, 47, 100, 111,
161–70, 179, 181, 182, 191,
195, 199, 204
multi-class, 180, 183, 189
socialism, 41, 48, 55, 97, 134, 170
socialist society, 7, 26, 27, 36,
90, 110, 125, 126, 188, 196,
211
social mobility, 34, 37, 38, 65,
78–9, 90–3, 101, 104, 146,
168, 170
social movement, 3, 54–5, 79–80,
82–3, 87–9, 104, 160,
179–83, 204–6, 209, 211–12
spontaneous housing settlements,
73, 77, 87, 142–7, 154, 159,
160, 180, 199, 233
state, 2, 37, 44, 50, 66, 82, 86,
87, 95, 109, 115, 125, 126,
146, 167, 170–3, 175–6,
178–82, 184–206, 210–11
authoritarian, 2, 39, 87,
185–95, 199–205, 211
bureaucratic-authoritarian,
187–8
corporatist, 188–91, 196,
200–1, 205
relative autonomy of, 191,
203–4
state bourgeoisie, 166, 184

state bureaucracy, 167, 175,
191
state capitalism, 197–8
state enterprises, 166, 167, 177,
197–8, 203
theories of, 54–5

theology of liberation, 88–9
Turner thesis, 144–6, 159

underdevelopment, 2, 7, 8, 11,
14–17, 24, 27, 39, 41–3,
45–7, 50, 53–5, 105, 152,
186, 209–13
unemployment, 1, 7, 15–16, 29,
45, 47, 54, 105, 118, 126,
149, 174, 185, 192–4, 205
'disguised', 149, 152
underemployment, 2, 15–16, 29,
47, 54, 105, 122, 149–52,
171, 185
uneven development, 7, 13, 28,
32, 36, 45–8, 55
United Nations, 7, 21, 22, 26, 28,
68–9, 92, 163
ECLA, 37–8
UNCTAD, 21
UNICEF, 209
UNRISD, 23
urbanisation, 29, 32, 100, 102,
137–60, 169, 171, 212

women, 4, 6, 74, 103–10, 115,
120, 131, 139–41, 153, 173,
214–32, 234
women's movements, 3, 55, 104,
181

Zapata, 133

254

Place Name Index